On Living in an Old Country

Patrick Wright is the author of a number of highly acclaimed and occasionally also reviled books, including *The Village that Died for England*, *Tank* (described by Simon Schama as 'a *tour de force*'), and *Iron Curtain*, which John Le Carré hailed as 'a work of wit, style and waggish erudition' and one disconcerted academic described as 'maddening.' Wright's first book, *On Living in an Old Country* is widely credited with having initiated a new understanding of the heritage industry. Its arguments were further pursued in *A Journey Through Ruins*, which reviewed the works of Margaret Thatcher's governments through their impact on East London, and is now also reissued in an updated edition.

Wright wrote *On Living in an Old Country* while working for the National Council for Voluntary Organisations. After many years as a self-employed writer and broadcaster, he is now a Professor at the Institute for Cultural Analysis at Nottingham Trent University and a fellow of the London Consortium.

Andrzej Krauze graduated from the Academy of Fine Arts in Warsaw in 1973. His early satirical drawings appeared in the Polish weeklies *Szpilki* (1970–1977) and *Kultura* (1974–1981). In 1979 he moved to London, where he continues to live. In 1981 he became a contributor to Solidarity's national weekly, *Tygodnik Solidarnosc*. Seven years later, he started drawing for the *Guardian*. His illustrations also appear regularly in *New Scientist* (London), *The Scientist* (Philadelphia), *Internazionale* (Rome), *Courrier International* and *Medecine/Sciences* (Paris), and in the leading Polish daily *Rzeczpospolita*, and the weekly *Wprost*. His character 'Mr. Pen,' introduced in this book's chapter on Mary Butts, now flourishes as a citizen of the world.

Praise for *On Living in an Old Country*:

'Patrick Wright is a sensitive, ultra-thoughful explorer...With a large torch and copious notes he invites the reader to a number of meandering guided tours well off the main footpaths.'
Tom Nairn, *The Guardian*

'A quite exceptional and richly rewarding book...You won't feel the same about the Heritage Industry after this devastating series of iconoclastic reflections.'
Colin Ward, *Times Educational Supplement*

'Wright is a brilliant analyst of cultural meanings and has uncovered...a central truth about the force of nostalgia in modern England.'
Paul Addison, *London Review of Books*

'In a rich and suggestive series of essays Patrick Wright explores the ways in which history itself has become the most powerful source of contemporary meanings about what Britain is and what it is to be British.'
Stuart Hall

On Living in an Old Country

THE NATIONAL PAST IN CONTEMPORARY BRITAIN

PATRICK WRIGHT
With drawings by
Andrzej Krauze

OXFORD
UNIVERSITY PRESS

OXFORD
UNIVERSITY PRESS

Great Clarendon Street, Oxford OX2 6DP

Oxford University Press is a department of the University of Oxford.
It furthers the University's objective of excellence in research, scholarship,
and education by publishing worldwide in

Oxford New York

Auckland Cape Town Dar es Salaam Hong Kong Karachi
Kuala Lumpur Madrid Melbourne Mexico City Nairobi
New Delhi Shanghai Taipei Toronto

With offices in

Argentina Austria Brazil Chile Czech Republic France Greece
Guatemala Hungary Italy Japan Poland Portugal Singapore
South Korea Switzerland Thailand Turkey Ukraine Vietnam

Oxford is a registered trade mark of Oxford University Press
in the UK and in certain other countries

Published in the United States
by Oxford University Press Inc., New York

First published in Great Britain by Verso 1985

This edition published by Oxford University Press 2009

British Library Cataloguing in Publication Data

Data available

Library of Congress Control Number: 2008943435

Typeset by SPI Publisher Services, Pondicherry, India
Printed in Great Britain
on acid-free paper by Clays Ltd, St Ives plc

ISBN 978–0–19–954195–9

1 3 5 7 9 10 8 6 4 2

For C.A.L.
(not forgetting *L'Assistance Publique*)
from the Laënnec

Contents

Preface to the OUP Edition:
Heritage and the Place of Criticism

Written between 1980 and 1985, the essays in this book set out to explore the presence of the past in British society at what seemed a pivotal and also startling moment of history. If I viewed the English scene with a somewhat dissociated eye, this was only partly because I had recently returned from Canada, where I had become familiar with a lingering expatriate imagery of 'the old country' that hardly correlated with the politically riven country in which I was now living. The question of national identity had also been cast into sharp relief by the recent election of Margaret Thatcher, who promised a radical break with the past, while simultaneously invoking a traditional idea of British identity and even destiny to be restored.

I was by no means alone in pursuing the theme of this book. For many years, Tom Nairn, the Scottish author of *The Break-Up of Britain* (1977), had been investigating the spectacular attractions, or otherwise, of the British state, and calling for a different expression of Englishness. The extent to which apparently ancient traditions could be synthesised around political and other purposes in the present had been demonstrated in the essays collected in Eric Hobsbawm and Terence Ranger's study, *The Invention of Tradition* (1982). Meanwhile, Zygmunt Bauman's *Memories of Class: The Pre-History and After-Life of Class* (1982), had opened a number of interesting questions about the role of historical memory in the British labour movement.

I was also stimulated by the Cambridge historian J.H. Plumb's suggestive study *The Death of the Past*, first published in 1969. Here Plumb describes 'the past' as the various myths, rumours, and omens that circulate through society at any given time, differentiating it from 'History' conceived as the 'intellectual process' with which historians attempt to 'cleanse the story of mankind from those deceiving visions of a purposeful past.'[1] According to Plumb, 'the past' is 'always a created ideology with a purpose, designed to control individuals, or motivate societies, or inspire classes.' The job of History, therefore, was to 'dissolve' and 'weaken' the past, and to replace its 'simple, structural generalisations'[2] with properly disciplined understanding. This seemed to me a defensible argument both in the superior truth and in the wider educational responsibility claimed for History. Yet it also seemed unlikely that the decisive 'cleansing' of public perceptions of the past would ever come. I concluded this partly because the elevated veracity claimed for 'History' has so often turned out to be chimerical,[3] but also because there is much more to be said about 'the past' than that its traditions are frequently invented or that its presentations of history often wander far from the actual facts. The past may indeed be harnessed to questionable purposes in the present. Yet to recognise this was surely also to suspect it of connections that even the most heroically truthful historian could hardly be expected to 'dissolve' merely by insisting on 'the way things really were.'

In writing these essays, I was interested in examining how ideas of the national past were sustained and articulated in the present. I approached 'heritage' as a cultural theme of wider reach than was necessarily the concern of archaeologists and museum curators in their specialist fields. Re-reading the book, indeed, I find that it refers to remarkably few museums at all. This may well be considered an oversight, but it also reflects how the so-called 'heritage debate' that took place in the years after 1985 refocused an argument that was earlier spread out over a far wider range of expressions of British identity.

In seeking to identify the factors driving questions of national heritage into prominence, I was hoping to deepen the theme, not to dismiss it as some critics later suggested. I tried to do this by connecting the phenomena I was describing to a consideration of the way various thinkers of the left had thought about history and tradition earlier in the twentieth century. In Britain as elsewhere, activists, writers and politicians have long been both claiming and fiercely rejecting the idea of 'heritage.' It was, for example, an evil thing in the mind of the anti-war campaigner, E.D. Morel, when he railed with passionate fervour against the Paris Peace conference in 1919. Denouncing the Allied leaders for blighting the future with their punitive policies against defeated Germany, Morel wrote of how they were burdening future generations with their 'indecent hatreds, their malignant passions, their contemptible egoism.' After condemning these 'old men' for setting out to 'league to posterity their insensate animosities and filthy lust,' he concluded 'the heritage must be repudiated.'[4]

'Heritage' could be seen in a similarly negative light even as it was being rallied during the patriotic emergency of the Second World War. In Rex Warner's novel *Why Was I Killed!* (1943), a recently fallen

soldier finds himself watching a group of visitors at the tomb of the
Unknown Soldier in Westminster Abbey. Asked how he would answer
a dead soldier who wanted to know why he had been killed, one of the
visitors, a chubby faced knight of the realm who is later revealed to
have made his money in the international arms trade, launches into a
speech about how patriotism is not dead, insisting 'We cannot but be
proud of our heritage.'[5]

If 'heritage' was fiercely opposed in some invocations (in Warner's
novel, a pragmatic factory worker quickly declares himself nauseated
by this stuff about 'Our glorious heritage!'), it could also be embraced
as an inheritance to be defended and carried forward into the present.
Attending a meeting of the International Association of Writers for
the Defence of Culture, held at Friends' House in London, June
1936, the French writer André Malraux spoke of a new International
Encyclopedia he proposed to create against the 'anti-rational and
anti-scientific emotionalism of Fascist reaction.' Speaking from the
left in that violently polarised decade, he declared that 'the cultural
heritage is not made up of the works that men must respect, but of
those only that can help them to live. Our heritage is made up of all
the voices that can answer our questions...'[6] This persisted in the
work of socialist historians, whose case for change in the present is
often presented as a vindication of history, and whose cause has often
been expressed as loyalty to a heritage—be it the English utopian tradition, Runnymede, the Diggers and Levellers, or the aspirations of the
industrial working-class.

It was Hannah Arendt, above all, who insisted that this tussle of
claim and rejection, in which 'heritage' was invoked as whatever
one likes or hates, was invalidated by the catastrophic events of the
twentieth century. Writing after the Second World War and with
the outrages of the Nazi holocaust burning in her mind, she saw
the western tradition challenged at its core. In the concluding para-
graph of the preface to her study, *The Origins of Totalitarianism* (1951),
Arendt reflected on the irruption of anti-Semitism, imperialism and
totalitarianism in a world that had so recently seemed assured of its
own progressive enlightenment. After that, she concluded,

> we can no longer afford to take that which was good in the past and
> simply call it our heritage, to discard the bad and simply think of it as a
> dead load which by itself time will bury in oblivion. The subterranean

stream of Western history has finally come to the surface and usurped
the dignity of our tradition. This is the reality in which we live. And
this is why all efforts to escape from the grimness of the present into
nostalgia for a still intact past, or into the anticipated oblivion of a better future, are vain.[7]

By the early 1980s, the British invocation of 'heritage' may have seemed
completely detached from the memory of the Nazi holocaust but it was
nonetheless, a present expression of discontinuity rather than its opposite. In this, I agree with David Brett, who has more recently suggested
that 'heritage' is 'a product of the process of modernisation which, by
eroding customs and expectations, forces us to re-articulate our sense
of the past.'[8] There were good historical causes to be defended in the
1980s, and there was still much claiming and condemning of 'heritage'
in the arguments of that era. Yet it seemed important also to recognise
that complicating factors were brought into play during the process
Brett describes as a 'rearticulation.' Though presented as a historically
formed legacy, the idea of 'national heritage' could be suffused with
contemporary class assumption or imperial nostalgia. It could be
aligned with a racist perspective, or wrapped around Westminster as
the epicentre of the unitary British state. It could be invoked against
a host of vividly imagined present-day bogeys: Europe, Modernism,
immigration, socialism and the welfare state. In its cruder forms even
then, it could serve as a form of environmental exploitation when
unleashed on a historical landscape or town centre.

That tensions might exist between wild articulations of history
and the disciplines of the public museum had already been imagined by Raymond Williams, who opens his novel *The Volunteers* (1978),
by staging an incident at St. Fagans National History Museum in
Wales, an open-air institution founded after the example of Skansen
in Stockholm. As Williams describes it, 'the idea that the museum
embodies is of an old Wales, still in part surviving, but with all modern realities left outside in the car park, or brought inside only in the
toilets which have replaced the privies. That is why it is called a folk
museum. Folk is the past: an alternative to People.'[9] Such is the setting
in which Williams imagines a Welsh nationalist assassination attempt
against a visiting English Secretary of State: a 'clash of scene and
action' in which the folkloric image of Wales is confronted with a
violent manifestation of 'material history.'[10] 'What this place offered,

after all, was a version of the life of a people: a version, characteristically, that attracted official visits. And then what had poured into it,
roughly and incongruously, with this lingering shock of surprise, was
another version, another practice, of the life of the same people.'[11] It
is an indication of how much museums have changed since then, that
this idea of history breaking into a closed and pristinely separated
display now seems curiously old fashioned. Assassination attempts are
surely still barred, but in more recent decades, many museums have
actively embraced a wider sense of historicity. The British Museum
may never have been an entirely inert reliquary but its director now
promotes it as 'the place where different cultures meet.'

With regard to the discussion that followed publication of this
book, I would like to recall two arguments in particular. The first
concerns the association of Margaret Thatcher's project with any
idea of an interest in history or a resurgent rather than merely new,
national identity. It has been suggested by various critics, that this
was a largely misguided claim. A number of reviewers doubted that
Margaret Thatcher gave a fig for history or tradition, and thought it
wrong to associate public interest in heritage with that cause. More
recently Peter Mandler has described this suggestion as 'rather per-
verse,'[12] implying that Margaret Thatcher was never anything like as
concerned about the past as was suggested. After all, her monetarist
policies were fiercely anti-traditional, and she could indeed seem most
interested in history as the dustbin into which to cast Arthur Scargill,
Michael Foot and her other socialist opponents.

Thatcher was a moderniser determined to use market mechanisms
to reconfigure British society. At the same time, however, she was a
characteristically 'reactionary' moderniser, who combined her monetarist economic policies with a rhetoric of national recovery, and
of true British identity organised around the Palace of Westminster
(which was regilded in more senses than one during Thatcher's years
as prime minister). This is why it does not seem to me inappropriate
that Anthony Barnett should have written what Mandler describes
as 'a whole book' (actually a long journal article later reprinted as
the short book *Iron Britannia*), about the Churchillian aspects of her
outlook. Contradictory as it was, the policy was both destructive of
tradition and dependent on it in order to legitimise its upheavals
in the minds of those affected. These tensions were central to the
political climate of the early eighties, and they became all the more

so during the privatisations discussed in my later book, *A Journey Through Ruins*.

Meanwhile, the argument associating 'heritage' with decline has certainly failed to thrive. It has been repeatedly dismissed on the grounds that conservation and heritage values have actually proved to be good for the economy, whether in terms of tourism or through their application to the redevelopment of historical quarters in towns and cities. If it really had been based on the suggestion that 'commerce and culture do not mix,' the argument might rightly be regarded as 'historical rubbish'[13] and there would be nothing more to say. However, the point even then was to indicate exactly that 'commerce and culture' did mix, and with interesting political consequences.

I remember being astonished when I first heard government figures proclaim that heritage and tourism would be developed as an economic alternative to heavy industries like steel-manufacture or coal mining. As I recall, there was a brief moment when everyone saw the insult: the miners of the Rhondda valley really were offered a 'Wild West' theme park in the place of their closing pits. Yet as I saw it, the argument about decline had a cultural rather than economic basis. Here and in the later book, *A Journey Through Ruins*, I was interested in tracing how an idea of endangered national tradition had shaped the public imagination in post-war Britain. It still seems to me that the polarised symbolic drama that I later named 'Brideshead and the Tower Blocks,' functioned this way, using architectural symbols to represent strongly opposed versions of what Britain was or had become. It was by no means the only version of history available in Britain at that time, but it was a powerful fixture of the imagination of the time. It could, I thought, be considered part of a 'culture of decline' to the extent that it worked to impose a closure on public thought, not least about the legitimacy and possibility of state-led attempts at social reform.

Some years after its first publication, this book would also be drawn up into a heated argument with Raphael Samuel, advocate of 'people's history' and a founder of History Workshop, which in its remarkable prime was both a journal and a movement that convened at a widely dispersed set of often highly disputatious conferences, seminars and less formal discussions that reached far beyond the confines of the university system. I knew Samuel, respected his prodigious knowledge, and enjoyed many conversations with him over

the years. I also wrote this book in a somewhat quarrelsome relationship to the movement with which he was so closely associated.
I attended History Workshop conferences, starting towards the end
of 1979, when the historian E.P. Thompson made his fiery assault
on Althusserian cultural studies in a freezing old church in Oxford.
I presented a first version of the Introduction at the London History
Workshop, where it was met with explosive hostility from feminist
historians who considered it an offence to venture any theoretical
remarks about everyday life. I first presented my discussion of Mary
Butts at the 'patriotism' conference in Oxford in March 1984. Two,
perhaps three, of the chapters in this book were considered by *History
Workshop Journal*, often after Samuel had invited their submission, and
then rejected by the editorial collective—a decision that would be
communicated, after the usual long delay, by Samuel himself or, in
one case, by Michael Ignatieff.

No doubt these articles might have been a great deal better, yet
there was also a broader tension in play from the start. As I came to
understand it, this lay between an approach holding that popular historical consciousness was to be cherished, respected and accessed as
much as possible through testimony, in the spirit of E.P. Thompson's
famous remark about saving the downtrodden from the 'condescen-
sion of posterity.' The other approach, with which I was associated,
held that public awareness of history was also shaped by factors that
demanded critical examination. This was, I think, a genuine complexity, and there were legitimate values to defend on both sides. At the
time, however, it was cast as a conflict between 'history' and 'theory'
or 'cultural studies.'

The argument was restated in 1994, when Raphael Samuel published his book *Theatres of Memory*. Samuel himself had previously written critical articles about the subject, but he now approached heritage
as a general good, associating its emergence and increased popularity,
so Neal Ascherson would point out in the dispute that followed, as 'a
victory for the democratic intelligence.'[14] In a chapter entitled 'heritage-
baiting,'[15] which I suspect was added to the book quite late in the compositional process, Samuel seemed to suggest that all criticism in the
area was motivated by reprehensible snobbery. Having unleashed this
accusation, with a slogan that seemed as much indebted to the medieval bear pit as to the 'Red-baiting' accusations rightly launched against
Senator McCarthy and his fellow anti-Communists in 1950s America,

Samuel went on to excoriate David Cannadine, Robert Hewison, Neal Ascherson and myself among others, and to allege that the critique of heritage was sourced in metropolitan literary snobbery, fear of 'trade,' a Puritan distrust of 'graven images,' and, with regard to the lavender bags and floral fabrics that travelled under the flag of heritage, possibly misogyny too.

I responded with a hostile review in the *Guardian*[16] and then kept my head down until 7 June 1996, when Samuel came to Lancaster University, where I then had a temporary toe-hold as a visitor. We discussed the issue further in a seminar also attended by Robert Hewison, John Urry and others who had been involved in the debate. Samuel was mortally ill by that time, but he remained impressively resolute. He looked Robert Hewison in the eye and repeated his charge that he was a metropolitan literary snob. He then turned to me, and recited a long and entirely convincing list of the various ways in which the recovery of the Mary Rose from the mud of the Solent (described in Chapter 5), had since contributed to historical understanding. This was, he suggested, an example of the difference between the perspective of the historian and that of the practitioner of 'cultural studies,' the latter, by implication, being all too keen to theorise airily about appearances and the way meanings are 'constructed' in the present but uninterested in the wider consequences or ramifications of its chosen images. At some point he also informed me that I had 'the mark of the convict' on me, alleging that it was this book that had made New Labour, then still in opposition, so contemptuous of history.

Though aware that Samuel had recently been much concerned with defending the History curriculum in schools, I doubted this attribution. I knew that New Labour had an aversion to the past, supported by the arguments of assorted consultants and branding advisers who condemned the traditional imagery of Britain as elitist, backward-looking and off-putting to potential international markets. So influential was the case for 'Britain™'[17] in the first months of New Labour government that, as Samuel would no doubt have noted had he lived to see it, members of the first Blair cabinet proved comically reluctant to be photographed near anything resembling an old building. Nevertheless, it seemed most unlikely that this aversion could reasonably be attributed to a far from programmatic book of reflections that was certainly not in Tony Blair's back pocket when he moved into Downing Street in 1997. If that accolade belongs to anyone, it should

go to Mark Leonard or Philip Dodd, who has claimed it for his own
Demos pamphlet, *The Battle Over Britain* (1995).

We met once again after that encounter at Lancaster, and Raphael
wrote me a gracious letter suggesting that we should argue more often
for 'the pleasure of making up.' Remembering this argument now,
more than a decade after Raphael's death, it seems plain that Raphael
had much on his side. His detailed account of the post-war rise of
conservationism, provided in *Theatres of Memory*, makes it quite clear
that there was a broad groundswell of interest, concerned with brick,
railways and every other imaginable entity. It is also true that the criticism of heritage had sometimes proceeded by mockery and dismissive
statement—although this seemed more characteristic of journalistic

comment of the 'a thousand words on anything' variety, than of the more considered critical arguments accused alongside it.

Meanwhile, Samuel's suggestion that the critique of 'heritage' was no more than a reflection of elitist disdain has stayed in place. By the time the argument was being repeated by Richard Weight, some eight years later, the endeavour to develop a critical understanding of the field could be dismissed as having no value except as proof of the liberal elite's 'continuing failure' to come to terms with 'mass democracy in the twentieth century.'[18]

This leaves us in a position that is frankly inadequate to the issues at stake. If heritage is an unproblematic good, and criticism only a product of petty social snobbery, then we are back at the starting point and the investigation has yet to begin. Instead of polarising argument in this way, we would surely do better to engage the issues raised by the French historian François Hartog in his recent consideration of the conversion of history into 'heritage' (Hartog's word 'patrimonialisation' is awkwardly Englished as 'heritagisation') that has, as he suggests, been such a marked feature of the 1990s. Reviewing the French experience, Hartog suggests that the presence of the past is shaped by the existence of distinct 'regimes of historicity,' a term by which he means to identify both the way 'a society considers its past and deals with it' and the 'method of self-awareness in a human community.'[19] In 'the modern regime of historicity,'[20] seen as prevailing through much of the twentieth century, hope was invested in the future, from which all light appeared to emanate and which seemed so superior to the present that time itself became a heroic actor and acceleration was conceived as a virtue. By contrast, Hartog suggests that the rise of heritage over the last twenty five years, is characteristic of a different 'regime of historicity' in which 'light is produced by the present itself, and by it alone.'[21]

'Heritage,' in other words, reflects the 'presentism' of a more recent age that has lost that earlier sense of the future. In our time the idea of the 'monument,' with which society once sought to impose values on its members, gives way to new forms of 'memorial' concerned with 'safeguarding heritage' and establishing a new 'calendar of public life' in which 'cultural memory' is cultivated 'like one cultivates a garden.'[22] According to Hartog, our 'regime of historicity' consists of a massive present, which is 'invasive, omnipresent [and] has no horizon other than itself,' and which is constantly in the business of 'manufacturing' the past around its own requirements.[23] His examples of the new pattern include the fall of the Berlin Wall, a destruction that was followed by 'instant museification.'[24] Like Philippe Hoyau, whose analysis is discussed in the Afterword of this book, Hartog also considers the rise of the 'ecomuseum': a new kind of 'museum without walls' in which heritage is linked to the ways of life of a particular territory. Far from seeking to imitate or capture the past, the ecomuseum sets out to escape both nostalgia and the passive gaze of tourism by establishing an 'interactive space' between past and future. Its appeal to memory is, so Hartog concludes, 'a response to the present,' even as it also tries to escape from the condition he describes as 'presentism.' Even though it may present itself as an enduring survival from days gone by, 'Heritage' is never 'nourished by continuity.'[25] It is actually, as Hartog suggests with Hannah Arendt in mind, a sign of rupture and a breach with the past. As for the projected idea of cultural identity,

> it is less a question of an obvious, assertive identity, more a question of an uneasy identity that risks disappearing or is largely forgotten, obliterated, or repressed: an identity in search of itself, to be exhumed, assembled, or even invented. In this way, heritage comes to define less that which one possesses, what one has, than circumscribing what one is, without having known, or even been capable of knowing. Heritage thus becomes an invitation for collective anamnesis. The 'ardent obligation' of heritage, with its requirements for conservation, renovation and commemoration is added to the 'duty' of memory, with its recent public translation of repentance.[26]

We may indeed feel inclined to question this schematic distinction between the modern 'regime of historicity' and its characteristically 'post-modern' successor. We may also suspect that the average city street nowadays belongs in several different 'regimes of historicity' all at once. Yet this attempt to understand the present articulation of heritage surely suggests a more useful way of thinking than seeking to measure the popularity of history by tallying the sales of history books over the decades, or by firing off polemical arguments along the lines of 'Heritage, for or against.'

If there is one lesson to be drawn from the British dispute over heritage, it is surely that the proper location for critical intelligence about these matters is within the conservation movement itself. When William Morris founded the Society for the Protection of

Ancient Buildings (1877), he was campaigning against the bad restoration practised by Victorian architects, who were in the habit
of 'scraping' historical churches back into conformity with what
they took to be a true period style: the aim, as David Brett has
argued, was to insist on 'repair, not restoration.'[27] A similarly critical perspective, as well as a wider social vision, was implicit in the
Ruskinian vision of the public interest that helped to motivate the
founding of the National Trust.

Coming forward into the twentieth century, we find fiercely critical arguments breaking out among those advocating a deeper public understanding of history. Peter Mandler reminds us that G.M.
Trevelyan, in an essay entitled 'Clio: A Muse,' first published in 1903,
had insisted that history was an art as well as a science, one that must
draw on a full range of narrative and emotional effect in his ambition
to interest and 'educate' the public.[28] Yet there would be other ways
of judging Clio before the twentieth century had advanced much further. An arresting condemnation was written in the wake of the First
World War by Violet Paget, a literary aesthete and Liberal cosmopol-
itan, who wrote under the name of Vernon Lee. Appalled by the war,
Lee set out to produce an analysis of the 'War Mind' and the way
the belligerent states imposed this propaganda-born outlook on their
divided peoples on both sides of the conflict. One of their assistants in
subordinating the minds of their subjects was 'the Muse of History':
described by Lee as 'a drama critic by vocation,' who made a series
of melodramas of the past and then offered them up as 'lessons' in
the present.[29]

Guilty of 'pandering...so-called history to our dramatic instincts,'
our vanity and snobbishness, the Muse of History presents the past
translated into 'the terms of the present,' thereby converting 'the
recorder of Events into a purveyor of ideal emotions...' Clio made
'hugged dolls' of past personages, and surrendered the past to a process of 'retrospective reincarnation' that favoured 'looking through
key-holes, listening behind curtains, tampering with correspondence
and generally behaving like blackguards with a perfect conscience.' In
Lee's view, the Muse of History has been 'the nurse of all the artifi-
cially incubated Nationalisms and Irredentisms' that have caused so
much havoc in Europe. If her emotional fables served to rally the
people to war, this was because they offered fantastic compensation
for miserable and oppressed lives—'granting their heart's desire to

those who have borne the brunt of reality's shortcomings.' According to Lee,

> the Muse has no use for flints and potsherds. What she wants are human personages to gape at on a puppet show or ferret out in the places where we keep rags and dirty linen. The Muse caters for our various imaginative needs, noble or base, giving us the heroes and martyrs and villains for whom our sentimentality, megalomania, and morbid passions clamour; personages great enough, abominable enough, pure enough, unhappy enough, to be the cherished companions, the hugged dolls, of our presumptuous day-dreams; also mean enough, dirty enough in all their splendour of royalty or genius, to comfort our own meanness with the thought: 'Well! They also were human (which often means brutish), just like ourselves.' Scaffolds and stakes, alcoves and backstairs; she provides them with all the detail which everyday life refuses, glory and filth to perfection; and often, and alas, as in some of her greatest ministrants (I am thinking of the incomparable Michelet), all mingled in nauseous or piquant concoctions.[30]

There is, I think, quite a lot to be said for revisiting this argument, folded away as it is at the back of one of the least-read books of the twentieth century. Lee's primary concern is that, by peddling the past as so much décor in the present, Clio cheats people of the one true lesson of history, namely 'Change, and our recognition of Otherness.' This may indeed be judged an extreme view, born of Lee's revulsion against the war in which her image of Clio was formed. There would, after all, be no such thing as history if the past really were entirely 'other' and all forms of present identification with it impossibly corrupt. Lee also goes further than J.H. Plumb would later do in yearning for a time when History would annihilate the past: 'no-one believes more than I do that History is destined to become an ever finer thing; and Clio to lose her footing in it, finally to vanish altogether, or turn, as other Goddesses have in their day, into some amusing little crone, Mother Hubbard or such like, for the delight of nurseries.'

Extreme as it is, Lee's insistence on the 'otherness' of the past is worth remembering in a time when 'heritage' is so often promoted as an experience of identification. It seems to me a useful corrective, for example, to Stephen Fry's suggestion, made at the launch of a campaign named 'History Matters' on 3 July 2006, that 'History is not the story of strangers, aliens from another realm; it is the story of us had we been born a little earlier.'[31] Fry was launching an educational

campaign, and could hardly do otherwise than insist on the acces-
sibility of the past to a wide range of people of different cultural and
educational backgrounds. And yet Lee's insistence on the 'otherness'
of the past might usefully serve to temper such calls for identification, which easily lend themselves to the idea of history as a kind of
costume drama which draws its measure from the present. One thing
that is certain, however, is that the Vernon Lee who wrote this furious
attack on the Muse of History was no enemy of history itself. Known
for her writings about the 'spirit of place,' she valued the way history
lived on in her favourite European locales and sometimes 'haunted'
the present in its otherness. She once commended the past as 'a shel-
tering spacious church, built by unpractical, imperious longings for
everything which reality denies.'[32]

A critical impulse would also motivate the emergence of new conservation bodies formed in the interwar years. The Georgian Group
was founded by Douglas Goldring, a pacifist long associated with the
National Council for Civil Liberties, itself set up in 1916 to protect
the legal rights of citizens during the war. Disturbed by the demolition of many Georgian buildings in London and elsewhere during the
early 1930s, he established the Georgian Group as a new committee
of the Society for the Protection of Ancient Buildings. Working with
William Morris's example in mind, he found the experience arduous,
and all the worse thanks to the landed aristocrats and Mayfair social-
ites he felt obliged to bring onto the committee. It is not clear how
much this group, chaired by Lord Derwent and including the young
Robert Byron, knew of Goldring's previous activities as a pacifist and
left wing 'propaganda novelist.' However, a working relationship was
never established and Goldring took his leave as soon as the Group
was established, convinced that it was pointless to try to reconcile his
idea of the public interest with the patrician assumptions of his committee members.[33]

This pattern, in which a critical perspective is articulated within
the conservationist movement itself, was repeated after the Second
World War. History Workshop itself was surely in this tradition,
and not only in its early connection with industrial archaeology: it
was founded to shift history writing in the direction of 'people's history' and quickly developed a feminist dimension as well. It was also
evident in the critique of what came to be known as the 'heritage
industry.' It has become customary to ascribe the phrase 'the heritage

industry' to Robert Hewison's book of this title, published in 1987.[34] The publicity blurb on the back of Hewison's sequel, *Future Tense: A New Art for the Nineties* (1990), claims that Hewison 'gave a new phrase to the language,' and the assertion has since gone into circulation as fact. Hewison is said to have 'coined the phrase' in Richard Weight's *Patriots* (2002),[35] but this is inaccurate.

In fact, the man who first spoke of 'the heritage industry' in this connection was the environmental campaigner and anarchist writer Colin Ward. He used it in October 1985, in a short review of this book published in *The Times Education Supplement*.[36] I mention this not out of any sense of self-importance, but to indicate that, in this case too, the critical view originated within the movement itself, and certainly not in the mind of some hostile outsider: be he the heroic champion of a future-orientated 'critical culture' (Hewison), or merely a 'grubby' mocker jeering at 'Disneyland Britain,' as Weight suggests.

By 1985, when Ward wrote his review, the word 'heritage' was circulating widely in connection with buildings and historical landscapes. For Ward, however, the associated 'industry,' had first come into view in the early 1970s. Ward was then a former teacher working as education officer at the Town and Country Planning Association. As a founding member of the new Council for Urban Studies Centres, he advocated teaching children about the environment through an approach that he and his deputy named 'streetwork': an urban alternative to 'field studies' that was 'mainly concerned with the environmental education of the non-academic child, in other words with the vast majority of the population.'[37]

City schools were encouraged to break out of their classrooms in defiance of an examination system 'originally designed as a selection filter for university entrance,'[38] and to follow the advice of Paul Goodman, the New York anarchist and novelist, who had urged educators to use the wider city as their school. They should develop their own alternative to the 'rural experience' often offered to urban schoolkids—a largely meaningless encounter, so Ward judged, that often consisted of 'a trip to a "stately home" to wander, like moujiks shuffling beneath the painted ceilings of the Winter Palace, through some fully certificated bit of "our architectural heritage", followed by a fleeting glimpse of the lions in the paddock. It has as much to do with environmental education as a visit to Snow White's palace in Disneyland . . .'[39]

Against this, Ward urged urban schools to take part in the development of interpretation centres and 'town trails,' which would enable learning in 'areas where the architectural heritage is less well known, or more badly damaged, and the contemporary environment is poor.' It was hoped that schools setting out to establish urban alternatives to 'nature trails' would be assisted by local architects and others 'with a highly developed sense of the *genius loci* and an ability to convey something of the excitement it can generate.' They should be aware, as Ward added later, that for many people, including some teachers, 'environmental education' meant having 'a positive antipathy' towards the built environment 'unless it is ancient.'[40] They must also be prepared to confront the related assumption 'that God made the country and Man made the town, and that the former is good, and worthy of reverence, while the latter is a regrettable necessity to be escaped from.'

If Ward and his colleagues had rising doubts about the values carried by the word 'heritage,' so too did the director of the Civic Trust, a voluntary association formed to protect and improve the urban environment, and which backed the urban studies initiative. In 2003 I talked with Michael Middleton, who had been director of the Civic Trust at the time. He recalled that the word 'heritage' had really seemed to take off in 1972, when the Council of Europe announced plans to celebrate 1975 as European Architectural Heritage Year. The Civic Trust was appointed to create and administer a series of events to mark the year in Britain: as part of the process, the first 'heritage centres' were set up in Faversham, York and Chester. Middleton also remembered how quickly the word had gone into wider circulation. Soon enough companies started offering 'Heritage' moth repellant and 'Heritage' ties, the latter bearing designs taken from the roof bosses of Westminster Abbey. Yet it was not from any professional fear of trivialisation that Middleton quickly became convinced that the designation 'heritage' was going to be 'a bloody nuisance.' He came to this conclusion because the term marked a new emphasis in public policy and therefore also threatened to redefine the activities of the Civic Trust, which had always been concerned not to appear backward-looking in its approach or 'preservationist at all costs.'

One person who appears to have had no such reservations about the new concept was the daughter of Barbara Cartland, a considerable lady who, on marrying Earl Spencer, came to be known as

Raine, Countess of Dartmouth. Now remembered as the stepmother of Princess Diana, she was a forceful committee lady in the 1970s. She served on the board of the recently founded British Tourist Authority (established in 1969) and she also chaired the British executive committee of European Architectural Heritage Year.

For administrative purposes associated with that occasion, Dartmouth argued that the urban studies initiative should be subsumed under the rubric of 'heritage.' The initiators resisted this suggestion, arguing that the class-ridden, past-orientated and spectacular perspective implied by this word was exactly what they were trying to escape. They, however, were the losers, and so too was the Civic Trust.

It was with the memory of these developments in mind that Ward started talking less than respectfully about 'the heritage industry.' His criticism, as Raphael Samuel would surely have understood (he wrote admirably and most admiringly of Colin Ward),[41] was not founded on literary snobbery, metropolitan arrogance or high-table contempt for amateur appreciations of the past. It was provoked by direct experience of the extent to which State-imposed relabelling could transform, and in some respects also undermine, the activities it claimed to advance. This, surely, is where the critical perspective should continue to reside—at least partly within the conservation project itself.

PW
May 2008
www.patrickwright.net

Acknowledgements

While this book has been written at a considerable distance from the beleaguered academic world in which I began to consider its themes, I have not had to work in frustrating isolation. My special thanks are due to the following people who have taken time to read and comment on some or all of the essays in this book: Michael Bommes, Richard Johnson, Cora Kaplan, Paul L. Harrison, James Donald, Bob West, Claire Lawton, Ferenc Fehér, Agnes Heller, Colin Mercer, David Held and Neil Belton.

The Institute of Historical Research has (for a small fee) allowed me to use its portals as an august kind of Tradesman's Entrance to the lending facilities of the University of London Library. Together with Birmingham University's Centre for Contemporary Cultural Studies, I would also like to acknowledge History Workshop (the forum as distinct from the journal), Comedia and the South Place Ethical Society for providing independent discussions which, in one way or another over the last few years, have helped me forward.

I have been most fortunate in having the collaboration of Andrzej Krauze over the period in which this book was written. My thanks to him for the drawings which do so much more than illustrate my essays.

I have incurred further debts while preparing the new edition. I would like to thank Neal Ascherson, who has drawn a number of more recent texts to my attention, Andrzej Krauze who unearthed copies of the original drawings and a few previously unused ones too, and Luciana O'Flaherty and Matthew Cotton at Oxford University Press. I am also grateful to Tim Putnam, for organizing and editing the 'Conversation' here included as an appendix.

PW

1985 and 2008

A Note on the Text

In preparing this new edition, I have been mindful of the extent to which the book belongs to the arguments of its time and is therefore not really mine to adjust. I have made some factual and stylistic corrections, and deleted a few asides that should not have survived into the first edition. New material is confined to the preface and also to the appended conversation with Tim Putnam, first published in the journal *Block* in 1989, which reviews some of the debates that followed publication of the first edition, and also anticipates arguments pursued in this book's successor, *A Journey Through Ruins*. It should be recorded that Miss May Alice Savidge, whose story is told in Chapter 6, died in 1993, leaving her transported house unfinished. The building was passed on to a relation, who has since completed the restoration and opened Ware Hall House as a bed and breakfast establishment. It has become a well-liked addition to Wells-Next-the-Sea, increasingly listed among the town's attractions. On a less agreeable note, I must also acknowledge that Miss Hilda Murrell, the murdered rose-breeder and conservationist of Shrewsbury, was not killed in the interests of British state security as I speculated, following Tam Dalyell MP, in the wake of the Falklands war. The falsity of this echoing conspiracy theory was finally proved in 2005, when the actual killer was convicted.

1

Introduction:
Everyday Life, Nostalgia
and the National Past

To articulate the past historically does not mean to
recognise it 'the way it really was' (Ranke). It means
to seize hold of a memory as it flashes up at a moment
of danger.

Walter Benjamin

1979 is well remembered as the year in which Margaret Thatcher
became Prime Minister of Great Britain. But 1979 was also the year
of a far lesser return to the old nation, for one day that summer
I made my own somewhat uncertain way through the arrival hall
at Heathrow having spent some five years living in North America,
mostly in Vancouver.

I had missed the Callaghan years in their entirety, but as a resident
of British Columbia I had seen the early phases of a Social Credit
administration which would soon be gaining more praise than either
Reagan or Thatcher from Milton Friedman and his fellows, as they
looked around to find something approaching worldly corroboration
for their monetarist economic theories. Was I equipped with foresight
as I stepped off that plane? I can scarcely answer in the affirmative,
not least because my overwhelming sense at that time was of reeling
with distance from a society which seemed to be making not just a
virtue but a new set of political principles out of hindsight. In short,
I felt as if I had stumbled inadvertently into some sort of anthropological museum.

I remember reading Tom Nairn's essay on 'The English Literary
Intelligentsia' shortly after my return and being especially struck by
the following remark which Nairn quotes in passing from Bernard
Bergonzi: 'As a cultural phenomenon the country has all the pathos
and unreality of an Indian reservation, full of busily cultivated
and exhibited native crafts and customs.'[1] Bergonzi may well take

a patronising view of Indian reservations, but the England of his description was certainly recognisable as the country to which I had returned.

Here indeed was Akenfield; here was Watership Down. I remember being impressed by the ritualised and highly mannered style of silent interaction forming the behavioural norm on a commuter train I took from Paddington station in the first year of Thatcher's Britain (fields full of dead elms). I recall visiting Fonthill in Wiltshire and finding that the artificial green world built by William Beckford in the late eighteenth century was being carefully re-established (if only in an old stable court) by Bernard Nevill, the designer of Liberty's fabrics who appears to have moved from the evocative (and doubtless also lucrative) world of reanimated William Morris patterns to become the custodian of English exotica in the more tangible form of culturally resonant real estate.

I remember renewing my acquaintance—one which had never been deep or habitual—with BBC Radio 4 and its extraordinary current affairs programmes. After yet another episode of 'The Archers' comes the conversational programme which brings us gently back to the real world. I recall one such documentary programme in which the views of a somewhat perplexed west-country smallholder (no representative of modern agribusiness, this stalwart character was himself thickset in aspic) who wanted to plough his field were held up against the arguments of articulate preservationists, eager to defend the last traces of some or other sacred remains. While the precise details escape recollection I remember that—whether it was Roman, Mediaeval or Elizabethan—this precious trace of England was already only visible from an aeroplane at times when the shadows were long.

I had come back to a country which was full of precious and imperilled traces—a closely held iconography of what it is to be English— all of them appealing in one covertly projective way or another to the historical and sacrosanct identity of the nation. Moreover, and whatever the contemporary stylisation may suggest, these were not simply residues that 'we,' the remaining inhabitants of this old country, were lucky enough to find still surviving around us. The national past is above all a *modern* past and, as the events of recent years have indicated very clearly, it is defined not just in relation to the general disappointment of earlier historical expectation, but also and more pointedly around the leading tensions of the contemporary political situation. Thus if 1979 was the year in which I started to think about the modern past and its national manifestation in British society, it was also the year in which Margaret Thatcher started to project her governmental mission not in terms of the merely political (and therefore changeable) consensus of liberal democracy but in the transcendent and eternalised measure of an imperial national identity which she alone could secure against the series of indefinite but nonetheless persistent threats which have played that conveniently demonic role in her public rhetoric.[2] While seeking to clarify some of the ways in which the past has been secured as a cultural presence in modern Britain, the essays in this book also try to follow this political development and to identify some of its more important preconditions.

In discussions over the last few years I have been accused of both anecdotalism and excessively abstract generalisation. As it happens, this book is made up of essays which I consider to be *occasional* rather than anecdotal in their orientation; they are focussed on particular eventualities in which considerable (if not always wider) significance can be found. The occasional essay offers a possibility and style of critique which I like; it has also suited my circumstances in these busy and untidy post-academic years. However, if the main six essays are linked by their preoccupation with a shared set of themes, there is also a recognisably theoretical perspective running through the book. My starting point here was hardly subtle. Borrowing an idiom from Tony Wilden (whose 'Imaginary Canadian' is different and has far greater adequacy) I postulated the existence of the 'Imaginary Briton'—as if the whole of British society was frozen over in an arresting display of the past: as if all social consciousness had been merged in the unitary symbolism of a publicly vaunted national identity.[3] While there is certainly a tendency to displace political tensions into the unifying perspectives of a dominant culture which is expressed above all in terms of the nation, it didn't take me long to realise that the 'Imaginary Briton' was a notion that really belonged to the airport arrival hall. In the eye of the returnee everything may seem identically familiar, identically strange. But this does not necessarily mean that the scene is actually all sewn up.

As the 'Imaginary Briton' disintegrated—becoming no more than a gestural metaphor which I still use occasionally if only for nostalgic reasons—I began looking to a number of theoretical sources in search of a more adequate analysis and understanding. I was impressed by

Ernst Bloch's ideas of 'non-synchronous' culture and utopian 'hope.'
I found Zygmunt Bauman's analysis of 'historical memory' useful,
and I also looked into Habermas—his work on rationality, communication and the lifeworld. But if all these influences were important,
I came across what would become my main source late in 1982 when
I read Agnes Heller's *A Theory of History*. Here was an analysis which
talked about historical consciousness in connection with everyday life
rather than either the perspectives of an insufficient class analysis (in
which economic position would be automatically reflected in consciousness were it not for 'ideology') or, coming in from a different
angle, the methodologies of historiographical research. The connection was already a live one from my point of view, and from here
things developed fairly steadily.

In some ways this seemed a strange influence. Heller's work, after
all, had been developed within the troubled tradition of George Lukács
and while this was evidently a tradition which would outlast its crude
Althusserian caricature, I had always felt it to be excessively austere
in its philosophical generality. Its positions on totality, expression
and History (with a very big H) seemed remote from—if not plainly
antagonistic to—the kind of empirical focus which I recognised as
my own. As it turned out, however, Heller herself had expressed such
reservations, and with far more consequential results than I realised at
the time. Heller's work is indeed philosophically expressed, but it also
provides an interpretative framework through which the national past
can be understood as far more than 'dominant ideology' and without disregarding its ambivalences or detail. Thus while my reading of
Heller pervades all the essays in this book, there are some preliminary
things to be said about this framework itself. While I have tried to avoid
unnecessary obscurity in this Introduction I am not without sympathy
for the reader who, finding theoretical writing heavy going, prefers to
turn a few pages at this point and to start with Chapter 2.

Everyday Life

Fairly late in a century which, in Guy Konopnicki's words, has already
seen the Balkans invade the entire planet, there need be little hesitation in granting that the unity of the nation is achieved at the cost of
considerable mystification.[4] Despite this, however, one cannot hope
to maintain an adequate relationship to the events of recent history

while also concluding from this mystification that the nation is simply unreal—a culturally derived illusion existing only to obscure a truth which continues most resolutely to reside elsewhere. This has been the crude Marxist view—that the nation is so much 'bourgeois ideology' laid on through a dominant media in a determined effort to obscure the deeper realities (the general interests) of the class struggle. I take it that there is little need to dwell on the inadequacies of this 'analysis,' persistent as it has proved to be.

The problem is not just that in dismissing the nation as a big fix such an approach leaves itself with absolutely nothing to say of those millions who have (with whatever ambivalence) lived, argued, hoped and died by the nation—except, of course, that they were all identically benighted dupes of the ruling illusion.[5] While there is indeed something resembling an omission here, this line of argument also asks us to collude with something far worse than any mere oversight: it asks us to accept a deformed perspective in which history, far from just failing to conform to the interests of its emancipatory inhabitants, also ceases to bear any reasonable relationship to their own self-understanding. If the culture of the nation is only so much wool, then the eyes over which it is pulled must belong to sheep. And so everything disappears, except the possibility of farming.

Cultural manipulation pervades contemporary British society—not least in endless public invocations of the national identity and tradition—and there is a lot to be said about it. But no value can remain to a critical analysis which has to define people as passive (if not always totally stupefied) in order to protect its theoretical core from crumbling on exposure to the very history in which it would offer a supposedly more active and democratic future. So the integrative capacity of the nation comes soon enough to pose another question, this one concerned not with falsity or illusion but with the actuality of the nation—with its practical *truth* as a cultural formation of enormous historical influence and power. What is the actual basis for the nation in contemporary experience and how can the forms of self-understanding which it promotes come to be shared by people of strikingly different situation and circumstance? I ask this question with specific regard to the sense of history, tradition and cultural identity which plays such an influential part in the British national imagination.

The essays in this book turn to a theory of everyday life in order to define the main characteristics of a vernacular and informal sense of history which is certainly not exhausted by the stately display of tradition and national identity in which it finds such forceful and loaded public expression. My argument does not seek to justify the national past by alluding to its popular basis in everyday consciousness. Neither is it my aim to suggest that the symbolism of the nation might in itself be rearticulated in a democratic or socialist direction (the kind of rearticulation advocated by some 'discourse'-orientated theoreticians and, more generally, associated with the constitutionalist pragmatism of leading Labour politicians). While the connection with everyday life certainly offers some explanatory account of the national past, it should also be seen more pointedly as its *project*—as the connection in which the prevailing symbolism of this old imperial nation works to establish its own over-arching constituency of support.

Customary intellectual usage identifies everyday life rather vaguely as mundane, as the world of regularity, habit and routine—a familiar and pragmatic world which, under normal circumstances, is taken for granted, neither questioned nor especially valued. As Karel Kosik has argued more precisely, everyday life is not a matter of privacy over public life, or of the profane as opposed to any 'exalted official life.' It is 'above all the *organising* of people's individual lives into every day: the replicability of their life functions is fixed in the replicability of everyday, in the time schedule for every day.'[6] Everyday life is replicable and pragmatic then, but it also has its special occasions, its rationality, its wisdom and, to the crucial extent that it is not limited to its role of social reproduction, its subjective and cognitive surpluses. Thus everyday life is not merely what stands in contrast to 'the unusual, the festive, the special, or to History.' The habitual idea which defines the everyday as routine and contrasts it with History (conceived as the exceptional or the significant) is in Kosik's words, 'itself the result of a certain mystification.' In more positive terms Kosik goes on to describe everyday life as follows:[7]

> In the everyday, the activity and way of life are *transformed* into an instinctive, subconscious, unconscious and unreflected mechanism of acting and living: things, people, movements, tasks, environment, the world—they are not perceived in their originality and authenticity, they are not tested and discovered but they *simply are there*, and are accepted as inventory, as components of a known world. The everyday appears as the night of indifference, of the mechanical and the instinctive, i.e. as the world of familiarity. At the same time, the everyday is a world

whose dimensions and potentialities an individual can control and calculate with his abilities and resources. In the everyday, everything is 'at hand' and an individual can realise his intentions. This is why it is a world of confidence, familiarity, and routine actions. Death, sickness, births, successes and failures are all accountable events of everyday life. In the everyday, the individual develops relations on the basis of *his own* experience, *his own* possibilities, *his own* activity, and therefore considers the everyday reality to be his own world.

Everyday life is the historically conditioned framework in which the imperatives of natural sustenance (eating, sleeping...) come to be socially determined: it is in the intersubjectivity of everyday life that human self-reproduction is welded to the wider process of social reproduction. Thus while everyday life may well be naturalised and taken for granted—indeed, while it may form a kind of second nature in which people orientate themselves without deliberate reflection—it is in reality socially formed and complex. At the heart of everyday life, therefore, is the interdependency of person and society. The social world always already exists to confront the people who are born into it, and it places demands which must be met if people are to make their way. There are values and norms to be appropriated and internalised, institutions and things to be understood, language and customs with which to come to terms. But if subjectivity is socially determined in this way, society also needs to be lived and put into action: its reproduction is dependent on a constitutive subjectivity, and determination can therefore be said to cut both ways.

This interdependency of subject and society is central to Heller's definition of everyday life as *objectification*: a process in which the subject is both externalised and constantly recreated—in which the social determination of subjectivity becomes in its turn (and through the agency of the subject) constitutive of society. Heller's theory of everyday life was first outlined nearly twenty years ago in *Everyday Life*, a book which stands closely and not at all unproblematically associated with Lukács's *Ontology* and *Aesthetics*—in particular with a teleological and essentialist conception of 'species-Being' which has been roundly criticised in recent years.[8] It is all to the good, therefore, that Heller—herself no blind follower of Lukács—should recently have returned to make a revised analysis of everyday life in a long essay called 'Everyday life, rationality of reason, rationality of intellect.'[9] In this later essay the Hegelian vocabulary is still present, but the implicit philosophy of history has been discarded. Similarly, the idea of 'spe-cies-Being' has lost its evaluative character, now being redefined as an empirical human universal in the open form, say, of rationality. In this introductory discussion I shall draw from both early and later writings with the aim not of elaborating or evaluating the theory per se, but of using it more strategically to trace the possible sources of a shared sense of history in contemporary everyday life.

For Agnes Heller everyday life is not an integrated system, but rather a heterogeneous complex of lived relationships. Everyday life is divided and formed in accordance with the developing division of labour; but while everyone belongs to a class, for example (and it should be stressed that Heller's is not a theory which is in any sense ignorant of class domination), the lived relationships of everyday life are not in themselves class relationships. The crucial point, then, is that while everyday life is indeed moulded and delimited by the social structure, it does not in itself simply express this social structure. Everyday life follows its own form, and Heller's concern is both to define this form and also to show the ways in which it is historically and politically determined.

Everyday life is always experienced in relation to the immediate environment. It is of pragmatic orientation and possessed of its own modalities—its own experience of time and space, for example, and its own patterns of presence and of contact between people (these are primarily face to face). It has its own modes of thought, its specific use of language and experience of institutions, and it has its own relation-ships to the norms and customs of external authority. Everyday life also has its own subjects—its own varieties of 'I,' 'we' and 'they'—for the experience of being one in a limited group (family, street, school, work place, village etc) is among its most basic terms. As Heller puts it in her earlier study, everyday life is above all *situated*. It always occurs in relation to a person's immediate locality: 'the terrain of a king's everyday life is not his country but his court.'[10] There is no total con-finement to this situation, however, for it is not as if everyday life were ever—even in pre-modern and more localised conditions—exhausted by its immediate locality or as if it amounted only to millions of little localisms. The point instead is that everyday life always starts with the person living it and that the anthropocentric perspectives of this start-ing point influence those aspects of everyday life which have a more general or universal aspect.

Particularity and Individuality

The fundamental distinction of Heller's *Everyday Life*, at least for my purposes, concerns the subject or personality of everyday life and is made between *particularity* and *individuality*. Far from representing different types of personality, particularity and individuality are initially theorised as different stances towards the social world which coexist within each personality.

Particularity may begin with nature, with the particular qualities and dispositions with which a person is born, but it doesn't stay there for long. As these endowments are cultivated and developed in accordance with the imperatives of the environment, the motivations and also the characteristically self-preserving viewpoint of particularity are also defined. This particularistic viewpoint follows necessarily from the fact that one perceives and seeks to manipulate the world into which one is born in a perspective which takes oneself as its origin. As a combination of qualities, motivations, feelings and viewpoint, particularity is not defined as a primordial self-interest which people must outgrow as they become adults. Heller goes to considerable lengths to argue that no human being can exist without some degree of particularistic motivation. She also insists, convincingly enough, that the particularistic viewpoint could not be defined without conditions of intersubjective generality: in other words, it is cultural rather than merely psychological.

In its cultural dimension the particularistic viewpoint includes recognition of those who share the same integration: thus, if it can be called solipsistic at all, its solipsism is one that rapidly extends from 'I' to 'we.' In Heller's words, the opposition between '*our* family, *our* town, *our* people, on the one hand, and "others" on the other hand—*their* family, town...—is as real and natural for the person as self-motivation itself.' Particularity therefore takes two related forms: it applies to the interests and endowments of the self but it can also be held in common as the cultural perspective of the group in which one comes to self-understanding. 'The "we" is that via which "I" am.'[11] This idea of a collectivity, of an integration with its sense of both insiders and outsiders, constituted *at the same level* as the personality is obviously worth registering firmly in an analysis concerned to understand the nation as a form of integration. So also is the idea (perhaps more emergent than fully expressed in Heller's early book) of particularism as a cultural perspective on social relations which are developing rapidly and with a disturbing impact on the habituated if not always precisely traditional ways of the everyday settlement in which one has grown up.

A man—and this figure is a caricature because no one is entirely particularistic—relating to himself and the world in a particularistic way does so primarily through *identification*. Motivated above all by the urge for self-preservation, he selects from the everyday environment in a way that suits his own particular disposition and viewpoint. In doing this he identifies himself with the norms and prescriptions of the environment in a direct and uncomplicated way. At the same time he develops and affirms a 'we' consciousness which, lacking as it does any critical distance from the given terms of his everyday community, is simply a generalised extension of particularistic 'I' consciousness to a group (family, town, nation and so on). This man may indeed swagger a bit. He may, in the example of Heller's *A Theory of Feelings*, claim that 'I am the best father, because I have brought up my children to become good businessmen or good noblemen or good Christians.' He is 'always right'; he does 'everything well' as long as the eye of others smiles back at him in agreement and approval, and his achievements in these two areas are only matched by his 'innocence'—an 'innocence' which is unshakeable precisely because, from the particularistic stance, authority and responsibility are always external. Far from agonising internally, the particularistic man 'obtains his justification from direct identification with the system of customs.'[12] And if his particular system of customs is threatened or questioned, the defensive response may certainly extend to bigoted demonisation and violence.

In contrast to this the individual stance assumes the existence of a critical distance between the person relating to the world in this way and his or her given qualities and environment. It is not just that a woman acting in an individual way is able to choose between alternatives, but that in doing so she leaves the mark of her own individuality on the choice which she makes.[13] This, according to Heller, is what differentiates 'autonomy'—properly autonomous and therefore individual consciousness—from a mere consciousness of alternatives. The individual stance, therefore, involves approaching one's own life—and indeed one's own particularity—as a conscious object and making a selection from the system of customs provided by the social environment. This selection is made on the basis of deliberately chosen values (ethical, moral, political) and it is accompanied by an equally conscious ordering and deployment of the particular cultural and personal disposition from which the person starts. It is quite possible, as Heller stresses, for a person to develop and follow an individual hierarchy of values which contradicts the dominant norms or values prevailing in the world at large.[14]

Everyday life combines the particular and individual stances, and for this reason it is not surprising that many of its characteristic formations are expressive of both. Thus, for example, Heller points to the experience of '*home*' which plays such a prominent part in everyday life, and which (as we will see repeatedly in the essays to follow) certainly also provides one of its primary and most expressive symbols. 'Home' is that 'firm position' which is 'integral to the average everyday life.' 'Home' is the familiar point at the centre of everyday life and as such it is not just a matter of bricks, mortar and a door to close on the world.[15] Without resorting to any closed essentialism, Heller stresses the intensity of human relations that are to be found here; she mentions the sense of security and also remarks that 'home' is the hub on which the everyday sense of space converges. Yet 'home' also has a more subjective resonance, expressing the coherence of a person's self-understanding and what Heller has elsewhere called the 'emotional household.'[16] Her point is that the subject of everyday life is constantly re-evaluating and rearranging itself—a process which is centrally concerned with the relationship of inner and outer, with 'the problem of the unity of the inner life and of feeling finding a "home" in the "world".'[17] Particularistic interests are harmonised (or otherwise) with the customs, values and norms of external authority, options are assessed in the light of conscience, experiences are remembered and reinterpreted in the light of age, feelings are framed and arranged (Heller speaks of 'gardening' in connection with the affects, of the 'education' and 'housekeeping of feelings') in a way that fits them to the historically defined tasks and demands of the external world.[18] 'Home' is therefore not just evocative of the familiar (if often agonising and also brutal) disposition of personalities in which so much everyday life is experienced; it is also the interior space in which some recognition can be given to endowments and potentials which have no opportunity for realisation in the world as it is outside—the space, indeed, in which disregarded potentials and needs may themselves find some limited 'home' in the world.

If the symbolic mobility of 'home' recalls the poem by Charles Olson in which a man carries a furnished house—'light as a basket'—on his head, it can also raise critical questions in relation to the rest of the world.[19] In this regard 'home' has a philosophical resonance, and not just in the Bachelardian sense of a 'poetics of space.' Heller quotes Novalis's saying that 'philosophy is homesickness': a saying which suggests that while the utopian symbolism of 'home' has certainly been used to romanticise the patriarchal family, to idealise domestic drudgery and to vaunt a national heritage of 'stately homes,' it also engages meanings and aspirations at the level of everyday life which are of a far more open-ended, critical and searching kind than any merely muck-raking definition of 'ideology' would be able to accommodate.[20]

If individuality is the name given to autonomous and principled decisions or actions, there are severe historical and political constraints limiting its development. As Heller writes:[21]

> It is a tough world into which we are born and in which we have to make our way. In this tough world, people work, eat, drink (usually less than they need) and make love (usually by the rules); people rear their children to play a part in this tough world and timorously guard the nook they have managed to corner for themselves; the order of priorities, the scale of values in our everyday life is largely taken over ready-made, it is calibrated in accordance with position in society, and little in it is moveable. There is little opportunity to 'cultivate' our abilities beyond, at best, narrow confines.

But while the development of autonomous individuality is limited by such a scarcity of opportunity, the upheavals of modernity have not simply reduced possibilities even further. Heller argues that particularity was indeed first made into an ideological principle with the development of bourgeois society—a society which, as she claims, made a value of egoism and which rationalised self-interest, defining it as in the long run identical with the general interest (this being Heller's definition of what is commonly known as 'bourgeois individualism'). This development is far from finished with, for the ideological enlistment of particularity continues not just in the moving rhetoric of demagogic nationalism but in the contemporary development which Raymond Williams has recently called 'mobile privatisation'—the cultivation in a decaying and abandoned public world of a life-style which prospers

in private, moveable and self-enclosed units ('homes'), and which owes its shape to a number of factors including the contemporary use of television and personal credit and mortgage facilities.[22]

However, this elevation of particularity to the level of general social principle is not all that takes place with the coming of bourgeois society. Indeed, Heller argues that the prospects for individuality were also vastly extended in the economic and cultural transformations that inaugurated western modernity. Where pre-capitalist society was tendentially stable and past-orientated, capitalist and industrial society is dynamic, future-orientated and full not just of disruption but also of new possibility. As traditional integrations were burst asunder, together with localised forms of community and status-definition, the apparently 'natural' correlation between people and the external norms of the social order governing their situation also comes apart. As Heller puts it:[23]

> Bourgeois society is the first 'pure' society; natural or blood kinship no longer determines the path of the individual. At the same time it is a dynamic society, and increasingly so; the tasks to be dealt with change continually from the point of view of every stratum and class, often even within the space of a generation. With the disintegration of community ties the individual becomes an 'accidental' individual (his class—or stratum—affiliation is of accidental character) but, at the same time he becomes a free individual as well, at least potentially.

While a dramatic increase of social insecurity follows in the wake of these transformations, there is also an increase in potential and possibility. As Heller writes, the 'emotional household' becomes individual—it is no longer a matter of the affects conforming to the prescriptions of customs and norms, but is instead now connected to the conscious evaluation of opportunities, inborn qualities and capacities.[24] But if this is the epoch of the 'problematic individual'—of anomie, a new awareness of 'dichotomy between potentiality and actuality,' and of the disintegration of traditional structures of social security—it is also the period in which universalistic values like freedom, equality and humankind come to be articulated along the heavily contested perspectives of a developing democratic logic. If consciousness is no longer primarily a matter of conformity to the prescriptions of a naturalised hierarchy of norms, and if cultural particularity and the social dynamics of a rapidly transforming world tend to conflict more sharply, the Enlightenment nevertheless lends strength to the 'internal' (although still intersubjective) authority which Heller calls *conscience*, with its evaluative and critical relation to external prescriptions.[25] Thus, and along with all the upheavals, there comes the celebrated and emancipatory claim that everyone is equally possessed of reason—this being the Enlightenment project which Heller incorporates into her own theory of rationality, equality and democracy.

Everyday Historical Consciousness

In Heller's analysis, everyday life has its own forms of historical consciousness. However, far from being concerned with establishing 'the way it really was,' Heller writes that 'historical consciousness is the consciousness of historicity.'[26] Historicity is a key concept in recent social and political theory, and Heller has herself made use of Alain Touraine's definition of historicity as a society's capacity to act on itself and determine the order of its representations. For Touraine 'historicity' is a 'symbolic capacity' which enables a society to 'construct a system of knowledge together with technical tools which it can use to intervene in its own functioning,'[27] but in Heller's conception 'historicity' also has a more existential dimension, relating as it does to fundamental questions such as 'where have we come from, what are we, where are we going?' Holding that these questions are concerns of everyday life, Heller sets out to characterise what she introduces as 'everyday historical consciousness.'

While claiming that 'everyday historical consciousness' forms the foundation for the more abstract and disciplined knowledges of his-

toriography and the philosophy of history, Heller nevertheless argues
that the two levels of knowledge remain qualitatively distinct. Just as
Gramsci could argue that everyone is a philosopher without claiming that everyone studies Aristotle, Heller's assertion that in everyday life we are all historians and philosophers of history obviously
does not imply that everyone is an academic specialist. In defining the
texture of everyday historical consciousness, Heller points above all
to the prominence of narratives. More specifically, she remarks that
everyday life is full of *stories* and that these (as Walter Benjamin also
knew) are concerned with being-in-the-world rather than abstractly
defined truth. Even when they are told of times past, stories are
judged and shaped by their relevance to what is happening now, and
in this sense their allegiance is unashamedly to the present. Stories
are repeatable and they make sense above all in terms of their *endings*. More than this, stories are assessed and appreciated in terms of
their *authenticity*, and 'the problem of authenticity is distinct from the
problems of objectivity and true knowledge'—indeed 'authenticity
and truth may collide,' and if this happens we often 'stubbornly resist'
the truth 'because we cannot "unbind the spell" of the "original".'[28]
While the authentic story may well negotiate with the truth, teasing it
and putting it at a distance, there are limits here and it is at the same
time unlikely to be flagrantly false. The essential thing for a story is
that it should be *plausible*; indeed, plausibility is defined as 'the veri-
similitude of everyday life.'[29] The authentic story is therefore *evocative*
in character, and by this Heller means that it expresses the personality
as a whole rather than the more specialised and intellectually disciplined subject of historiography.[30]

In Heller's account stories play a prominent part in the everyday
activity of *making sense*.[31] They help to bring things into the order of
our world—to thematise events, making them explicable in a way
which also defines our present relation to them. Making sense is a
fundamental activity of everyday life and, while it can obviously lead
to different conclusions in different situations, it tends to follow the
same basic form. It works, for example, by *naming* things and events,
and it accounts for phenomena in terms, say, of *analogy* or *causality*. It
explains happenings in terms of the machinations of *fate* or in terms
of voluntary *intention*, and it has a powerful sense of what is *probable* or
possible—'irrespective of whether the event happened in the past or is
going to happen in the future.' Similarly, we make sense of things by

employing *general sketches*—maxim-like formulations which work like proverbs, preparing our comprehension of the world and implying an evaluation as they do so.

It is also worth mentioning Zygmunt Bauman in this connection, for he has recently stressed the connections between what he calls historical memory and the everyday process of 'making sense.' The historical memory of a group, as he writes, is institutionally carried and it certainly doesn't always surface 'to the level of verbal communication': it 'finds its expression in the group's proclivities to some rather than other behavioural responses' and 'is not necessarily recognised by the group as a particular concept of the past.' Embedded as it is in everyday consciousness, historical memory is 'determined by the very structure of the life-world,' and for Bauman this means among other things that it follows an interpretative schema—one which is 'daily reinforced by micro-social individual experience'—which explains sociopolitical processes by locating a self-interested group which is motivated to promote and benefit from them.[32] Thus, as Bauman sees it, everyday life can sustain those historical (rather than merely retrograde, as Bauman insists) 'memories of class' in which a nineteenth-century model of class-struggle lives on to inform understanding of a contemporary world in which exploitation—courtesy, not least, of the welfare state—takes different forms.

But if everyday historical consciousness has a persistent and fairly continuous formal repertoire, it is certainly not just a static and unchanging characteristic of everyday life. To put this differently, everyday historical consciousness is not merely a formal matter of style or expression. It also includes a sense of historical development or change as it impinges on everyday life: a '*sense of historical existence*' as Heller calls it. While defining the historical transformation of everyday life Heller writes that 'in a homogeneous and static world humans usually accept the ready-made reality without further ado. "Making sense" is a mere subsumption.'[33] If this static pre-industrial world with its traditional and external hierarchy of values ever existed in a pure state, modernity has certainly seen its disruption. If meaning was once 'given' and no specific effort or intention was needed 'for making sense of one's *own* life,' this has changed with the development of the capitalist and industrialised economy.

In modernity the forms of life are open to interpretation and 'Man's life is no longer written in the stars.'[34] Society is no longer traditional or past-orientated, and in its unstable equilibrium it now looks forward along the perspectives of a dream of progress which itself seems progressively deranged. Heller revives Feuerbach's fast-moving figure of Captain Forward to describe the dynamic and future-orientated nature of modernity, suggesting that his is indeed a hard ship on which to be sailing as it plunges along its uncertain course. Everything that may have been stable is caught up into transformation and development; all that is solid, as Marshall Berman has recently reminded us with such brilliance, melts into air.[35] No wonder that the everyday 'sense of historical existence' becomes progressively anxious, searching more intently for answers which—in the dislocated experience of modernity—seem to be less and less readily forthcoming. No wonder that 'historical memory' should sometimes seem to slip out of kilter with the present, continuously raising ghosts and anxiously holding old answers up against the disorientating light of new questions. No wonder either that while Heller's *Everyday Life* attends especially to the bourgeois enlistment of particularity as an egoistic ideological principle, the social upheavals of developing bourgeois society should seem to emphasise the second meaning of particularism as *the cultural form in which a group faces the destabilising demands of social transformation.*

It is this sense of particularism (ie not a merely psychological one) which I take up from Heller's work and explore in this book. While I prefer to leave closer definition of the concept to the empirically focussed essays which follow this introduction, it should nevertheless be stressed from the start that particularism varies in its relation to social development from one group or situation to the next. Thus, while the particularism of marginal or subordinated groups may be closely and defensively held *against* the political and social mainstream, it is characteristic of dominant particularism to permeate the fabric of social life as if it were a universal legitimising principle in itself—the bourgeois-imperial sense of national identity and belonging is often projected as the absolute essence of a social life which it also places conveniently beyond question.

For Heller, the upheavals of modernity are not simply to be assimilated to the developing capitalist economy. While there is no denying the massive impact of capitalist development, these transformations also testify to the (limited and contested) development of democracy and to the disintegration of religion as a meaningful and legitimating world-view along with its only partial replacement by science. Certainly, the impact on everyday life as it is caught up in this unprecedented scale of transformation is both formidable and complex. The traditional hierarchy of socially binding values is eroded and replaced by a far from morally regulated emphasis on the overriding bourgeois value of success.[36] As for the self-evident world of everyday life, this seems to lose its significance and meaning. To indicate this, Heller cites modernist developments in art, music and the novel which, at about the time of the First World War, severed the connections linking these forms or genres to traditional everyday modalities (styles of realism or systems of tonality) in gestures of revolt which dismissed the everyday as empty of unity or meaning—altogether without significance. The same transformations have their influence on the everyday sense of historical existence: with the changing status of everyday life, History can indeed seem to hang overhead like a whimsical power in the air.[37] Its impact is unquestionable but, like everything else of any actual influence, its source is to be found outside an increasingly devalued everyday life. Thus dawns the era of anxious irresponsibility in which everyone seems both helpless and innocent—not just of what happens to themselves, but of the fate of others both near and also at the farthest reaches of an increasingly instantaneous world system.

Crucial to Heller's explanation of these changes in the experience of everyday life is the argument that science, as an abstract and universal form of knowledge, implies no lifeworld and that it therefore owes nothing to the everyday life over which it nevertheless presides as legitimating world-view. To indicate this partial devaluation of everyday life which comes with the rise of science Heller cites Kant who (perhaps already against his better judgement) could still refer to contemplation of the starlit sky as a source of knowledge. The legitimation of everyday life achieved by science is significantly different from that which existed under the religious world-view. Where religion legitimised both norms and rules, Heller suggests that science can only secure rules. It can demystify and provide a great increase in knowledge, but it has no moral capacity and cannot give meaningful sanction either to life or to the social order (with its differentiation of groups and their experience of everyday life) in the same way that religion could. In its rationalisation of social practice science makes new demands on the subject of everyday life. Hence, as Heller puts it, the marionette syndrome characterising so much modern activity—an experience of specialised activity which has no connection with a person's individuality and seems entirely dictated from outside.

Science doesn't imply a lifeworld; it also draws knowledge away from everyday life into the specialised spheres of reproducible know-how, only returning it to everyday life in the form of rationalised and mechanical practice. In these transformations everyday life may well seem to lose its adequacy and necessity as experience. To grow old, in Heller's poignant example (itself a rather romantic ode to the individual producer of the preindustrial craft world), is no longer to grow wise: in a world where skill tends to be replaced by entirely reproducible technique to age is only to become redundant and used up—some kind of exhausted relic at best. As Heller puts it, 'if our actions do not throw roots down into our character as a whole, we are bereft of soul, and life slips through our fingers without having been lived at all.'

As a universal form of knowledge, science also tends to devalue the local and situated aspects of everyday life. People encounter science above all in its institutionalised forms—rationalised places of work, education, and the bureaucratic agencies of the welfare state. As an ability to work within the terms of such institutions becomes a prerequisite for survival, it becomes necessary for people to become competent (and entirely reproducible—that is, non-unique) subjects of institutional and rationalised routine. In this way people are drawn into a world that is governed by 'Research Institute facticity'—Heller's name for a consciousness which has no truck with values and which reduces rationality to mere problem-solving.[38] As for the familiar social character types deriving from the traditional division of labour, these are said to be eroded while (with meaningful world-views now being produced by specialised professionals) the fundamental socio-economic groups and classes tend to become more and more pragmatic in outlook. Heller also argues that the rise and increasing intellectualisation of science has given shape to a contemplative and non-pragmatic relation to nature—a relation to nature which has gone on to become the material for a million pastoralising adverts. Hence, perhaps, the wide and continuing appeal of the seigneurial type of 'pleasing prospect' that Raymond Williams has traced among the landowners of eighteenth century England.[39]

Modernity, in short, has seen the dislocation, the devaluation and also the disenchantment of everyday life. Habermas speaks of the 'colonisation of the lifeworld' at this juncture.[40] With Heller the issue is theorised in terms of everyday life (which, like Habermas's lifeworld is intersubjective and culturally defined) rather than the lifeworld (which Heller prefers to define—with Husserl and Schutz—as a phenomenological attitude). Similarly for Heller there can be no straightforward colonisation here, if only because everyday life was already 'colonised' by religion before its submission to science occurred. There are other substantial differences between Habermas and Heller, but for my present purposes the common ground is enough: both would agree not just that rationalisation and the accompanying dislocation of traditional forms of self-understanding has been extensive, but also that this has had a major influence on the political and cultural situation in western societies.

The Nostalgia of Everyday Life

While Heller herself is in no doubt that modernity holds—not least in the development of science—positive potentials, she argues that the transformations just sketched are widely experienced in terms of loss rather than gain. Given the dislocation of memory and traditional integration which has occurred, and given that the various (and in some cases antagonistic) futures projected within modernity seem also to have fallen like so many broken idols in its path, it is perhaps to be expected that anxious revaluation of the past should also take place. This is to say that Western modernity has its nostalgia—a nostalgia

which, while it may indeed be differentiated according to the division of labour, also testifies in more general ways to the destabilisation of everyday life. For the purposes of this introduction it remains only to indicate some of the forms taken by this nostalgia—something which is best done through discussion of a few examples.

Presenting as it does the image of a plentiful life without conflict or colliding self-interests, the idea of the golden age or the rural idyll seems always to have spoken to the constrained condition of everyday life—if only as what Heller calls a 'charming intermezzo in life's drama.'[41] This 'charming intermezzo' obviously takes different forms in different historical circumstances, and its projected freedom has doubtless always been better suited to some people than to others. In William Morris's critical utopia, to take an obvious example, the idyllic 'home' is one in which women's domestic labour goes on only scantly changed if at all—even though it finds greater respect among the brothers of the Pre-Raphaelite household.

Similar things might also be said about Stephen Graham's well-received book *The Gentle Art of Tramping*, which was first published in 1927.[42] This idealisation of 'tramping' sets out to redeem many of the activities of everyday life (eating, walking, sleeping, meeting people, preparing food, wearing chosen clothes, conversation, companionship, pragmatic knowledge and skill) by portraying them in an existential dimension rather than a social or political one; it presents them as uniquely personal rather than routine, and it does this by defining them within a contemplative relationship to nature ('the starry sky is the emblem of home') rather than in the predominantly urban situations of the modern division of labour. While Graham can certainly be ingenious in his attempt to reanimate modern everyday life (proposing, for example, the 'zigzag' walk—take the first turning to the left, the first to the right, the first to the left and so on—as a way of making the modern city declare itself anew), his anti-political 'tramping' idyll is definitely one for the upper-class adventurer: women are welcomed as long as they adopt 'rational attire ... and a stout pair of shoes,' but Graham (whose favourite tramping companion seems to have been the American poet Vachel Lindsay) makes it quite clear that he is 'not writing of the American hobo, nor of rail-roaders and beachcombers or other enemies of society—"wont works" and parasites of the charitable.'

Just as the pastoral world of Graham's tramp is idyllic, the modern past often has that idealised air of the golden age: it is formed according to the well developed perspectives of a romantic orientation which responds to modernity by asserting that the true potentialities of human development must be seen in the light of traditional (Heller speaks of 'natural,' but not in a way that implies any pre-historical state) and deeply settled communities that have already been destroyed.[43] Further definition is given to this modern past by the increasing independence of science and its effective knowledge from everyday life, for this opens a space in which a non-practical relationship to nature has developed. If, in Kant's phrase, contemplation of the 'starry heavens' no longer offers knowledge, the contemplative and non-practical relationship to nature becomes open to reformulation in, say, contemporary ideas of ruralism (ranging from high-cultural romanticism—at least in the British case—to the 'green roads' of interwar meditation and on to the desperately conjured 'ley-lines' of the 1970s' Avalon). Similarly, while everyday life is more and more dominated by the repetitive thinking demanded by various rationalised and routinised activities, the more intuitive and analogical modes of thought don't simply cease to exist—even though they too may wander off to imagine the signatures of natural meaning in the past and countryside.

So the thematic repertoire of the modern past comes to be defined in close relation to everyday life. In a world where values are in apparent disorder and where the social hierarchy has lost its settled nature, it is not so surprising that old forms of security become alluring (the upstairs/downstairs style of traditional integration where everybody in the house—servant or 'family'—has an unproblematic place at the beginning and end of every day). With the family being less solely the agent of socialisation (since the expansion of the state into new areas), the idea of the old more authoritative and sufficient family may indeed loom up in the soft-focus of the modern past. With the rationalisation and bureaucratisation of everyday life the past—especially in its imperialist dimension—becomes a theatre in which adventures of personal action can still be played out (a development which, while it can certainly testify to imperial and economic decline, also reflects the diminished radius of action available to the specialised subject of so much modern activity). In the same way, a modern interest has developed in the lost crafts of foregone times when the traditional techniques and understanding (the practical reason) of everyday life were apparently still sufficient to the world and when, as can fondly be imagined, age brought wisdom rather than meaningless decrepitude. Likewise comes a yearning for character types of the sort associated with the division of labour as it existed in the earlier stages of industrial capitalism—or before the industrial and bureaucratic extension of science. This may well be expressed in the nostalgia which, as Heller puts it, is 'a typically bourgeois feeling: the problematic individual looks back with painful yearning and respect to the non-problematic individual' of earlier times.[44] But there is also a nostalgia of the left to be found here: one which cherishes the romantic memory of a time when the working class could more easily produce its own meaningful world-view: the unproblematic community of the 'general interest.'

Many other aspects of the modern British past could be approached through Heller's analysis but I shall limit this opening sketch to a further two. The first is that the rationalised and specialised experience of contemporary everyday life gives rise to a sense of the unique—of the auratic (possessed of 'aura') object and the place or site which seems to bear meaning in itself. Far from being a merely high-cultural imposition, this emphasis on the unique is an expression of subjective surplus—of subjective experience which finds no realisation in the constrained and rationalised activities of much modern everyday life—and by now, as I will suggest in more detail, it surely forms a powerful motivation even for fairly high-cultural tourism. However, if the modern sense of the 'unique' has a strong subjective resonance, its cultural elaboration is often also directly related to a deliberate celebration of traditional everyday life, or of the customary lifeworld which is now so threatened and disregarded. Thus the classical revivalism of a contemporary architect like Quinlan Terry is certainly expressed against the Modern Movement (state-led social reform discredited with the collapse of every dismal towerblock; Nikolaus Pevsner—the man who traced what he called 'Englishness' through every county in the land, and whose use of the discipline of architectural history to create a public map of England's grand buildings should be counted among the more significant acts of cultural democracy in post-war Britain—reviled as an alien cultural totalitarian). But this architecture also lays claim to traditional commonsense as it might linger on in popular understanding. Terry's advocacy of limestone and marble over aluminium, stainless steel and laminated plastics, his assertion of old-fashioned skills and a craft-style of apprenticeship over theoretical and 'professional' training, his apparently elitist personal cosmology ('I have always wanted to work, sleep and worship in the same half mile')—these aspects of his architectural vision rest on affirmed loyalty to what he sees as a God-given (and in modern times betrayed) lifeworld. As Terry has decreed, all good architecture stems from the Tabernacle and 'So long as the sun shines and the clouds rain and buildings are subject to winter and summer, as long as people eat and drink, marry and are given in marriage, as long as they require *separate rooms* in which to eat, talk and sleep, then the buildings they will want most of all will be in [the classical] tradition.'[45]

The second point concerns the fascination of remembered war. Abject and manipulative as it undoubtedly is, the public glorification of war can express the real counterpoint which the experience of war has provided to the routinised, constrained and empty experience of much modern everyday life. In war—and surely not just for men—personal actions can count in a different way, routine can have a greater sense of meaning and necessity, and there can be some experience not just of extremity (avant-garde pleasure), but also of purpose. In this undoubtedly limited respect war can indeed be recollected as both more meaningful than normal everyday life and also as a purification. As Stephen Graham noticed in the mass carnage of the First World War, when the battle is on it becomes possible to muse on the old national character types again: 'In England and Scotland also, it is noticeable that the war has given us a truer perspective and cleared away the Lilliputian obstructions of modern life. We see Shakespeare great and wonderful again, and our mockers of Shakespeare shrink to figures like those men made of matches that used to appear on Bryant & May's match-boxes.'[46]

This 'quickening' effect of war may indeed be much loved by Conservative nationalists, but it is not entirely of their invention. The Second World War may well have been redeclared against a new enemy by Margaret Thatcher, but this is only possible because there is something there to redeclare.

The National Past and the Re-enchantment of Everyday Life

Genuine tensions and aspirations of everyday life find expression in the modern past, and in this respect there is certainly no wool being pulled over any sheep's eyes. Nevertheless, a political conscription of the past goes on—sometimes with stark crudeness—and it is certainly no intention of mine that this should be forgotten. However 'plausible' the glorification of remembered war may be in present everyday life, it still takes a particular cultural interpretation to insert Shakespeare into the momentarily enlivened world of modern matchstick men as they stumble off into the mass slaughter which a transcendent destiny has generously prepared for them. The nation is the modern integration par excellence, and it is in the service of the nation that public images and interpretations of the past circulate. If many traditional and community-based forms of cultural integration have been eroded, the nation which replaces them is not simply abstract; it works by raising a dislocated and threatened—but none the less locally experienced—everyday life up into redeeming contact with what it vaunts as its own Absolute Spirit. The rags and tatters of everyday life take on the lustre of the idealised nation when they are touched by its symbolism. There is therefore no simple *replacement* of community by nation, but rather a constant—if also always momentary, fragile and partial—redemption of its unhappy remains. Where science in Heller's definition can only legitimate rules and (just as crucially) where so much contemporary experience in this period of economic and imperial 'decline' can only disappoint or frustrate, the symbolism of the nation can still provide meaning. In this respect the nation works to re-enchant a disenchanted everyday life.[47]

Of course there is extensive negotiation between the austere symbolism of the idealised nation and everyday life. Just as everyday life is formed and developed by its symbolic interpretation, the superior public symbolism of the nation—however aloof and essentialised it may seem—responds to its own expression in everyday life. Thus, for example, the attentions of everyday life have facilitated the transformation of Crown and Monarchy into the Royal *Family*, just as they have also provided the ground on which the national heritage—with its aura and its cult of the uniquely expressive object—has been expanded in fairly recent years so that it now includes the local scene alongside the capital city, the old factory alongside the municipal art gallery, the urban tenement or terrace alongside the country house, the vernacular alongside the stately and the academically sanctioned. Likewise, the power of the nation to involve people in a common sense of identity—its capacity to work as an inclusive symbol—derives in no small part from that anxious sense of historical existence which can to a significant extent be generalised across the social structure at the level of everyday life.

In the end, however, we come back to history in a more familiar sense, for the national past is formed within the historical experience of its particular nation-state. Among the factors which have influenced the definition of Britain's national past, therefore, are the recent experience of economic and imperial decline, the persistence of imperialist forms of self-understanding,[48] early depopulation of the countryside, the continuing tension between the 'nations' of Britain (Wales, Scotland and, most obviously, Ireland), the continued existence of the Crown and so much related residual ceremony, the extensive and 'planned' demolition and redevelopment of settled communities which has occurred since the Second World War, and indeed the still living memory of a righteous war that 'we' won (even though 'we' may no longer have any doubt about the cheap little ruse with which history subsequently turned 'our' short-lived victory into long-term defeat). Similarly, while an anxious readiness-to-receive the past exists as something of a generality in modern everyday life, closer historical attention will also reveal that very different versions and appropriations of the past continue to emerge from different classes and groups—even if these sometimes seem to compete within a shared romantic orientation.

In its connection with everyday life the national past addresses the question of *historicity*, of cultural authenticity and security in the face of change. While this is certainly a historical question, it should not be confused with the question of historiographical truth or of 'the way it really was.' One answer to this question of historicity is offered by Conservative authoritarianism: here is a strategy that would freeze the whole of social life over, raising a highly selective image of British particularity to the level of Absolute Spirit and presenting it as the essential identity of the betrayed nation to which we must all return. Here is the national identity to which the modern subject must be encouraged to submit, and if like Arthur Bryant we are a 'historian' of this tendency then we will happily dignify the vaunted image by calling it 'The Spirit of England' and tracing it back into the very rocks of these islands (rocks which, of course, are 'different').[49]

If we are to consider this Conservative nation carefully, it must surely be with a view to discovering other possible articulations of

cultural particularity, articulations which are respectful of the heterogeneity of contemporary society and also capable of making a
coherent political principle of difference. Perhaps we should start in
the knowledge that the 'national past' doesn't exhaust or fully express
everyday historical consciousness, and that everyday nostalgia therefore has a critical and subversive potential as well. The subject of
modern everyday life may be like the poet Geoffrey Grigson as he
stalks around his Wiltshire landscape making a record of all the places
which bear an echo; but if there is a craving for re-enchantment this
is certainly not a craving that can only find satisfaction in the unitary
and exclusive image of the imperial nation.[50] While it can indeed be
expressed jingoistically, the everyday sense of historical existence also
testifies to radical needs which—finding neither realisation in present
everyday life nor recognition in the complacent grandeur of official
symbolism—may still be reaching out to 'seize hold of a memory as
it flashes up at a moment of danger' (Benjamin). If the utopianism of
the national past is not merely a formal utopianism which might be
considered implicit in all ideology, then it is also worth asking not so
much whether the culture of the nation could itself be rearticulated to
democratic ends, but whether everyday historical consciousness might
be *detached* from its present articulation in the dominant symbolism of
the nation and drawn into different expressions of cultural and historical identity. But considering that 'hope' has already been theorised
(and with real historical magnificence) within a Marxist philosophy of
history, perhaps it behoves us also to remember that while the English-
speaking world is familiar with the idea of hoping against hope, there
is also a more plain-talking Polish saying which translates as 'Hope is
the mother of fools.'[51]

2

Trafficking in History

> According to traditional practice, the spoils are carried along in the procession.
>
> *Walter Benjamin*

The National Heritage Lost and Found

> The content of cultural conservatism has undergone fundamental changes as well. It can no longer find a circumscribable social *topos* whose morality and especially whose taste could be conserved as an unimpaired paradigm. Its essence lies rather in the protective gesture itself.
>
> Fehér and Heller (1984)

Mentmore Towers

In May 1974 the sixth Earl of Rosebery died. Millions of pounds in death duties promptly fell due, and the future of the Rosebery estate came into question just as quickly. At the centre of this estate stood Mentmore Towers, a florid country house near Aylesbury in Buckinghamshire. Mentmore was built for Baron Meyer Amschel de Rothschild in the mid-nineteenth century and designed by Sir Joseph Paxton—an architect then at the height of his controversial eminence as designer of Crystal Palace. There was also a massive collection of furnishings and works of art (French eighteenth century and Italian sixteenth century pieces from the old Rothschild connection, while a formidable clutch of English paintings had been gathered under Rosebery ownership). Here, as Marcus Binney put it in 1977, was 'one of Europe's greatest treasure houses'—'the only outstanding High Victorian house to survive intact'—under threat of dispersal and liquidation.

The next Lord Rosebery came out of his counting house and looked around, knowing that if Mentmore Towers was not sold by

May 1977 (within three years of his father's death) further estate duties would become due. His mother moved into a comparatively humble residence in Aylesbury and Rosebery offered both house and contents to the nation for £2 million in lieu of death duties. There the matter sat for months and even years as time ticked fatefully away on all the grandfather clocks in England. After long delays the Department of the Environment eventually refused the offer, claiming that it might have cost over £80,000 per year to maintain the house and that this would have been an unjustified drain on public resources—especially at a time when public expenditure (courtesy not least of the International Monetary Fund) was severely constrained. The government—and these of course were the years of Callaghan's Labour administration—looked into the possibility of using the National Land Fund (then standing at some £17.5 million) to purchase the house and its contents, but here again it refused to go beyond a certain point, stipulating that private funds must be found to fill the large remaining gap. These were not forthcoming. So the three years passed in fruitless bureaucratic wrangling. As Marcus Binney protested, many options weren't even explored and by the beginning of 1977 the room for manoeuvre was gone—even though neither the National Trust nor Buckinghamshire County Council (nor even the nearby new town of Milton Keynes) had been consulted by the government.

By January 1977 Sotheby's (where, incidentally, a real live Rothschild was hidden among the directors) had announced what they hoped would be 'the most important sale of the century,' and for the rest of the year Mentmore was in the news. In February Save Britain's Heritage (Marcus Binney's pressure group) issued a leaflet called *Save Mentmore for the Nation* which argued for a two year holding measure, claiming (truthfully enough as it turned out) that this need not cost the government a penny.[1] Sotheby's estimated that the contents alone would fetch £3 million and, eager to get the hammer out just as soon as possible, withdrew advertising from *The Connoisseur* when the editor of this normally acquiescent magazine sided with Binney. At about the same time Mentmore Towers was reassessed and declared a grade one listed building, but the fact that the Department of the Environment now had to give permission before any alteration or demolition could take place didn't make Lady Birk or Peter Shore (then Ministers for the Environment) any more flexible.

The National Trust wrote to *The Times* expressing deep interest in the house if only an endowment could be arranged to cover its ever steeper running costs, and Lord Rosebery again bent over backwards to arrive at a solution. He extended the deadline beyond which the auction could not be avoided to April 5th, welcomed the National Trust's interest and gave the impression that, even if the government wouldn't act in the best interests of the nation, he himself certainly intended to do so: some works of art and the Marie Antoinette furnishings would, as he said reassuringly, go to the Treasury to be placed in national collections. On April 4th there was still no solution, although the heritage lobby had certainly tried hard enough. Patrick Cormack (Conservative MP for Southwest Staffordshire) announced that Rosebery had agreed to extend the deadline for a final twenty-four hours: as it was put dramatically, 'the deadline will expire on Wednesday at midnight.' In the words of *The Times*, 'Conservative and Liberal MPs are known to be concerned.' Peter Shore agreed to reconsider, although he probably knew already that nothing would come of it.

On the eve of destruction there was parliamentary discussion which did not follow simply along party lines. Michael English, Labour MP for Notts West, took the parochial view that Mentmore was merely a nineteenth-century copy of sixteenth-century Wollaton Hall, which stood in his constituency, and that priorities were evidently wrong: 'if there is any public money to spend on a building of architectural merit it should be spent on the original and not on the copy.' Andrew Faulds, also Labour and a prominent advocate of heritage legislation, dismissed English as a 'lower browed twit.' The Conservative Norman St John Stevas, who was of a mind with Patrick Cormack on this matter as on so many others, warned not only of 'a grave loss to the national heritage' but of how the government stood to lose 'the bargain of the century.' Peter Shore muttered on about priorities and how there were many claims on scant resources, while Stanley Newens (Labour MP for Harlow) stressed that 'it would be a bad thing to allow the temporary situation to cause us to lose this national asset.' Nobody even dreamed of Céline's provocative suggestion that 'you don't lose anything much when your landlord's house is burnt down.'[2]

Intent on reminding its readers that Mentmore was above all a stately and magnificent 'home,' *The Times* set its archaeological assistants to work and by February 1977 they had unearthed an unpublished manuscript by the Marchioness of Crewe. The Marchioness may have died in 1967 but here, nevertheless, was an account from someone who remembered living in Mentmore at its peak. In an excerpt printed on the 26th, under the title 'Memories of the grand

life in the vast treasure chest of Mentmore,' the recollections of a well-positioned child were displayed: 'a riot of beauty and richness was everywhere; carving, embroidery, marquetry and bronzes dazzled and bewildered...' After dwelling on this 'strange sense of the exotic,' the Marchioness quotes Disraeli, who apparently once said 'I hope prosperity and happiness hover over the Towers of Mentmore.' Neither Disraeli nor the Marchioness of Crewe, whose article closes with the prayer that this wish 'will forever be fulfilled,' are likely to have been overly impressed by the events of the 1970s. But just in case a few slower readers missed the point, *The Times* reiterated it on April 6th, publishing an article called 'Days of Delight at Mentmore' by Robert Rhodes James. Tory MP for Cambridge, James was also biographer of the fifth Earl of Rosebery, and he mused on his visits to this 'palace-museum.' Mentmore had been a 'happy home' and, even though 'to separate the collection and the house is impossible,' James sees this inconceivable dismemberment of one of the nation's greatest homes looming: 'Now it appears as a result of almost incredible indifference that this gem is to be destroyed... Very soon a glittering chapter of our history may have gone for ever.'

The hammer was eventually raised by Sotheby's and it didn't stop falling for ten festive days in May, except at those moments when the loot which had been sold had to be cleared out of the auctioneer's marquee so that more could be shovelled in. Prices rose above all estimates, and by the end of the month £6 million had changed hands—three times what the government had refused for all this and the house as well. Recriminations were immediate and bitter. Lady Birk confessed from her Ministerial position that there were lessons to be learned from this 'agonising affair.' A Drouais portrait which was bought by the National Gallery for £380,000 had apparently been offered to the Treasury at a fraction of this price in lieu of estate duty and turned down. John Hale, Chairman of the National Gallery trustees, came out against the Treasury and Denzil Davis (Minister of State at the Treasury) was publicly grilled—accused of lying as well as of general incompetence, with many of the questions coming from members of his own party. By December, Lord Penarth (Tory Chairman of an all-party reviewing committee on the Export of Works of Art) had announced what was clear to many: 'the Mentmore sale should never have taken place, and the Government and the Treasury must bear the blame.'

Mentmore was the Callaghan government's stately home, and there was nothing remotely modest about it. The house 'glittered with gold,' as one anonymous 'expert' put it in *Save Mentmore for the Nation*, and its collection had been gathered from the rarest heights of cultural tradition. If details of the contents had not been published before 1974, this was only because Lord Rosebery was already spending thousands of pounds a year on burglar alarms. Similarly, there was nothing peripheral or of merely particular interest about the position of either the Rothschild or the Rosebery family in British history—both were dynastic.

Here indeed was the national heritage, and it was lost to a bungling and bureaucratic government which could have 'saved' the heritage *and* made a handsome profit at the same time (and in this Binney was proved right). Here also was Lord Rosebery, the good and patriotic aristocrat, who even withdrew a few items from the sale in order to present them as gifts to faithful but now sadly departing servants, doing everything he possibly could to ameliorate a situation which was—as he was careful to stress—completely beyond his control. And here was a ruinous Labour government refusing to act and—at least for much of the public—finding yet another sphere in which to call the question of its own adequacy to the nation. Two years later this last question would return in a general election. By that time the Mentmore story was complete, shifted irreversibly into the past tense. In December 1978 the empty house was bought for £240,000 by the Maharishi International College, an organisation concerned with transcendental meditation. G.K. Chesterton could not have done better: there were the traditional glories of an imperial nation; there was decline and betrayal; there was the empty shell of a building occupied by acolytes of an alien creed. Transcendental 'bliss' can hardly have been the happiness which Disraeli hoped would 'hover over the Towers of Mentmore.'

Calke Abbey

Charles Harpur-Crewe died a few years later, in 1981. Since the eighteenth century his family had occupied Calke Abbey, a country house in Derbyshire, but with Charles's demise, £8 million in capital transfer tax fell due, and son Henry found himself offering the house (together with its contents, the park and enough agricultural land to endow the place for the National Trust) to the government in lieu of payment. Once again there were lengthy negotiations, with the Treasury eventually agreeing everything but the essential endowment. The National Trust couldn't accept the house without endowment, so destruction and dispersal loomed in their familiar way.

The pattern of response was also repeated. In November 1983 *Save Britain's Heritage* published a 'lightning leaflet' called *This Magical House Must Be Saved Intact. Now!* and once again the National Trust communicated its interest in the house through the correspondence page of *The Times*.[3] On this occasion it was Conservative Minister Neil Macfarlane who repeated the refusal over and again, suggesting also that, like himself, the supposedly independent trustees of the National Heritage Memorial Fund (which had since taken over the role of the National Land Fund) could not see the priority of Calke. On December 9th 1983 *The Times* slipped into its 'heart of the shires' mode and printed the deep lyric—a sonorous leading article pleading that Calke should be 'saved' intact. There was some argument in which Calke was claimed to be of lesser interest and Lord Vaizey even suggested that its contents were little more than two centuries' worth of junk. On March 13th, however, and as the last hours approached, rescue was announced by Nigel Lawson in his first budget speech as Chancellor. Extra money had been made available for the National Heritage Memorial Fund to make the endowment possible. So Calke was 'saved' for the nation, represented as so often in such cases by the National Trust.

If Mentmore was Callaghan's country house, Calke is certainly one of Margaret Thatcher's. Of course there have been many other rescues and losses under both governments, but political symbolism doesn't worry over details like this when it comes to designating the representative case. Calke is significantly different from Mentmore, and not just because it was 'saved' so dramatically. By any orthodox assessment Calke was a lesser establishment than Mentmore— nobody would have called it one of Europe's greatest collections, for example. There were indeed some valuable paintings (Landseer, Linnell, Ruysdael etc) among other traditionally precious items, but both house and contents lacked the massive distinction and opulence of Mentmore. As for the Harpur-Crewes, who beyond a handful of cousins had ever heard of them?

Calke was valued in completely different terms than Mentmore. The major virtue of the house was declared to be precisely that *nothing* had happened here, and that almost no one knew about the place. Where the Rothschild and Rosebery families produced people who went out to write their name in large letters over the surface of the whole world, the Harpur-Crewes were more reclusive and eccentric types who poked about Derbyshire and stayed close to their stately pile (which itself, in the words of *The Times*, 'sits low in the seclusion of its deer park'). Some Harpur-Crewes were natural historians who collected stuffed birds and mammals; but they seem by and large to have been tweedy gentlefolk, better fitted to wandering around setting mole-traps in the greensward than to the increasingly specialised subtleties of aristocratic tax avoidance (*The Times* leader of December 9th 1983 found their failing in this area especially touching). Where Mentmore was apparently notable from the start for its advanced amenities (hot water central heating throughout and artificial ventilation in all rooms), the Harpur-Crewes, again in the celebratory words of *The Times*, had been contrastingly 'slow to embrace the amenities of modernity.' Indeed, they were reported as having resisted the motor-car until 1949 and electric light until as recently as 1960.

Along with their reluctance to face historical change, it is the Harpur-Crewes's anachronistic irrelevance to the modern world that makes them so deeply 'historical' in the approach to 1984. In the 1980s the Harpur-Crewe family is distinguished precisely because it lacks any distinction, and Calke Abbey is of historical value because it too is sufficiently unremarkable to have survived unnoticed. The attraction of the house was only peripherally related to the value of its artefacts or to its architectural merit. The point instead was that Calke had not been cleaned up (by, say, the 'new wife' who Lord Vaizey thought might have helped reduce those 'skiploads of junk') and that its continued existence had gone unknown. Unlike Mentmore it was not for security reasons that this country house had never been written up and displayed, but rather for lack of sufficient interest. Like the family's want of historical distinction, it was only the house's oblivion which made contemporary rediscovery possible. The Harpur-Crewes, it was said, had not thrown anything away and Calke as a result became 'the house where time stood still'—just draw back the curtains, blow off the dust and every little particular of the Harpur-Crewes's previously unregarded world is there to be found. Here was a time-capsule, a 'little piece of England' which had shown such remarkable resistance to the march of time that it seemed to *The Times* like 'the outcome of a successful experiment with time'—a phrase which could equally well be applied by the same newspaper to other aspects of the ongoing Tory project.

The myth of historical recovery is complete. When journalists from the *Observer* went up to Calke early in 1984 they found no servants remaining and a singular Henry Harpur-Crewe living alone—indeed, camping out—in two of the house's eighty rooms. That left some seventy-eight rooms on which curtains and doors had been closed at some time over the last 150 years. There was the room of Richard Harpur-Crewe, who died in 1921—his car manuals, model ships and copies of *Jane's Fighting Ships* still lying there to be photographed by the newly admitted cameras. There was a bird lobby filled with specimen cases, while the tools and equipment in the outhouses were so well preserved that the National Trust's surveyor apparently likened the densely packed timber stores to a 'scene from Diderot's *Encyclopédie*.' And above all there was the Victorian drawing room, furnished and redecorated in 1856 and scarcely used since—the colours still brilliant after a century under wraps.

In a sense Lord Vaizey was right to remark that Calke contained 'skiploads of junk,' and the defenders who rushed in to point out the

I don't know why, but I prefer this old towerblock...

really valuable items in the house were certainly further from the real point than Vaizey himself. For, beyond any question of conventionally valued artefacts, Calke proved that household junk can indeed also now serve as the stuff of a national past which is valued for surviving secretly against the insidious drift of recent history. The mere endurance of 'England' is miraculous in the midst of all this recent decline and, as the Calke story showed, its survival can now be associated with the familiar bits and pieces of a private and above all *interior* life which still goes on behind some closed curtains and doors even though the more general public experience is of destructive modernisation, bureaucracy and continuously announced decay. The brilliant and cluttered Victorian drawing room discovered at Calke was photographed and displayed widely. A remarkable survival indeed, this preserved and rediscovered room was also the somewhat ethereal realisation of thousands of carefully designed historical interiors from recent television productions. Here in our midst is the world that we thought was lost; it survives only as a miraculously neglected fragment or as obsessive reconstruction in the contemporary electric theatre, or in the case of Calke as a bit of both. Far from any conventional consideration of architectural or cultural value, Calke is how one dream of old came true in the anxious climate of 1984. If the national heritage was lost at Mentmore in 1977 it was rediscovered in a different expression seven years later—still home at Calke.

The National Heritage Act (1980) and the Redeclaration of the Second World War

> It is best to have a supply of memorials to guard against accidents. I mean to have an assortment of tombstones myself.
>
> Mark Twain

Between Mentmore and Calke came the National Heritage Act (1980). This legislation was the culmination of considerable parliamentary discussion and agitation, much of it prompted directly by the Mentmore affair. Deliberations over the national heritage and the measures necessary to ensure its preservation occurred during Labour's term of office. A White Paper proposing legislative reform was produced in February 1979, but by this time the writing was already on the wall. A few months later Thatcher would defeat these hesitant and bureaucratic vandals in a general election and start to consolidate her project of bringing national pride and other old values back to the country at large. The national heritage was in the air during that election campaign and, while there were certainly also larger issues about, there can be little doubt that, like Dutch Elm Disease, the Mentmore fiasco played its part in forming public opinion of the Labour Government.

As it happened, then, the legislative reform which was planned under Labour was modified and enacted under Tory rule. The National Heritage Bill was introduced into both Commons and Lords with considerable patriotic clamour on all sides. At its second Commons reading in December 1979 Norman St John Stevas announced that this Act alone would justify his career, claiming that the Government would be remembered for this legislation long after its other achievements were forgotten.[4] St John Stevas has doubtless had plenty of opportunities to savour the retrospective irony of his remark, for as a victim of one of Thatcher's early cabinet reshuffles his ministerial career was too short to find any other possible justification. Nevertheless Stevas's speech is worth quoting in the full glory of its parkland metaphors, for it gives a vivid impression of the evocative rhetoric which in its very vagueness seems so central to the definition of the national heritage:[5]

> What has for so many years been a dream of visionaries and enthusiasts is about to become a reality. It is a measure of the importance that the Government attach to the preservation of our heritage that, despite all the pressures for the reduction of public expenditure which the government are quite rightly exerting, they have found room for the extra investment needed in this area. It is not an extravagant beginning, but it is not a derisory one either. 'Tall oaks from little acorns grow.' I believe that in future the branches of this fund will spread over the heritage ever more widely, protecting it from the economic storms and changes that make it especially vulnerable.

The arboreal metaphor is peculiar to St John Stevas but a comparably inflated language seems to have risen from all sides of both houses. Labour's Andrew Faulds spoke of his honourable colleagues in the House of Lords (Lady Birk and Lord Donaldson) who 'took up cudgels' for the heritage, and Patrick Cormack, Conservative MP and author of *Heritage in Danger*, celebrated the fact that the Bill came forward with all-party support, announcing that 'it is vital for the preservation of our heritage that it should never become a political football.' Andrew Faulds agreed: 'it is not often—indeed in this Parliament it is exceptional, probably unique, that we in opposition can positively welcome any legislative intention from this benighted government.'

While there was no outright opposition from any quarter, there were some minor silences. For reasons which will shortly become clear, Enoch Powell (a true champion of the nation) wasn't in the House of Commons to be heard. Similarly, while this legislation was clearly adopted as a cause by the more moderate, traditionalist and (in subsequent Thatcherite rhetoric) 'wet' wing of the Conservative Party, Francis Pym also stayed out of discussion. Here again there may have been a little embarassment to avoid, for Pym was already embroiled in difficulties over his particular piece of 'our' national heritage. Eleven months and a public enquiry later he would be refused permission to demolish Hazells Hall, his listed family seat in Bedfordshire, a refusal which was announced in November 1980 and which came hard on the heels of a Repairs Notice served by Bedfordshire County Council.[6] Although there were little cracks like this in its noble edifice, all-party agreement over the National Heritage Act (1980) was still strong. St John Stevas certainly saw this as the beginning of great things, for in July 1980 he remarked that 'Margaret Thatcher has shown herself, in just over a year in office, to be a national leader as well as a party leader.'[7]

No doubt the nation was moved by these measures to protect its increasingly vaunted heritage, but a far more forceful presentation of national unity was approaching and one of a kind that St John Stevas is unlikely to have anticipated. With the Falklands adventure the politics of national identity and concord shifted dramatically. The sovereign heritage now needed a curiously military form of preservation as this old fox-hunting nation sailed out to be blooded once again. As for St John Stevas, by this time he himself had become a minor and indeed rather quaint piece of the past—suffering neglect if not absolute dereliction on Thatcher's back benches.

Like most of the preservation legislation preceeding it, the National Heritage Act (1980) has two main co-ordinates: it is concerned with the preservation of that range of property which it defines as 'the heritage,' but it also seeks to secure public access (of an acceptable sort), to ensure that 'the heritage' is available for cultural consumption and that it is *displayed* as such. In itself the National Heritage Act (1980) is a threefold measure: it eases the means whereby property can be transferred to the State in lieu of capital transfer tax and estate duty; it provides indemnity to museums which might otherwise be unable to afford the cost of insuring objects loaned to other exhibitors; and it establishes the National Heritage Memorial Fund.

The National Heritage Memorial Fund was grafted onto the remains of the National Land Fund, which had itself been established in 1946 under the guidance of Labour Chancellor Hugh Dalton. The National Land Fund was set up with £50 million which came into the Exchequer from the sale of surplus war materials. Dalton's idea was for the fund to work as a 'thanks-offering and war-memorial' for the Britons killed in the Second World War: 'the beauty of England, the famous historical houses, the wonderful stretches of still unspoilt open country,' surely it would be a fitting memorial that these 'might become part of the heritage of all of us.'[8] But while the words were undoubtedly fine the reality was rather less forthcoming. The National Land Fund never achieved any practical existence as an emergency or contingency fund and there was even some argument as to whether it existed at all, except as a bureaucratic accounting device within the Treasury. In 1957 it fell to Enoch Powell, that august lover of the English countryside, to supervise the reduction of the National Land Fund to £10 million. Acting on behalf of the Tory government, in which he was then serving as a junior Minister, Powell justified this reduction by claiming that the Fund didn't really exist; as he put it, in 1946 the Exchequer had merely lent itself £50 million. Dalton disagreed, but his moment was already past.

The National Heritage Memorial Fund was established on the rather optimistic expectation that it would take over the £16.6 million which remained in the National Land Fund and that each subsequent year it would receive an additional income initially planned as £5.5 million. This is not a vast sum of money, as St John Stevas admitted, but the National Heritage Memorial Fund is a redesignation of more than just money. First, and as was claimed in parliamentary debate, this fund was established to redress earlier breaches of promise. The previous 35 years may have failed to honour Dalton's intention that the National Land Fund should have a real rather than merely notional existence, but there was also a more general feeling that the period had failed really to honour those who had fallen for the nation during the war. Had the Fund not been cut in 1957, moreover, there would by now be enormous sums available on an annual basis. Some MPs speculated out loud on this theme, one even claiming that if the National Land Fund had not been reduced in this way there would be some means of resisting the cultural predations of the massively wealthy Paul Getty Foundation, with its grotesque galleries in Malibu. The details may seem relatively trivial, but it should certainly be recognised that the National Heritage Memorial Fund represents one of the Thatcher government's first (and perhaps less than fully conscious) attempts to revive the spirit of the Second World War and to set up its own patriotic measure against that long drawn-out betrayal known in more polite circles as the post-war settlement. For in Conservative rhetoric the Second World War has been redeclared—not against Hitler this time, but against the kind of peace which followed it: if Spitfires and Lancasters are in the skies again, they now fly against 'socialism' and the 'overweening state.'

In taking over the memorial function of Dalton's National Land Fund, the National Heritage Memorial Fund also transformed it. In the 1980 Act those Britons who actually died in the Second World War are completely lost, submerged in the even mistier invocations of a fund which (in the words of the National Heritage Act) stands as 'a memorial for those who have died for the United Kingdom.' When? Where? How? And on which side? How is it possible to die for this bureaucratic entity 'The United Kingdom' except perhaps by having a coronary on an expenses account in Whitehall or Brussels? Where Hugh Dalton's memorial still had a hortatory intention, indicating (however imprecisely) a specific loss or sacrifice, the National Heritage Memorial Fund gestures only towards its own existence in the present. As Lord Mowbray and Stourton put it in the House of Lords, 'the heritage is a memorial to everything in the past always.'[9] There is nothing hortatory about the National Heritage Memorial Fund; all it invokes is a generalised and everyday sense of the way things used to be, and in this respect it stands as an early engagement with that anxious and vernacular sense of historical existence which Thatcher has deliberately gone on to make the ground of so many spuriously 'historical' gestures and pleas.[10]

If the memorial function of the National Heritage Memorial Fund was shrouded in mist from the start, the actual heritage which is to be protected or saved was hardly figured out in fine detail either. The Fund is administered by a group of independent trustees whose chairman is appointed by the Prime Minister. These Trustees were decidedly not to be experts, but rather people of the right general understanding. As St John Stevas put it to the Commons, the trustees would be 'a group of what I call cultured generalists, reflecting the whole British heritage rather than experts in particular fields.'[11] Or, as Lord Mowbray and Stourton would later tell the Lords, 'the trustees are people of great commonsense in the world of art.'[12] It was left to the trustees to arrive at 'a working definition' of the national heritage, and like other working definitions this one has never been formulated. As the trustees put it in their first annual report, 'we could no more define the national heritage than we could define, say, beauty or art,' and for this reason it was decided to 'let the national heritage define itself' by awaiting requests for assistance to come in.[13]

So one is left wondering what cultured generalism and common-sense in the world of art actually amount to in practice. The individual grants awarded over the first two years told a fairly predictable story: awards are made to museums, trusts, universities and even to the British Film Institute. They aim to cover the cost of works of art, archaeological recovery (the generously funded recovery of the Mary Rose, a project at Ironbridge Gorge . . .), the preservation of buildings, nature reserves and even (in the BFI's case) old film stock. Behind these often worthy dispensations there is also a more general, and indeed well connected, sense of what the nation and its inheritance actually amount to.

Thus Lord Charteris of Amisfield, appointed Chairman of the trustees by Margaret Thatcher in April 1980, also turned out to be the Provost of Eton College—a quarter from which other interesting views on the national heritage have emerged. During a strike which closed *The Times*, Michael McCrum, then headmaster of Eton, wrote to the *Guardian* contesting the view that public schools should not have charity status. McCrum described the use made of foundation funds, saying that 34 per cent was spent on scholarships, religious services and 'other charitable activities.' He then went on to remark that: 'Most of the rest was spent on the upkeep of the foundation buildings and grounds, only parts of which are used by those whose parents pay full fees, the oppidans. The college chapel and ancient buildings are part of the national heritage and were visited during the year by more than sixty thousand tourists.'[14] The establishment, then, is not only shored up by charity status but also held above all question by the gaze of rubber-necking tourists. In July 1984, and following a decision which itself went a long way towards defining cultural generalism, Michael McCrum was himself appointed a trustee of the National Heritage Memorial Fund.

No matter how striking they may be, however, the trustees' personal connections can scarcely be the main point at issue. As it was phrased in the debates which surrounded the National Heritage Act (1980), the national past—'our' common heritage—seems indeed to be identifiable as the historicised image of an instinctively conservative establishment. While the Great Tradition of bourgeois culture was frequently invoked in the debates, the interests of property are also more pragmatically expressed. Anyone doubting this might take a wander through the pages of *Historic House*, the quarterly journal of the Historic Houses Association. In amongst the adverts for burglar alarms, minstrels, elaborate and outsize greensward cutting machinery, heritage estate management agencies and horse boxes, there is relatively little on the aesthetic or cultural aspects of ownership. The important news is all about prices fetched at recent auctions, ways of getting cheap Manpower Services Commission labour to trim the verges or touch up the paintwork and, above all, ways of operating the ever-changing tax system to the best possible advantage.

But the deft manoeuvring of historic house owners cannot provide an adequate account of the National Heritage Act (1980) either—and not just because the dispossession of a few well-heeled 'guardians' of 'our' national heritage would be hopelessly inadequate as any kind of political goal. While the interests of property are undoubtedly in play, the cultural motivation for the National Heritage Act (1980) is the important issue to understand, and this as we have seen was broadly shared. The crucial questions, therefore, concern this public valuation of the national past which seems to be so widely held in common. What is this sense of nation and past which serves as cultural background to measures like the National Heritage Act (1980)? What is its evidently changing interpretation of the history-to-be-saved, and how has it come to win such wide support? In order to define the character and institutional basis of this public sense of history—one in which a public is defined every bit as much as a past—I shall now give two historical sketches. The first of these is concerned with the emergence and development of preservationism from the late nineteenth century onwards, while the second deals with the ruralist advertisements which Shell has produced in Britain over the last sixty or so years.

Preservation and the National Trust

> Bertram's Hotel. So many memories…The past fused itself with the present. A French phrase came back to her, *Plus ça change, plus c'est la même chose.* She reversed the wording. *Plus c'est la même chose, plus ça change.* Both true she thought.
>
> Agatha Christie (1965)

The impulse to preserve landscapes and buildings is an insistent cultural tendency within western modernity, but it does more than naively plea for old calm and settlement in the midst of contemporary turmoil and change. In Britain a fairly diverse preservation lobby has been working with recognisable historical continuity since the second half of the nineteenth century. The early moments are increasingly well known, often as the inaugural dates of influential voluntary organisations which were formed in the later decades of the nineteenth century. Thus in 1865 the Commons Preservation Society was formed, while 1884 saw the founding of the National Footpaths Preservation Society. Responding to the threatened 'restoration' of Tewkesbury Abbey, William Morris helped press the Society for the Protection of Ancient Buildings into existence in 1877.

There were also more specifically civic initiatives, such as the London Survey Committee, which became active in the 1890s and secured the support of the London County Council in 1897. As for the more general background to these developments, a number of recently suggested factors should be acknowledged. Michael Hunter has pointed to the increasing influence of historicist values, which at this time came to be articulated against Enlightenment ideas of progress and reason, while others place more emphasis on an aesthetic and neo-pastoral impulse which turns into a demand for preservation as it recoils from the rampant urbanity of a brutal industrial capitalism.[15] Alongside these influences, emphasis should also be placed on the consolidation of the imperial nation-state; for whatever else it may involve, preservationism has certainly played its part in a nationalisation of history which enables the state to project an idealised image—never fully achieved, but there is a tendency never-theless—of its own order against a geographical and historical back-ground of its own selection.

Patrick Cormack, one of the many advocates who has also outlined a history of preservationism, finds the story beginning in 1854 when John Ruskin submitted a proposal to the Society of Antiquaries, sug-gesting that an Association be established to maintain an inventory of 'buildings of interest' threatened by demolition or the wrong kind of restoration.[16] The 1860s saw legislation to protect wildlife from the ravages of the fashion for plumage—a fashion which had numerous bourgeois women sporting half a seagull on their hats (and many others protesting)—but the first parliamentary manoeuvre on the preserv-ation of monuments seems to have come a decade or so later, when the Liberal MP Sir John Lubbock drafted his National Monuments Preservation Bill. Influenced by Ruskin's earlier initiative, this pro-posed the establishment of a National Monuments Commission along with a schedule of those monuments which the Commission would protect. This Bill was rejected on its second reading in 1875, as were Lubbock's next two attempts to get preservation legislation enacted in 1878 and 1879. The opposition to preservation may have been enhanced by anti-aestheticism, but one fundamental objection was raised again and again: the enactment of any of Lubbock's Bills would introduce into 'the law of the land' a principle which elevated public interests above private property rights. This transformation was resisted heavily, and the resistance was expressed clearly by the Tory, Francis Hervey, who asked: 'are the absurd relics of our barbar-ian predecessors, who found time hanging heavily on their hands, and set about piling up great barrows and rings of stones, to be preserved at the cost of infringement to property rights?'[17]

In 1882, with Gladstone in power, a Bill prepared by Lubbock was enacted as the Ancient Monuments Protection Act. It was, as Cormack comments, a weak affair which established a schedule of some twenty-one monuments which the nation might take into guard-ianship or purchase. The 1882 Act was strengthened in 1900, but even then it was not sufficient to resolve the conflict between growing pres-sure for public intervention in matters of preservation and the private property rights which were so heavily represented in both Houses of Parliament. The Act provided no compulsion and it didn't apply at all to inhabited monuments. While Parliament hesitated at the brink of infringing property rights the extra-parliamentary preservation lobby continued to expand its activities. It was in the institutionalisation of this lobby that a working solution to the conflict between public interest and private property was eventually negotiated. This negotiation is clearly at work in the early history of the National Trust.

The National Trust was formed in 1895, but the impetus for its formation lies in the 1880s with the experience of the Commons Preservation Society which had campaigned successfully over Hampstead Heath, Berkhamsted Common and Epping Forest. Because the Commons Preservation Society did not have corporate status it was legally barred from acquiring land and could consequently not purchase common rights. In 1884 Robert Hunter, solicitor with the CPS, proposed the creation of a body which would be incorporated under the Joint Stock Companies Act, and therefore able to buy and hold land and buildings 'for the benefit of the nation.' As Hunter said, 'the central idea is that of a Land Company formed...with a view to the protection of the public interests in the open spaces of the country.' Hunter was supported by Octavia Hill who apparently suggested that the name include the word Trust rather than Company so that the benevolent side of the operation would be stressed. The third founding figure was Hardwicke Rawnsley, a friend of Ruskin's who was also Canon of Carlisle. Rawnsley had been active with the Lake District Defence Society, an organisation which had been rallying the ghosts of Coleridge and Wordsworth in order to oppose the construction of railways and the closure of traditional rights of way in the Lake District. The Lake District Defence Society was caught in the same impasse as the Commons Preservation Society: it might try to 'save' threatened beauty spots with money raised by public subscription, but there existed no body that could hold land for the benefit of the nation. In 1894 the constitution of the National Trust was drafted and a meeting resolved: 'that it is desirable to provide means whereby landowners and others may be enabled to dedicate to the nation places of historic interest or natural beauty, and to this purpose it is expedient to form a corporate body, capable of holding land, and representative of national institutions and interests.'[18]

In 1895 the Association was registered as 'The National Trust for Places of Historic Interest and Natural Beauty'; it was registered under the Companies Act, but because it was not profit making the Trust was not obliged to include the word 'Limited' in its title.

Especially during the first twenty years of its existence, the National Trust worked as a campaigning pressure group. This brought it into explicit conflict with private capital and government on occasion. Nevertheless, in its concern with what it has helped to define and create as at once the 'public' and the 'national' interest the Trust has also had a ground in common with government. At the institutional level, the Trust has achieved results precisely by working in close relation to both capital and state. Within two years of its formation it was advising County Councils on the listing of historic buildings, and in the same early years it was attempting to unite and organise preservation groups; in 1900, for example, archaeological societies and field groups were brought into affiliation. This organisation of the preservation lobby was double-edged: it brought about a more concerted and effective lobby at the same time as it produced a more corporate and therefore, under certain circumstances, a more manageable one. In 1907 an Act of Parliament made the Trust a statutory body, giving it the right to hold land 'inalienably'—that is to say, it was protected so that no one could acquire Trust property without permission from Parliament. Legally instituted in its novel way under the Companies Act, the National Trust seems to have provided the state with a way out of the conflict between public interest and private property. The two are now negotiated, if not wholly reconciled, but at a displaced level: as a registered company the National Trust holds property privately, and yet it does so in what it also works to establish as the national and public interest. Indeed in some respects this national public interest occupies a position analogous to that of the shareholder in an ordinary limited company. One doesn't have to take a completely negative view of the National Trust to see that the inalienability of the Trust's property can be regarded (and also staged) as a vindication of property relations: a spectacular enlistment of the historically defined categories 'natural beauty' and 'historic interest' which demonstrates how private property simply *is* in the national public interest.

With preservation established as a public concern within the relations of private property, the tone of Conservative thought on the matter appears to change. As the century turned, Hervey's pompous complaints about relics and barbarians gave way to an almost opposite assertion. This can be heard in the words of the Tory

Lord Curzon, who spoke against his party's previous opposition to preservation law in the debates which surrounded the extension of the Ancient Monuments Protection Act which became law in 1913: 'This is a country in which the idea of property has always been more sedulously cherished than in any other, but when you see that to get that Bill through Parliament it had to be denuded of its important features, and only after many years was it passed in an almost innocuous form into law, one feels almost ashamed of the reputation of one's countrymen.'[19]

How is one to account for this shift in emphasis? While it may not be wholly determined, the shift does accompany a change in the role of the dominant classes. In the mid-nineteenth century the bourgeoisie was transforming the whole fabric of society. By the end of the nineteenth century, and more acutely as the twentieth developed, this position of dominance was less secure. Economic crisis, various challenges to imperial power, the rise of working-class organisations and war all threatened it. Aside from any questions of endangered landscape or monument, a growing concern with the preservation of the social order develops in this context. The endeavour to preserve landscapes and monuments is obviously not identical with this wider conservatism, but close and sometimes crudely instrumental connections have been made nevertheless. In 1929, for example, Arthur Bryant sought to identify the spirit of political Conservatism with the kind of patriotism which he associated with the preservation of rural England. For Bryant the rural scene was an 'educative influence' which needed to be preserved 'in the service of the state.' As he put it more fully:[20]

> From the plain man has been taken away the home smoke rising in the valley, the call of the hours from the belfry, the field of rooks and elms. His home is now the grey land of the coal truck and the slag heap, and 'amid these dark Satanic mills,' his life is cast and his earliest memories formed. And the spirit of the past—that sweet and lovely breath of Conservatism—can scarcely touch him. It is for modern Toryism to recreate a world of genial social hours and loved places, upon which the conservative heart of Everyman can cast anchor.

Anyone choosing to glance at Patrick Cormack's *Heritage in Danger* will see that the game goes on, and that Conservative ideologues are still presenting their political project in the moving vocabulary and imagery of the national heritage. But for all the persistence there is no easy or final settlement here, and the relation between capitalist property interests and the preservation of heritage sites has remained fraught throughout the century. Capitalist property relations can only be preserved if they are reproduced through new accumulative cycles, and preservation of these relations seems in this sense to necessitate the constant transformation of life in both town and country. The preservation of capital is therefore predicated on widespread social change and, indeed, actual demolition. Summarily stated, this is the dereliction which brings capital into conflict with the preservation lobby—a conflict which, however deeply buried, still underlies the publicly maintained serenity of 'our' national heritage.

In pointing to an appeal like Bryant's I am not suggesting that the preservation movement is class-determined in a mechanical way; indeed, it should be stressed that preservationism is certainly capable of internal differentiation and conflict. Thus, for example, in 1900 there was argument over Stonehenge. After peering, with understandable anxiety, into the future, two of the upright stones had fallen during the last night of the nineteenth century, and the Society for the Protection of Ancient Buildings clashed with the Commons and Footpath preservationists when the owner, Sir Edmund Antrobus, took protective measures which included the introduction of a turnstile and an admission charge. The preservation of monuments is one

thing, but it is quite another to limit public access to places where, as Hardwicke Rawnsley of the National Trust put it, 'men's feet all up the ages have been as free as air to come and go.'[21] And, indeed, while preservationist idealisations of country and past certainly merged quite explicitly with Baldwinite Conservatism in the twenties, and while they also supported massive attacks on popular 'plotland' development in the thirties, preservationism never lies simply in the pocket of the state.[22] The contest over public access to land and traditional rights of way continued with real intensity through the twenties and thirties, and in organisations like the Federation of Ramblers Clubs (precursor of the Ramblers Association), the Woodcraft Folk and even perhaps the proletarian-taming Youth Hostels Association it had a recognisably working-class base. Preservationism continues to involve resistance to the inroads of state and capital on traditional towns and landscapes, and it does this in the name of a powerful national interest which can express itself in socialist as well as Tory terms.[23] Nevertheless, in the early decades of this century there does seem to have developed an increasingly stable means of negotiating the emergent conflict between preservation and property. Crucial to this is the organisation of the preservation lobby in close relation to Parliament and the state.

The growing complex of extra-parliamentary pressure and amenity groups concerned with preservation, and the activities of this complex in relation to the various apparatuses of the state, has played a major part in defining the National Heritage. This contribution can be identified initially by indicating the conjunction of 'historic interest' and 'natural beauty' which is to be found in the full name of the National Trust. Obviously this conjunction does not originate with the National Trust, and one place where it exists before 1895 is in the academic Fine Art tradition. The National Trust may work to preserve landscapes and buildings but it is also an organisation through which class-specific academic culture has been generalised and more widely disseminated. It should be remembered that John Ruskin figures in the background, that there are links between the early National Trust and the Pre-Raphaelite Brotherhood, and that in 1900 three out of four Vice Presidents of the National Trust were members of the Royal Academy.

The preservation lobby has been active in bringing this coalescence of 'historic interest' and 'natural beauty' into prominence in national public life. Both categories were historically constituted to start with, and their coalescence has produced a merger in which a conventional realism can be used to naturalise a bourgeois interpretation of history and society. This coalescence is a basic constituent of the National Heritage, and it continues to play an important part in generalising bourgeois into 'national' culture. Members of the heritage lobby sometimes speak of the country house as the 'soul' of Britain, and it is true that since the Second World War (in the years of Labour and the welfare state) the National Trust has been picking up threatened country houses at a dramatic rate. More generally, the country house is certainly the classical instance of such a coalescence: it combines its own 'historic interest' with the 'natural beauty' of what are actually heavily landscaped and aestheticised surroundings: the 'soul' of a nation or just the perfect naturalisation of a hegemonic view of the nation which has needed special preservation in the years of progressive taxation and state-led social reform, or both?

In recent years all has seemed very quiet on the National Trust's many expanding fronts. Well over a million people are now members, but it has to be said that even if the National Trust is also now one of the largest landowners in the country, this is a giant which, at least when it comes to politics rather than national-historical reverie, merely snores. In 1982 it was slightly roused by those of its members who were angry at the way 'inalienable' National Trust land in Buckinghamshire was quietly leased to the Ministry of Defence so that an anti-nuclear bunker could be built to house the Command Headquarters of the NATO Air-Forces. But normally the sleep is unbroken: with its million communicant members The National Trust has become an ethereal kind of holding company for the dead spirit of the nation.

Indeed, it is so busy managing its own vast and illustrious assets that other more active organisations have been formed fairly recently to campaign more noisily for threatened buildings. This is where Marcus Binney has come in, together with SAVE Britain's Heritage— the pressure group which he helped form in 1975. It may well seem unlikely given that Binney emerged from the customarily placid pages of *Country Life* (the magazine of which he is architectural editor), but SAVE Britain's Heritage works by emphasising the *dereliction* of property. Even though its adopted buildings are often in public rather than private ownership, SAVE is therefore an organisation whose activities contrast interestingly with those sedate National Trust sites in which private property, the public interest and the national imagination seem to be so perfectly harmonised. Perhaps Canon Rawnsley would have approved this return to old themes, although he may also have regretted that those old liberal (but still political) questions of public access seem to have little place in these more recent and architecturally defined activities. While such speculation on Rawnsley is idle, this is as good a place as any to indicate how the National Heritage Act (1980) redefined these questions of access and use, turning them into administrative questions of *exhibition* and display.

Reinstating the Land (Arcadia according to Shell)

> Is there life beyond the posters? When a train takes us outside the city, we do see a green meadow—but this green meadow is only a poster which that lubricant manufacturer has concocted in league with nature in order to pay his respects to us in the country as well.
>
> Karl Kraus (1909)[24]

Diverse as it is, preservationism has played a forceful part in producing mass public ideas of the nation with its valued past and countryside. But if the rise of preservationism needs to be understood in its developing relationship with the state, there are also well-made connections with private capital to be taken into account. This is evident in the advertising which has been produced in Britain by Shell—a company whose publicity has had connections with preservationism since the early 1920s at least.

An advertisement which Shell placed in the trade magazines in October 1973 carried the heading 'Do you know any other petrol company which encourages motorists to walk?':[25]

> Last year once again, thousands of people got out of their cars and started walking. Along cliff-tops, through deep rich woodlands and down by the seashore. They were following Shell–National Trust Nature Trails. A trail followed by thousands of motorists before them. For Shell and the countryside are old friends. No other company since the invention of the motor car can claim to have done so much to help open up the countryside to the ordinary motorist. Or to have helped preserve it for future generations of motorists to enjoy. Whether

tramping the nature trails, reading about it in the Shell Guide, or listening to it on Shellsound guides, the Shell name is constantly in front
of them. For the Shell name is one of the most continuous and rewarding of promotions in the history of advertising. It helps Shell sell more
petrol than any other petrol company in the UK. And it's yours the
moment you become a Shell dealer. Along with 73 years of goodwill,
advertising and promotional activity second to none. You'll have to
walk a long way to do better than that. *Shell. The name every other petrol
company would like to have.*

Nature and preservation are evidently good for business, both as a
direct inducement to consumption (on the brink of what would come
to be known as the energy crisis) and also in the more general terms
of public relations. But above all it is the stylised sense of paradox
which is indicative of Shell's recent advertising strategy. It is aimed
at the general public now, at the driver rather than the garage owner
or tenant. One such advertisement appeared on a full page in the
Guardian on 13 September 1979. Most of the page was occupied by
a spellbinding colour photograph the quality and effect of which can
usefully be described in Walter Benjamin's terms. In 'The work of art
in the age of mechanical reproduction' Benjamin discusses a photographic naturalism which is both profoundly technical and at the
same time apparently free of all technical mediation. He then commented that 'the equipment-free aspect of reality here has become
the height of artifice; the sight of immediate reality has become an
orchid in the land of technology.'[26] This says quite a lot about the
image which burst into a certain area of public consciousness from
that Thursday's *Guardian*.

The photograph makes an immediate impact; indeed, it is designed
to leap off the page. Stunningly 'natural,' the image shows a river
meandering across the page and into the distance: green grass, trees
and hedges in the foreground, with a climbing landscape of fields
and foothills into the distance. There is no sign of humanity, except
that of course this is a singularly worked form of 'nature.' We are in
Snowdonia National Park, and the sky is a deep dark yellow: a thunder-
ing effect, a sense of strangeness and menace, but also a photographic
cultivation of the wild. As for the point of view and the perspectives
which it introduces into the image, this too is strangely unaccountable:
slightly higher than might be expected of the regular tourist's glance
from the driver's window, and yet lower than the customary aerial

photography. Nature is strange, an 'other,' a place to go or goal for the city-dweller. The somewhat unreal position which the national culture offers the tourist is embodied in this image. Dislocated and caught in a constructed sense of the 'natural' view, the reader of the *Guardian* can only answer 'Yes' to the slogan which appears beneath the image: 'Wouldn't you protest if Shell ran a pipeline through this beautiful countryside?' But, as the text goes on to say, 'They already have.' Beside a comforting mugshot of an expert, of the distinctly 'rural' looking Shell horticulturalist, comes the authoritative elaboration:

> When Shell proposed a pipeline from the North East coast of Anglesey to Stanlow refinery, seventy eight miles away in industrial Cheshire, people were worried. The line would run through part of the Snowdonia National Park and have to pass under the rivers Conwy, Elwy, Clwyd and Dee. What scars would remain? It is five years since the line was laid, and as I fly along the route today, even I can see no sign of it. On the ground, the course of the pipe can be followed by a series of small unobtrusive markers. Apart from these there is nothing to tell you that the top of a pipeline runs one metre beneath your feet. The sheer invisibility of the line surprises visitors but not me. I was responsible for reinstating the land and well know what unprecedented lengths we went to. Every foot of the way was photographed before digging started, and the vegetation restored the way the record showed it... even to the exact varieties of grass. Sometimes, I agreed deviations in the line to avoid disturbing rare trees. In addition, a team of archaeologists preceded pipeline contractors to make sure that the route would avoid cromlechs, barrows, earthworks and other historical sites. We are proud of the result, and it shows the way for other conservation projects.

For all the appeal to 'nature,' it is above all a political landscape which is displayed and defended here, one which owes its existence to the legislative measures which culminated in the establishment of this National Park. While it is well marked with stone walls and other boundaries characteristic of pre-modern agriculture, there is nothing to define this as a functional landscape in any contemporary sense. If there is no mark of agribusiness here, there are also no makeshift shacks, no caravans, no trace of the amenities of public leisure.[27] Here indeed, is the preservationist's dream, a moving but also frozen countryside with powerful 'historical' and 'natural' appeal—a sacred geography to which the public has no legitimate relation except through an appreciative and increasingly educated visual imagination. Shell can commit the outrage of breaking these rules, but only because it can also put the entire scene back together as it leaves. In the words of the slogan which has been kept in public consciousness since at least the 1930s, 'You can be sure of Shell.'

On 15 October 1980 another full page advertisement in the *Guardian* went to work on the contemporary theme of the suburban fox: a fox in the foreground and scrub grass leading up to an oil refinery silhouetted against a reddish and slightly smokey sky. 'A Shell refinery alive with wildlife' reads the slogan, and then comes the reassuring narration from the horse's mouth; this time it is one of Shell's 'Environmental Technicians' who begins by saying: 'An oil refinery is not the first place you'd look for herons, or a marsh harrier, or a kingfisher, or a fox. Yet, strange as it may seem, the open spaces in and around Shell's Stanlow's refinery literally abound with wildlife.' More recently, in December 1980, a colour supplement to the *Observer* contained a Shell advertisement in which the photograph presented a modernised yeoman, a rather stalwart agricultural worker standing behind some harvesting machinery. The fields lead back to a sky which is blackish-green, and the slogan breaks in as follows: 'To you, it's a barley field. To us, it's a battlefield.' Turning back to the *Guardian*, on 12 August 1981 a full page advertisement announced that 'This, believe it or not, is how Shell goes recruiting its marine ecologists.' The photograph shows an outdoor type scrabbling around under another freakish sky (this one was blackish-red). He is 'recruiting' mussels with a sack from among green kelp on the shores of what the text announces as 'beautiful Dornoch Firth.' The mussels are to be installed around North Sea oil rigs (which 'crouch like enormous spiders on the horizon') and monitored for signs of pollution.

The same insistence permeates these four advertisements: that those two constructed neutralities 'nature' and 'technology' walk hand in hand through this progressive, if slightly bizarre, modern world.[28] It is not only that, as in the advertisement addressed to garage owners, 'nature' and conservation are good for business. More significantly, 'nature' provides the final layer of insulation around the pipeline: the wilds are literally wrapped around the oil company's operations. It is certainly remarkable that Shell, a company whose entire operation has been premised upon that vast transformation of relations to the environment which accompanies the development of the automobile, can not only present itself as the guardian of 'nature' and 'historical sites,' but can also secure the assistance of the preservation lobby for the sake of this presentation. The sense of this paradox was flaunted towards the end of 1984 when Shell's new pipeline in Fife was completed. The presentation was the same in these later advertisements. Under the title 'A rambler's guide to our new pipeline,' Shell showed photographs of 'ancient ritual stones' along the undisturbed castles and landscapes—£400 million sunk without trace into 'the hillsides of Mosmorran.'[29]

With the exception of a period during and after the Second World War, when petrol distribution came under state control and advertising was consequently suspended, Shell has been producing advertisements which work on the themes of 'nature' and 'history' since before the First World War. There have indeed been other themes (in the thirties, for example, a series of advertisements likened other petrols to the restricting clothes worn by Edwardian women—'She's a hiker, but…' 'She can swim, but…' 'It's no use William, these skirts get in the way'). Similarly, the constraints on what can be said or suggested have obviously changed—in recent years, for example, it has not been possible openly to promote profligate consumption of petrol—but the advertisements produced over the last sixty years show a remarkable consistency. The recent examples just described draw and elaborate on a well-established repertoire which extends far beyond the well-publicised slogan 'You can be sure of Shell.' The ruralism going alongside a celebration of technology, the perspectives of the images, the almost parental claim to care for both 'nature' and 'history,' the reassuring text with its mixture of comfort, expertise and good common sense, the cultivatedly pedagogical relation between text and image: these and other characteristics of the advertisements can be traced through the developments of five decades.

Through the early part of the twentieth century Shell was operating in sharp competition with other oil companies, and more than in other areas of industrial production this competition was heavily concentrated on the control of markets. Shell's early growth was partly due to its access to Russian oil and its ability to subsidise one market by setting it off against another. The fundamental question within the British market, however, seems to have been different. How does a company strive to control a market when there is no visible difference between its merchandise and that of rival companies?

From the twenties onwards—and alongside a whole series of 'secret ingredients' and measures to control outlets—Shell appears to have found a strategy to deal with this problem through advertising, which served to redefine the countryside in terms of tourism and leisure.

Because so much of the target population was dissociated from traditional relations to the land, Shell could represent the country-side in strikingly abstract terms. The countryside is equated with cyclical time, with colour and the seasons, and as such it is repossessed in bright advertising images and with a marketing campaign that differentiates 'Summer Shell' from 'Winter Shell.' In the more homogenised space of modern communication, distance is no longer experienced in any traditional sense: indeed, Shell restages it as 'the measured mile' with which the motorist causes the countryside to pass in review, as so many miles per gallon.[30] The countryside is a place of strange allure now, a utopian zone which in its 'historical' capacity still holds residues of a former world: traces of an Albion in which time is still cyclical but to which the motorist can still make his progressive way. History, progress, the time of travel all lead to a timeless Gestalt of earth with 'nation,' and the touristic 'visit' is sublimated in advertising which makes oblique references to an earlier and less predictable

kind of travel which, after Debord, can be called the 'journey.' But if
the tourist is the questing hero, motorised and on wheels, 'visits' are
nonetheless quantifiable for that; they can be calculated, anticipated
and managed in advance. In 1974, for example, 47,600,000 visits
were apparently made to historic properties—9.5 million by people
from overseas. In 1983, to quote the English Tourist Board's figures,
there were 174 million visits to the tourist attractions in England alone
and at least £200 million was raised.[31]

It would be wrong to assert a total continuity of development in
Shell's advertising, but there are noteworthy characteristics nevertheless. In the late 1930s, for example, the car tends to be removed, taken
out of the ruralist image (the growing tension between motoring and
preservation seems to encourage this).[32] Over the same period of time
the road, which has always been carefully positioned in relation to
landscape, becomes evident as a principle of perspective. In numerous advertisements it provides the continuity between foreground
and viewed distance, and in many of the advertisements its passage
through landscape is likened to that of a river: as if, as indeed is the
case in one sense, the countryside takes its shape around the passage
of the motor car. In a series produced in the early sixties and called
'Explore the Roads of Britain with Shell' the road itself becomes pre-
historic, natural and immemorial: the series is concerned with ancient
roads such as the Fosse Way or the Roman Steps in Merionethshire,
and although the perspectives are identical to those of earlier images,
the roads are now green or of natural stone. The tarmac has gone and
the road has become a primordial pathway, 'natural' and 'historic'
combined. Nothing is left of the contemplative relation to nature but
a primitive and 'timeless' pact with the earth.

It is as an agency in the reproduction and elaboration of hegemonic culture that Shell is of interest in this discussion, and two aspects
of this process are worth identifying more closely. The first concerns
the involvement of the preservation lobby in Shell's advertising; while
the second has to do with Shell's use of established 'Culture' to lend
its advertising campaign substance, resonance and credibility.

Shell's involvement with the preservation lobby is some sixty
years old. In 1929 an advert was formulated under the title 'Shell
and the Countryside.' The text read as follows: 'Shell began removing its advertisement signs from the countryside as long ago as 1923.
In 1927 they also asked their garage owners to remove Shell enamel

plates from their premises. Many thousand such plates were, in consequence, abolished, and the work is still in progress. Shell's ways are different.' This piece of publicity, directly related to the start of 'lorry bills' (fairly large posters which were exhibited from the sides of Shell delivery lorries), led into a concerted advertising campaign in the early 1930s. The campaign moved in two related directions, the first of which involved publishing facsimiles of letters sent to Shell by organisations such as the Royal Society of Arts and the Scapa Society for Prevention of Disfigurement in Town and Country. These letters acknowledge Shell's endeavours to protect the countryside from disfiguring advertisements, and were published under the sign of Shell in periodicals like the Tatler and the Royal Society of Arts Journal. The second direction is taken through rather more generally distributed adverts featuring photographs of beauty spots and the following text: 'The proprietors of Shell do not advertise their petrol in places like this.'

In the 1950s and 1960s Shell's involvement with the preservation lobby takes on a far more emphatic pedagogical aspect, involving any number of calendars and nature guides which were taken up largely in schools. The images in these advertisements tend to follow an identifiable form: they show a collection of bits and pieces—feathers, cones, berries and suchlike—fragments of 'nature' which are singled out for pedagogical identification. These items are gathered together for the purposes of a nomenclature which forms the substance of the text, and they are displayed in the foreground of the image. A long view stretches out behind them to a landscape in the distance. The emphasis throughout is that one 'knows' nature in order better to appreciate and care for it. In these later advertisements it is knowledge and education—often the act of naming or, more generally, of what Heller describes as 'making sense'—rather than the car and the road which bridges the distance between near and far.

To a significant extent this educational approach to the countryside is continuous with earlier preservationist initiatives. Thus, for example, during the Second World War Batsford published a series of books with titles like *How to See the Country* or *How to Look at Old Buildings*—all part of an endeavour to cultivate the brutalised and (at best) indifferent senses of town-dwellers who had been displaced into the countryside by the upheavals of war.[33] As Harry Batsford wrote in the 'Introductory Note' to the second edition of *How To See The*

Country: 'It is hoped that all these migrations will render it possible for all but the hopeless urbanites to learn to "see" the country—to get to understand, appreciate and realise something of the message of its outward aspect, its changing seasons, its people and their life and work...No-one is a true Englishman, or has lived a fully balanced life, if the country has played no part in his development.'[34] While Batsford himself didn't necessarily express all of it, an extensive demonology has been elaborated around the urban working class and its 'uneducated' relationship to the countryside. Here are people who break fences and leave litter, who play radios and shout while others are trying to commune with nature, who pick the wild flowers (even the threatened orchid) rather than appreciating them in their natural habitat, who frequent tea-shacks and lack stout shoes; who (as the century moves on) drive their vehicles way beyond the invisible boundaries where (at least according to the tacit agreement of more cultivated society) everyone should start to walk—sometimes even onto the sacred 'green roads' themselves...

Shell has made extensive use of established cultural practices in developing its advertising repertoire. In terms of 'Art' this is evident in the still-famous series of 'lorry bills' which were produced throughout the 1920s and 1930s. These 'lorry bills' nearly always featured paintings, and while some of the earlier images certainly did work in terms of a conventional realism it is much more significant that the series also makes continuous appeal to what begins to look like a conventional unrealism.

Considering these images one is not, for example, dealing only with an art which seeks to efface itself, to bury all trace of its production in the view which it sets up as 'natural' and 'real.' The commissioned paintings which were reproduced as 'lorry bills' also tend to stress their character *as* paintings. One result of this is to lend the reproducible aura and authenticity of 'art' to those sites of 'natural' and/or 'historic' interest to which the advertisements encourage the motorist to drive. But there is something else at work here too, and this can be described as the identification of heritage sites and the countryside, not with any constructed sense of 'reality' so much as with *style.*

'Lorry bills' were produced in the thirties by artists such as McKnight Kauffer, Duncan Grant, Barnett Freedman, Paul Nash, Graham Sutherland and Ben Nicholson. Many of these later images, and especially those of the American expatriate McKnight Kauffer, tended to situate an assertively modernist style in the historically transforming disjunction between the urban motorist/viewer and the countryside. They use a modernist style to link the unfamiliarity with which the countryside appears to the city-dweller with the 'strangeness' of what, for all its oddity, is actually accepted as proper to 'modern art.' The invocation may still be nostalgic and pseudo-pastoral in many cases, but like motoring it is also stridently modern. The countryside is thus caught up in a tense movement in which a traditionalist and non-instrumentalist imagination of 'nature' is displayed against a stylised celebration of the machine—a movement which asserts both the cyclical time of the seasons, of the eternal return of 'nature,' and also the irreversible historical time of progress, the time which has brought us the motor car. This tension, which has itself become a fairly basic figure in the image-repertoire of National Heritage, often embodies progressive time as the road while the cyclical order of time is presented as scenery, the pastoral landscape through which the road sweeps. The same tension between different conceptions of time facilitates another development which is at work in Shell's images during the 1920s: in this sequence the slightly bemused but still organic horse is lifted out of the traditional rustic field, transformed into a futuristic and metallic image, and then returned to the countryside as the abstract horse-power which gets the driver out of the city.

It is not only a developing battery of images that Shell has used to weld ideas of countryside, the visit and the national past to the brand name. These connections are also attempted through an identification of a recognisable vocabulary and text. In the early 1920s Shell's advertising is not particularly articulate, its utterance being limited mostly to short and rather flat slogans. However, by the 1950s a characteristic language has been developed: a language full of cultural assumption, irony (even self-mockery) and display. In the early 1960s, for example, advertisements started to announce that 'here you can relive legend and history on the spot,' or, in the same scene-of-the-great-event vein, to celebrate 'Glen Trool: where Bruce fled his own bloodhound.' But there is also a more evocative gibberish of authenticity, represented by the ridiculous text which accompanies a washed-out painting of Lower Lough Erne: 'Wrapped in morning mists of centuries, monks still hide.' A little bit of 'history,' some 'beauty,' a touch of 'artistic' and 'literary' style: these are among the basic elements of Shell's deftly constructed national archaism—an archaism which is evocative, spectacular and approachable by road.

It is worth outlining some of the more evident stages in the development of this vocabulary with its pseudo-literary edge. In the late 1920s a series of 'historical' cameos appeared in the *Listener*. These featured quite lengthy dialogues which were written in supposedly archaic language and which mixed 'historical' figures (for instance, Pepys and Nell Gwynne) in discussion about places held abstractly in common (for instance, Whitehall). The dialogues always stacked time and space up on the well-publicised platform of Shell. In the thirties there were at least three noteworthy developments. The first is an extensive series of advertisements which made a stylised and 'witty' use of limerick structures to link places with the name of Shell: 'Stonehenge Wilts but Shell goes on forever'; 'Lover's Leap but Shell gets there first'; 'Stow on the Wold but Shell on the Road'; etc. In the late 1930s Shell also introduced a series of 'Valentines' consisting of 'poetic' twitterings printed in the centre of closely drawn ruralist friezes:

> STOP FAIR MOTORIST DIVINE
> HERE I AM
> YOUR VALENTINE

Third, in the mid-1930s Shell started to publish a series of County Guides under the general editorship of John Betjeman at the *Architectural Review*. The first of an immensely influential range of publications which still occupies a central place in the heritage canon, these were written, as the company announced, by authors 'who are generally poets or artists with a bump of topography.' Joined by Paul Nash, Robert Byron and John Piper, Betjeman's group tended to be both modernist and conservative in orientation but still reminiscent, perhaps, of those 'cultured generalists' who were later to be the trustees of the National Heritage Memorial Fund.

In sum, Shell draws on an asserted practice of Literature in much the same way as it draws on Art. Acceptable if not always completely soft poets of a middle-class and rural inclination—figures like John Betjeman and Geoffrey Grigson—were used extensively in the 1950s, for example. The significance of this cultural connection becomes evident if one considers the shifting audience to which Shell's advertising is addressed. It is evident, for example, that the earliest advertisements mentioned in this discussion—those from the early 1920s—derive from a time when motoring was only available to a small and wealthy social fraction. It is the culture of this fraction which influences the formation of Shell's advertising repertoire: its vocabulary, its images and also what develops increasingly explicitly as a pedagogical relation between image and text. This influence takes two forms. First, it is directly at work in the formation of Shell's early images in the 1920s; but if it played this role in the initial formation of Shell's advertising repertoire, developing bourgeois culture also provided the relatively constant milieu from which later copywriters and artists were drawn, and in terms of which potential advertisements could be judged before general dissemination. An example of this latter kind of cultural regulation (perhaps one that makes it all seem too unified and crude) is clearly described in Vernon Nye's unpublished 'Recollections of Shell and BP advertising.' Nye, who worked in Shell's Publicity Department during the thirties, describes how new advertisements were first published in pre-booked space on the 'Imperial and Foreign' page of *The Times*. In this way what Nye calls 'Management and Top People' would see the advertisement in question and it would then be possible to consider their reaction when it came to deciding whether the advertisement should be distributed more generally.

As the automobile became available to a wider public, Shell's advertising was orientated towards a wider audience. By the 1960s and 1970s the automobile is well within the reach of members of all social classes. By this time the advertisements have become general, or rather 'national,' in their appeal. They are now addressed to everyone: the citizen as motorist. In this shift of address, the repertoire certainly goes through some changes, but the overall effect is, nevertheless, the generalisation as 'national' of cultural values which, in origin and also in their subsequent refinement, are specific to earlier bourgeois culture. For a consideration of public ideas of the nation then, Shell is significant as an apparatus of cultural reproduction. This can be seen very clearly in Shell's early entrance into television advertising with a series called 'Discover Britain.' As Vernon Nye recalls, 'the first advertisements were really an extension into television of the kind of advertising Shell had found so successful in the press and on posters':

The method chosen was to invite John Betjeman to select places worth visiting and talk about them. To do this effectively required the use of three minutes of time, whereas the limit allowed by the regulations was only two minutes. However, the agents Colman, Prentis and Varley, were able to persuade the authorities to allow three minutes. Research conducted by the London Press Exchange after commercial television had been operating for a time showed that the Shell commercials helped to make TV acceptable to the public who felt that if television advertising was to be like this then it did not mind at all.

Rented Culture didn't just please 'the public'; it evidently also eased its transformation into a sphere which would be defined increasingly by the new mass media. However, if we are to draw such a conclusion, we should also register that developments of this kind also produced vehement High Cultural and neo-aristocratic rejections of the emergent mass pastoralism. Thus, for example, J. Wentworth Day would probably have considered Betjeman little better than a traitor. In 'The Most English Corner of All England'—an essay written during the Second World War—Day celebrates his own particularistic Norfolk and especially the aristocrats with whom he likes to go shooting. Where the weather hasn't kept the offensive town-dwelling masses out ('the trippers and the peering photographers with their museum-minds and long-focus lenses disappear as soon as the northeast wind whistles down from the Arctic'), the 'great landowners...have saved this corner of England which the speculative builder, the tripper-exploiter and the sprawling holiday camp might so easily have ruined and reduced to untidy "bungalows" and marine slumdom, as they have so many other miles of coastland.'[35] But we will come to a far more interesting version of this rejection in the essay on Mary Butts.

Taking the Measure of the National Past

She went to places and shops she remembered from her young days sometimes merely with the curiosity of seeing whether they were still there.

Agatha Christie (1965)

The foregoing discussion of the National Trust and of Shell's advertising indicates how extensively rural and 'historical' conceptions of the nation have been elaborated within the changing public spheres of twentieth century Britain. As for the all-party rhetoric which surrounded the passage of the National Heritage Act (1980), this displayed many of the assumptions of a public sense of history in which stately and even academic elements find themselves aligned with the more vernacular emphasis of everyday historical consciousness. Some of the prominent characteristics of this sense of history can now be identified directly.

The Abstraction of History

National Heritage involves the extraction of history—of the idea of historical significance and potential—from a denigrated everyday life and its restaging or display in certain sanctioned sites, events, images and conceptions. In this process history is redefined as 'the historical,' and it becomes the object of a similarly transformed and generalised public attention. That 'history' can become its own justification under these circumstances was indicated by an advertisement which the Sun Alliance Insurance Group issued in 1980. As the text of this advertisement announced, 'Better bring your insurance problems to us. People have since 1710.' A similar presentation of 'history' as the time of a certain kind of national test informs the memorable Bicentennial chorus line of *Nashville*, Robert Altman's film about American populism: 'We must be doing something right to last two hundred years.'

That this abstracted sense of history stands as more than just the proof of the pudding can be seen in an advertisement issued in the same year for *The Times Atlas of Western History* ('The book that puts history on the map'). This image combined four devastatingly 'historical' faces, including those of Gandhi, Elizabeth I and Hitler. History is presented as a gloss, as the light touch of a dab hand, an impression of pastness which can be caught at a glance. This moonlit impression of history can actually submerge the differences between the figures or presences through which it declares itself, leaving only a multiple invocation of the same sense of 'the historical.' In this respect it is reminiscent of the memorial function of the National Heritage Memorial Fund.

Abstracted and redeployed, history seems to be purged of political tension; it becomes a unifying spectacle, the settling of all disputes. Like the guided tour as it proceeds from site to sanctioned site, the national past occurs in a dimension of its own—a dimension in which we appear to remember only in order to forget. 'History' is stressed to the same measure that active historicity—the possibility of any historical development in the present which is not simply a matter of polishing old statues with ever increasing vigour—is denied to a consequently devalued and meaningless present day experience.

History as Entropy; the new Biedermeier

> Past inner life is turned into furniture just as, conversely, every Biedermeier piece was memory made wood. The interior where the soul accomodates its collection of memoirs and curios is derelict.
>
> Theodor Adorno, *Minima Moralia*

If temporal endurance stands as some sort of measure of achievement, value and quality, this sense is certainly intensified when history is widely experienced as a process of degeneration and decline: like people, countries grow old and decrepit. In this lugubrious perspective the future promises nothing except further decline and one can only hope that ingenious stalling measures will be contrived by necessarily Conservative governments. As that rather embittered stager of ideology Wyndham Lewis put it after the Second World War, Britain is now little better than a rabbit warren on top of a burned-out coalmine.[36] In this vision human dignity and cultural value are nonsynchronous residues, sustained only by an anxious and continuously publicised nostalgia not just for 'roots' in an imperial, pre-industrial and often pre-democratic past, but also for those everyday memories of childhood which are stirred by so many contemporary invocations of this better past. In Flann O'Brien's words, 'I do not think the like of it will ever be there again.'[37]

This sense of history as entropic decline has gathered momentum in the sharpening of the British crisis. National Heritage is the backward glance taken from the edge of a vividly imagined abyss, and it accompanies a sense that history is foreclosed. With organic history in the last stages of degeneration we enter more than just a commemorative age of dead statues. Under the entropic view of history, supported as it is by various High Cultural paradigms, 'the past' is revalued and reconstructed as an irreplaceable heritage—a trust which is bestowed upon the present and must be serviced before it is passed on to posterity. In this process owners are transformed into 'custodians' or 'trustees.' The land or country house owner, for example, emerges as the 'steward'—a public servant who does 'us' and the future a favour by living in the draughty corridors of baronial splendour and tending what he cannot simply consume. One can hear some of the key accents of this transformation in the Duke of Edinburgh's stupefying Introduction to the Department of the Environment's booklet *What is Our Heritage?*.[38]

> The great achievement of European Architectural Heritage Year has been to draw attention to the shortcomings of our generation as curators of the European Architectural collection.

The status quo becomes objective reality in a new sense. All Western Europe is now a museum of superior culture and those citizens who are not lucky enough to be 'curators' of 'the collection' shouldn't worry that they have been left out of the action, for they are still subjects of this new archaism. Their position is to look, to pay taxes, to visit, to care, to pay at the door (even when entering cathedrals these days), to 'appreciate' and to be educated into an appropriate reverence in the process. In this connection it is worth recalling that one of the objectives of the National Heritage Act (1980) was to increase the exhibition of 'the heritage.' In this age of dead statues stately display surely provides access enough.[39]

. National heritage makes numerous connections with what was initially an aristocratic and high-bourgeois sense of history as decline but it also moves on into new areas. As the *Spectator*'s review of Cormack's *Heritage in Danger* announced, 'Physical decay, rather than politics, is Mr Cormack's main theme.'[40] Comparably, during the second reading of the National Heritage Bill (1980), W. Benyon, Tory MP for Buckingham, made a curious statement in which he defined the national heritage as *that which moulders*. While this remark may have been intended to get preservation funds directed more towards property owners than towards the conservation of landscapes and wildlife, it also testifies to an expansion which has recently taken the national heritage beyond its traditional high-cultural definition. Alongside the customary valuation of artworks, country houses and landscapes, these mouldering times have—as Lord Vaizey said of Calke Abbey—seen fairly ordinary household junk included in the repertoire. Alongside the stately museum and the National Trust mansion there now comes the vernacular pleasure of the junk-shop. Here is an altogether more secular amusement in which worn out and broken rubbish can be appreciated at the very moment of its transformation into something worth saving—a bargain, perhaps, but more significantly something resonant of an ordinary and more hand-made yesterday which is just becoming precious as yet another lost world. While the poor have always visited junkshops in search of serviceable items with a little life in them yet, they now jostle with others who are there for more alchemical reasons. These are the ones who pick things over in order to savour the minor pleasure of deciding what shall be allowed to continue on its decline towards the rubbish heap and what will be reinstated in the light of a new attention which values, say, interwar clothes, early synthetic materials or a collection of hand-picked plates and glasses—unmatched but no less newly auratic for that. This, of course, is George Orwell's territory and in due course I will have more to say about his fascination with the modest and cast-off remains of other people's everyday lives.

While the definition of the national heritage has been expanded in the recent sense of decline, this hasn't only involved the inclusion of previously secular contents in an initially sacred repertoire. For if the aura of national heritage hovers over a widening range of objects it has also been relocated, increasingly orientated towards *interiors* and their organisation or design. Like the 'technostyle' interior design which became fashionable in the United States during the thirties, this intensification of private space is occurring at a time when public life seems to be in irreversible decline and when doors are surely there to be closed behind one rather than opened onto the world.[41] In his recent suggestion that Britain is seeing the coming of a new *biedermeier*, Roy Strong refers to early nineteenth-century developments in the Austro-Hungarian Empire when the '*ancient regime* was reinstated and the liberal middle classes, denied power, turned in on themselves and created a style of living whose basis was the cultivation of domestic virtues in the form of all aspects of family life, the home and the garden.'[42] Along with Laura Ashley wallpapers and fabrics, Strong cites the success of a magazine called *Interiors* as evidence of this contemporary shift, and high on the list of factors which have contributed to this development we should certainly place both the continuing extension of home ownership and also the rise of television with its transformation of the relationship between 'home' and 'world.'

The new interior is not invariably 'historical' in style. Indeed, Terence Conran's vastly successful range of interior furnishings (Habitat and the revamped Heals) balance tradition with modernity in a way that leaves little doubt what the main point is—no matter how bad it gets out there you can still turn the lights down low and pull a passable duvet up over your ears. But for all this, the interior provides a main site for the contemporary restaging of history. The rediscovery of Calke Abbey showed how the mere survival of undisturbed interior life can be powerfully moving in the 1980s. The same contemporary orientation is witnessed by the hyper-'realistic' historical interiors of so many 'quality' electric-theatre productions—interiors which are partly 'realistic' and partly televisual projections of what rooms must have looked like before the coming of television itself. The same tendency is also at work in the changing world of museum technology. While the austere display of celebrated objects against an acreage of empty (if statutory) space is indeed slipping out of fashion, the most significant new displays are as much reconstructions as exhibitions; they use the interior space of the museum to construct *scenes* rather than to display objects. The Yorvik Viking Centre at York, for example, uses audio-visual techniques to conjure up its recently opened Viking wharf, smells and all. For many tourists these new 'time-capsule' displays may just give boredom a mildly interesting new form, but they surely also mark a developing perception of history as a miraculous impression that can best be sensed within separate and hermetically sealed enclosures.

Heritage and Danger

Given an entropic view of history, it is axiomatic that 'heritage' should be in danger. To the extent, moreover, that threat defines the heritage as valuable in the first place the struggle to 'save' it can only be a losing battle. The 'stewards' struggle valiantly on behalf of their trust, but a barbarian indifference is all around.

It is against this indifference that the urgent tone of the parliamentary conservationist tends to be directed: 'legislation designed to preserve the best of the past has often come too late.' Of course the country house is given to decay, but there is a development on this theme which brings in the larger question of property and inheritance: 'The problems of the country house are not only fiscal, but physical.

The owner has to do more and more physical work for himself, with the result that a large country house is no place for elderly people: hence the need to be able to hand on to the next generation—and the next generation will need just as much income, and probably more, than at present.'[43]

Claims such as this leave no doubt that the national heritage is far more than an accumulation of threatened objects. Like Debord's spectacle, national heritage still mediates social relations through its ideas, edifices and artefacts. Quite apart from any matter of physical decay, it is also these social relations that get carried forward and secured against threat. Hence (if only in part) the curious style of presence which is so often characteristic of the national heritage—a presence in which cultural authenticity and a rather more corrupt motivation are closely (if sometimes almost indiscernably) connected.

The reality of the national heritage is like that of Bertram's Hotel, an institution of Agatha Christie's invention which survives in the London of the 1960s as an imperilled fragment of High Edwardian life. Intensely and preciously authentic, Bertram's Hotel is also theatrical in atmosphere—real and yet also unreal. The unutterable question has eventually to be asked: 'Could there really be anything seriously wrong with a place that served old-fashioned afternoon teas?' And the answer is that there certainly could be, for behind the manically traditional scenes of Bertram's Hotel there is a multinational conspiracy going on: 'These people; decayed aristocrats, impoverished members of the old County families' are indeed 'all so much *mise en scène*.'[44]

National Geography: The Past That Simply Exists

Considering the merger of history and landscape that lies at the heart of 'our' national heritage, it is consistent that 'the past' should be treated as if it were a simple existent. This emphasis takes two forms: 'the past' is there both to be dug up and also to be visited.

The first of these two modes of presentation derives from antiquarianism and archaeology. In this presentation it is as if one only had to kick a stone in the vicinity of Ironbridge Gorge to uncover early industrial society. What might start as an (industrial) archaeological emphasis opens up a perspective in which 'the past' is defined entirely as bits and pieces which can be recovered, commodified and circulated in exchange and display. This emphasis on tangible remains tends to decontextualise the very objects through which it presents 'the past.' After all, and even though the point can be generalised too far, it is difficult to 'recover' social relations—to auction them off or fit them inside glass cases. Industrial archaeologists and museum staff may well appreciate this as a problem of exhibition (as the Education Officer at Ironbridge Gorge put it, 'skills, techniques and machines, yes, but how does one exhibit social history?'), but this rendering of the past as buried and recoverable bric-a-brac or treasure is not confined to the museum.

With the advent of the cheap metal detector, the past has become the quarry of a bizarre field sport. The resulting protest is to be heard in the voice of 'Stop Taking Our Past,' an organisation which was founded in March 1980 to prevent Britain's archaeological heritage being wiped out: 'We are appalled by the thought that one of the biggest threats to our heritage now comes not from the building of motorways, not from the building of new towns, but from hundreds and thousands of people with metal detectors.'[45] This comment is more than just the record of an existing problem (the updated barrow thief who leaves gaping holes in the verdant surface of historical sites). The hyperbole also ushers us back into that state-subsidised theatre in which middle-class images of the urban working class are played out. The passage works on the transforming theme of the great unwashed, taking it far beyond even the later image of the urban proletariat spilling back onto the land in charabancs to leave litter and broken fences to mark the incomprehension of days of leisure. The barbarians have now enlisted technology in their search for the past, and if something isn't done soon they will surely dig it all up.

This quasi-archaeological sense of the past as recoverable and talismanic bits and pieces is linked with a second supposition which lies at the heart of contemporary tourism: that the past is really there to be visited. Many television presentations of history have contributed to this rendering of the past as an existent, and not just the documentaries that celebrate old remains. One might, for example, recall the BBC's reconstituted 'Iron Age Village' in which ex-hippies were paid to live out a year in the practically imagined life of their primitive ancestors. As much publicity and journalism announced, this reanimated 'village' was not just a faithful recreation of the past; it was also real—hidden away 'somewhere' in the south of England between 1978 and 1980.

If the main point about the past in this definition is that it is still 'there' to be seen or visited, what happens when past and present meet in the exquisite encounter which forms the achieved experience of national heritage? I quote a representative passage from a narration given by George Melly in a BBC2 programme entitled 'Shakespeare in Perspective.' As Melly stands in some of the older streets of Shrewsbury he remarks: 'The city traffic may roar past outside...but here for a moment the real estate agent from Dallas, the insurance clerk from south-east London may enjoy an hour or two in a simpler more gay world.' A similar sense of sudden change was evoked by Esmond Knight in his programme on the English Archer. Two actors strolled the pastures of modern agribusiness and a narrator mustered the strengths of the mother-tongue to transform this green scene into another one: 'And suddenly the whole scene is transformed into a seething mass of horse and steel and swirling colour.'[46]

It is this imagined transformation that needs to be understood, and one needn't worry unduly that it applies equally to Texan and Londoner (there is a whole industry of genealogists giving white American and post-Commonwealth tourists access to the national heritage via 'roots'). A national heritage site must be sufficiently of this world to be accessible by car or camera, but it must also encourage access to that other 'simpler' world when the tourist or viewer finally gets there. This publicly instituted transformation between prosaic reality and the imagination of a deep past is central to the operation of the national heritage.

National heritage has its sites, but like amulets to believers these sites exist only to provide that momentary experience of utopian gratification in which the grey torpor of everyday life in contemporary Britain lifts and the simpler, more radiant measures of Albion declare themselves again. This publicly instituted passage into the past can sometimes be understood in terms of Sartre's description of the primitive community of anti-Semitism.[47] As can be seen from the following letter which was sent to the *Birmingham Evening Mail* by an expatriate now resident in Africa, the pleasure of this ideology can involve the pseudo-poetry of a 'national' and implicitly racist *gestalt*:[48]

   I received a copy of the *Evening Mail*'s Our England special today. A curse on you.
   I had just (after 12 months) convinced myself that I was well rid of the rotten weather, football hooligans, unions, dirt, inflation, traffic,

double standards of politicians—and suddenly it's back to square one. The grimy facade is lifted, and the real England comes flooding back.

Long winter walks through the Wyre Forest ending at the George at Bewdley, chestnuts roasted on an open log fire and swilled down with a pint of mild, house hunting round Ludlow for the mythical half-timbered home, the joy of finding one at a price I could afford and trips to auctions to furnish it for £60...

Summer evenings at the Royal Shakespeare, scents wafting across the river...The sounds and scenes of England.

Thanks for helping me regain a sense of perspective.

The expatriate view has the false and wishful clarity of distance. It is from afar that the 'memory' of woodsmoke and the old counties, of thatch, live elms, threepenny bits and steam engines is most pungent, and no one should be surprised that the most rabidly nostalgic heritage publications are those like the quarterlies *This England* or *Heritage: The British Review* which incorporate an expatriate perspective and which in their reaction seem to assume that the purest Britons are those who simply couldn't stand the decline any longer—superior white subjects who finally realised that the last act of true patriotism must be to take that lucrative job in one of the old colonies.[49] Only from outside can one be the truly loyal custodian of a nation which has declined to the point where it exists only in memory and distant imagination. In these magazines the tables have turned and it seems to be the expatriate Briton who restores 'a sense of perspective' to the inevitably rather clouded residents of the perishing realm. Franco Moretti has remarked of liberal England that 'only those who saw Britain from afar were truly capable of understanding it.'[50] Further down this tumbling century, many patriotic readers of *This England* would willingly concede the point.

National heritage is visitable, but it also provides access to another world. Hence not only the British Tourist Authorities' slogan 'Go away to Britain,' but also a saying from the Irish Tourist Board: 'Take a small step sideways and find yourself in another world.' British Rail hasn't missed out on this theme either. In 1980 BR advertised a special train of 'historical' carriages under the slogan 'In the high speed world of today it's nice to have a quick look back.' With some of the Inter-City trains now moving at 120 mph, it doesn't seem entirely facetious to suggest that this 'quick look back' is increasingly just a glance out of the window. For isn't the very look of rural Britain now publicly identified with 'the historical' itself? Isn't that the eighteenth century which can be seen flying past outside the window? Or has agribusiness won the field and landed us all in the prairies?

The Accommodation of Utopia

In its historical repertoire National heritage borrows many of the trappings of the English utopia (of Arthurian legend, of Blake and Samuel Palmer, of Morris, and Pre-Raphaelitism...), but it stages utopia not as a vision of possibilities residing in the real—nor even as a prophetic if counterfactual perspective on the real—but as a dichotomous realm existing alongside the everyday.

Like the utopianism from which it draws, national heritage involves positive energies which certainly can't be written off as ideology. It engages hopes, dissatisfactions, feelings of tradition and freedom, but it tends to do so in a way that diverts these potentially disruptive energies into the separate and regulated spaces of stately display. In this way, what much utopianism has alluded to or postulated as the challenge of history—something that needs to be brought about—ends up behind us already accomplished and ready for exhibition as 'the past.' Where there was active historicity there is now decoration and display; in the place of memory, amnesia swaggers out in historical fancy dress.

The 'Timeless' Authenticity of Historical Remains

Restaged and reappropriated as the past, history is often also appreciated for its 'timelessness.'[51] This paradoxical sense of timelessness existing where one could be forgiven for expecting to find a stress on historicity and change is in part a measure of endurance: the object or traditional practice which has 'come through' the trials of centuries. However, it can also reflect the immobility which descends on the present when history is eternalised and worn self-consciously as finery over the merely ageing body of society. In order to become spectacular—something separate with which the public can commune in regular acts of appreciation—history must in one sense be something that is over and done with. In its stately connection, history becomes 'timeless' when it has been frozen solid, closed down and limited to what can be exhibited as a fully accomplished 'historical past' which demands only appreciation and protection.

'Timeless' history is often also petrified history in another sense, for what survives is usually what was made and intended to survive: the edifices and cultural symbols of the powerful, structures of stone rather than wood, the official rather than the makeshift and vernacular. However, if the survival of historical objects can mark the power of those who have been in the position to determine both history and the evidences which remain, it would certainly be wrong to reject the apparent 'authenticity' of surviving objects as emblematic of domination alone. Donald Horne has recently argued against the 'senseless reverence given to objects merely because of their authenticity,' citing the many museums which confront their visitors with 'objects without social processes.'[52]

The point is not hard to see; indeed, I have already made a similar one with regard to Ironbridge Gorge. But while anyone who has gone out systematically to visit the major museums of all Europe should perhaps be forgiven a degree of exasperation, it should also be recognised that the meaning of historical and cultural authenticity differs widely from one situation to the next. The ruins of Ancient Rome meant one thing in Mussolini's Italy but the famous ruins of Zimbabwe meant something rather different to anti-colonialists in British Rhodesia. Similarly, in some of the European countries under Soviet domination the relics even of a fairly recent old world (say, for example, the democratic First Republic of Czechoslovakia) have an aura and significance which is not generalisable—least of all in terms of museums and their conduct of exhibition.

Against Horne's suggestion that 'the very didacticism of the Communist museums makes them superior, in principle, because they do not assume that the objects tell their own story,' it should be insisted that there are societies in which no public evidence can exist, and in which no story of the past can be told, except in the interpretation of the state and its colluding hacks. In situations of this sort memory is bound to find mute but still evocative presences to sustain itself and 'authenticity' (whether or not it be in a museum) will communicate more than even the most rigorous exposition of 'social process.' Similarly, Horne claims that many museums have such reverence for the authenticity of objects that it is as if 'historians stopped writing history' and merely displayed their archives: 'What can these museums do that books cannot do better?' And yet people flock to see the reviled object-in-itself (far more than buy history books) and it would take massive arrogance to argue that people only do this because as tourists they are under the false spell of the past as fetishised bits and pieces.

Cultural traditions do not (except in the very crudest of reductions) exist only to be explained and administered as ideology. Similarly, and for all the manipulation, the sense of the 'unique' in modernity cannnot be written off as merely elitist. At the vernacular level, the 'unique' gains in importance and meaning with the rationalisation and disenchantment of everyday life; and despite the many problems implicit in the institutional restaging of history there is at least the possibility that real cultural creation—albeit of a kind connected to mourning—can occur in the public appropriation of historical remains. Rather than sneering at the much abused figure of the tourist (who unlike the full-time sociologist of museums, can always go round the corner for a drink or muse, as Mark Twain did at Saint Paul's, on the railings rather than on the sacred edifice they enclose), we should instead be considering whether all those millions can really be so entirely mistaken in their enthusiasms.[53]

Against Horne's plea for exposition rather than authenticity we should (with Heller) remember Rilke's archaic torso of Apollo (that Greek statue which persisted not just as a fetishised relic in the Louvre

but as a critical auratic presence in the early twentieth century) and also the possibility that Rilke, the High Poet who wrote complex Sonnets to Orpheus rather than rousing odes to the industrial proletariat, may well have been nearer to everyday historical consciousness than is any easygoing demystifier of the 'authentic.' In this far preferable perspective the tourist appears less as fool than as pilgrim journeying between two poles of everyday historical consciousness: childhood remembrance and history as it is appreciated in the collection, the tour or the visit.

Agnes Heller has written that 'in the world of conventions uniqueness is an obstacle. There one must conform.'[54] Against the rather too familiar conventions of Horne's analysis, let us remember those 'timeless' ruins of Zimbabwe as they burst through layer after layer of European and colonial false 'exposition': how, after all, could the primitive 'Kaffirs' of Mashonaland ever have built temples of this magnificence—temples, as the 'exposition' put it so clearly, which must obviously have had a whiter, more northern origin?[55] Let us also remember the enraged crowd which broke into the Cathedral Close at Lincoln in 1726, determined to prevent the reconstruction work which—as popular fear had it—would leave the Cathedral without spires.[56] A pre-touristic approach to 'authenticity,' perhaps, but this story from an old world should still help to persuade us that however problematic the restaging of history may be, 'authenticity' is not to be dismissed as a universally constant confidence trick. In this case a little bit of real history may be just what we need to bring into the picture.

The Vagueness of Deep England

Where the trustees of the National Heritage Memorial Fund deflected the difficulty of defining the national heritage into the pragmatics of their Fund's administration, pundits and enthusiasts have long tended to plunge into a language of vague and evocative gesture. The resulting sub-lyricism is well represented by the following passage from Patrick Cormack's *Heritage in Danger*:[57]

> When I am asked to define our heritage I do not think in dictionary terms, but instead reflect on certain sights and sounds. I think of a morning mist on the Tweed at Dryburgh where the magic of Turner and the romance of Scott both come fleetingly to life; of a celebration

of the Eucharist in a quiet Norfolk Church with the mediaeval glass filtering the colours, and the early noise of the harvesting coming through the open door; or of standing at any time before the Wilton Diptych. Each scene recalls aspects of an indivisible heritage, and is part of the fabric and expression of our civilisation.

In resting his case on what is self-evident to the cultivated senses of the Imaginary Briton, Cormack also writes in a well established and broadly Conservative tradition. The *ur-text* (and Cormack writes like a man who knows it well) seems to come from Stanley Baldwin who evoked England in this way during the twenties—and not just when he reminisced on Bewdley, his 'native town' in Worcestershire. Baldwin didn't think any more of dictionary definitions than Cormack does: for him too 'England' was to be evoked or recalled 'through my various senses—through the ear, through the eye and through certain imperishable scents.' Thus in a much cherished passage the floodgates burst open and a deeply held ancestral world pours in:[58]

> The sounds of England, the tinkle of the hammer on the anvil in the country smithy, the corncrake on a dewy morning, the sound of the scythe against the whetstone, and the sight of a plough team coming over the brow of a hill, the sight that has been seen in England since England was a land, and may be seen in England long after the Empire has perished and every works in England has ceased to function, for centuries the one eternal sight of England. The wild anemones in the woods in April, the last load at night of hay being drawn down a lane as the twilight comes on, when you can scarcely distinguish the figures of the horses as they take it home to the farm, and above all, most subtle, most penetrating and most moving, the smell of wood smoke coming up in an autumn evening, or the smell of the scutch fires: that wood smoke that our ancestors, tens of thousands of years ago, must have caught on the air when they were coming home with the result of the day's forage when they were still nomads, and when they were still roaming the forests and the plains of the continent of Europe. These things strike down into the very depths of our nature, and touch chords that go back to the beginning of time and the human race, but they are chords that with every year of our life sound a deeper note in our innermost being.
>
> These are the things that make England, and I grieve for it that they are not the childish inheritance of the majority of the people today in our country.

Other interwar examples could easily be quoted from writers like G.K. Chesterton, or even Ramsay MacDonald for that matter, but illustration enough is to be found in the following passage from H.A.L. Fisher's essay on 'The Beauty of England':[59]

> The unique and incommunicable beauty of the English landscape constitutes for most Englishmen the strongest of all the ties which bind them to their country. However far they travel, they carry the English landscape in their hearts. As the scroll of memory unwinds itself, scene after scene returns with its complex association of sight and hearing, the emerald green of an English May, the carpet of primroses in the clearing, the pellucid trout-stream, the fat kine browsing in the park, the cricket matches on the village green, the church spire pointing upwards to the pale-blue sky, the fragrant smell of wood fires, the but-terflies on chalk hills, the lark rising from the plough into the March wind, or the morning salutation of blackbird or thrush from garden laurels. These and many other notes blend in a harmony the elements of which we do not attempt to disentangle, for each part communicates its sweetness to the other.

This interpretative stress on the senses, on the experience of meanings which are vitally incommunicable and undefinable, may only seem clear as an example of what Hermann Glaser once described—albeit in a very different national context—as the 'deadening of thought through mythicising vagueness.'[60] All three passages celebrate their 'indivisible heritage' as a kind of sacrament encountered only in fleeting if well remem-bered experiences which go without saying to exactly the extent that they are taken for granted by initiates, by true members of the ancestral nation.

There is certainly some similarity between this England and the incommunicable France that Sartre traced out in his investigation of war-time anti-Semitism. Here is another deep nation founded on an imagined participation immemorial rather than any mere legality, and demonisation or exclusion can indeed be as intrinsic to Deep England as it was to Sartre's France. If discussion of the anti-Semitic potentials of interwar 'England' must wait until the next essay, it is certainly worth indicating how clarifying a sense of threat is to the definition of the deep nation. As Peter Scott, later of Slimbridge and the Wildfowl Trust, put it in a radio broadcast on Easter Day 1943:[61]

> Friday was St. George's Day. St. George for England. I suppose the 'England' means something slightly different to each of us. You may, for

example, think of the white cliffs of Dover, or you may think of a game of bowls on Plymouth Hoe, or perhaps a game of cricket at Old Trafford or a game of rugger at Twickenham. But probably for most of us it brings a picture of a certain kind of countryside, the English countryside. If you spend much time at sea, that particular combination of fields and hedges and woods that is so essentially England seems to have a new meaning.

I remember feeling most especially strongly about it in the late Summer of 1940 when I was serving in a destroyer doing anti-invasion patrol in the Channel. About that time I think everyone had a rather special feeling about the word 'England.' I remember as dawn broke looking at the black outlines of Star Point to the northward and think-ing suddenly of England in quite a new way—a threatened England that was in some way more real and more friendly because she was in trouble. I thought of the Devon countryside lying beyond that black outline of the cliffs; the wild moors and rugged tors inland and nearer the sea, the narrow winding valleys with their steep green sides; and I thought of the mallards and teal which were rearing their ducklings in the reed beds of Slapton Leigh. That was the countryside we were so passionately determined to protect from the invader.

Patriotism is obviously quickened in wartime and the results can be peculiar as the nation is reinvented around the imperatives of the present situation. Where people like Arthur Bryant have long been deliberately renovating the history of Britain, there are also accounts of the nation's prehistory and geography which are actually con-temporary projections of an endangered Deep England. Thus, for example, the following passage from Rex Weldon Finn's *The English Heritage* says far more about the imagination of the time in which it was written than about any early settlement of Britain. First published in 1937, the book was republished in a revised edition in 1948; this time with a dedication to 'The men and women of the Royal Air Force and Women's Auxiliary Air Force who helped to preserve the English Heritage, and more especially to the dead of those Squadrons in which I had the honour to serve.' This is a book in which one hears that 'Britain indeed attracts the primitive immigrant':[62]

The view obtained from the seas to the south and east suggests a plenti-tude of agricultural land; such hills as are visible are neither alarming or steep; there is the certainty of isolation from the disturbed Continent. Save for occasional occurrences of chalk cliffs and marsh in her south coast, there are few obstacles to an easy landing on her shores.

Equally, the immigrant finds it possible, even easy, to penetrate the hinterland.

If a sense of external threat has played a crucial part in the definition of Deep England, the threat itself is more likely to be buried in the foundations of the nation than to be figured out with any historiographical accuracy. In Finn's case one senses that the 'immigrant' travels in a coracle or long-boat made by Messerschmitt, while the 'disturbed' nature of the Continent gathers a similarly contemporary resonance.

There was an unquestionably good cause to the Second World War (though this is far more than can be said for the redeclared version through which we are living now), and these fragile patriotic utopias should be respected to the extent that they are connected to a popular defence of democracy, perhaps even along with the claim that 'In an age of destruction there is a reawakened interest in the things that "endure".'[63] Certainly, I am not quoting these passages simply to accuse their authors of implicit anti-Semitism, or of cynically creating a mythical England out of nothing. Aside from the democratic cause of the Second World War, there is also a practical core to the patriotic fantasy—one which is real enough even though it lies at the level of everyday life rather than historiography. This can best be defined by asking what one must be to become a communicant of the essentially incommunicable deep nation.

To be a subject of Deep England is above all to have *been there*—one must have had the essential experience, and one must have had it in the past to the extent that the meaningful ceremonies of Deep England are, above all, ceremonies of remembrance and recollection. More specifically one must have grown up in the midst of ancestral continuities and have experienced that kindling of consciousness which the national landscape and cultural tradition prepare for the dawning national spirit. The stress on the incommunicable nature of such indivisible moments is fitting since these eulogies to England seem to celebrate both childhood amnesia (or rather the fact that conscious memory only becomes possible once a certain cultural and intersubjective formation has taken place) and also what Heller describes as the mutual *inherence*—the indivisibility—of the different constituents of everyday life. If one must have had the right experiences, therefore, the truly national subject will also have had them at the right time—at the threshold of conscious memory and self-understanding.

In Sartre's language, it is not enough to have been to the wood a few times: 'one must have made notches in the trees in childhood' and one must then be in a position to go back and find them 'enlarged in ripe old age.'

The movement into racism is certainly real enough, and the normative tone—the 'ought'—has already crept into my account. However, it is vital to distinguish particularity itself from the brutal visions in which a certain particularity is elevated to the status of absolute principle. Thus while an imperialist image of British particularity has been foisted on millions of subject-peoples in the school-houses of Empire, and while the same symbolism of the British nation continues to inform the British experience of particularity, it should be recognised that particularistic experience is not *in itself* identical with imperialist experience—even though the latter, which is always normative and asserts its ruling image over others, depends so fundamentally on its imagination of the former.[64] However, if the passages quoted are not all necessarily to be treated as entirely cynical attempts to raise everyday particularity to the level of Absolute Spirit (this was, perhaps, the special gift of Baldwin and, later, Churchill), they certainly work within a select and privileged repertoire of (predominantly green) images. Deep England can indeed be deeply moving to those whose particular experience is most directly in line with its privileged imagination. People of an upper middle-class formation can recognise not just their own totems and togetherness in these essential experiences, but also the philistinism of the urban working class as it stumbles out, blind and unknowing, into the countryside at weekends.

Yet there is also reason to suggest that writers like Baldwin and Bryant needn't really have worried so much that the privileged particularity of the rural scene was no longer the 'childish inheritance' of the majority of people. For no matter how loaded its favoured images, Deep England also speaks to other experiences. Beyond the favoured images, in other words, it is also formally expressive of some of the basic conditions of modern everyday life, almost regardless of the social situation in which it is lived. Just about anyone who, in the developing turmoil of modern society, has ever had cause to look back and wonder about old forms of security will surely be able to find meaning in Deep England, just as will anyone who has ever fallen under the spell of his or her own intersubjective formation—for there is a narcissism in this love of the green moments underpinning and resonating at the incommunicable heart of an 'inner-most being' that also happens to be secretly shared by others of the same cultural formation. It is not just a poet like Rilke who has some experience of memories which 'have turned to blood within us, to glance and gesture, nameless and no longer to be distinguished from ourselves,'[65] and it is certainly not *only* in the desire of racist or imperialist fantasy that such memories are experienced as existing in a communal dimension while at the same time being cradled in the atomised heart of the modern individual. In periods of dislocation, moreover, there will probably be a greater poignancy to the secret glances and gestures which pass between members of the same cultural formation, and there is no reason to believe that such keen glances and gestures—expressions of a cultural particularity held passively and defensively in common—will only pass between those with neo-aristocratic roots in the Shires either.

While the particular images and ideas privileged by Deep England are of relatively narrow social provenance, there is also a celebration of particularism *in itself* in these passages, and here an extension into different social worlds becomes possible. All everyday life is situated and includes the sense of belonging to a particular culture, place and group; just as all personal consciousness accumulates within a cultural matrix which itself goes on to become the ground (both 'ours' and 'mine') of inevitably moving memory—the 'unwinding scroll' of Fisher's description. These aspects of all everyday life can find expression in a Deep England which is none the less loaded for its formal generality.

The approved and dominant images of Deep England are pastoral and green, but there is also something 'green' about everyday life, whatever the situation in which it is lived. Deep England makes its appeal at the level of everyday life. In doing so it has the possibility of securing the self-understanding of the upper middle-class while at the same time speaking more inclusively in connection with all everyday life, where it finds a more general resonance. The vagueness of so many of the eulogies of our 'incommunicable' and 'indivisible' national heritage is partly testimony to the inherence of everyday life and to the interrelated nature of its constitutive experiences; but vagueness works in the more political connection too: making it possible for images to remain true to their privileged constituency at the same time as they grant a stirring and practically-based image of threatened belonging to the urban working-class and even to other peripheral subjects who might choose to take it up.

3

Coming Back to the Shores of Albion: The Secret England of Mary Butts (1890–1937)

THE CRYSTAL CABINET

The Maiden caught me in the Wild
Where I was dancing merrily
She put me into her Cabinet
And Lockd me up with a golden Key

This Cabinet is formd of Gold
And Pearl & Crystal shining bright
And within it opens into a World
And a little lovely Moony Night

Another England there I saw
Another London with its Tower
Another Thames & other Hills
And another pleasant Surrey Bower

Another Maiden like herself
Translucent lovely shining clear
Threefold each in the other closd
O what a pleasant trembling fear

O what a smile a threefold Smile
Filld me that like a flame I burnd
I bent to Kiss the lovely Maid
And found a Threefold Kiss returnd

I strove to seize the inmost Form
With ardor fierce & hands of flame
But burst the Crystal Cabinet
And like a Weeping Babe became

A weeping Babe upon the wild
And Weeping Woman pale reclind
And in the outward air again
I filld with woes the passing Wind

William Blake

A Particular Preoccupation with Home

Mary Butts was born in 1890 and spent her early childhood in
Salterns, a house overlooking Poole Harbour. No small house either,
even though the garden (and it would probably be more accurate to
speak of 'grounds') apparently came to 'less than one hundred acres.'
It was 'the kind of house the Dorsetshire gentry lived in,' so Butts
would write in an autobiography which, after Blake, she named *The
Crystal Cabinet.*[1]

In this book (a work in which memory is also imaginative reinvention—the garden was actually nearer 20 acres), Mary Butts
recalls woods, an orchard, terraces, kitchen gardens and the customary
retinue of attendants: maids, cooks, gardeners, a coachman who wore
the livery colours of the family. There was a room full of drawings
and watercolours by William Blake which had come into the family
through Thomas Butts, friend and patron of Blake. It was, as Butts
claims with the grieving hindsight of the 1930s, a 'profoundly English
life; in the very last years of the old Queen, little had been changed
since her accession.'[2] In this 'wood and wind-lulled' place, then, there
was a family, and as often happens with families of position there was
also a quasi-mystical sense of history in which notions of ancestral
continuity and family identity are expressed in terms of genetic stock,
hallowed possessions and eternity itself:[3]

> My home was not one that had been for long in our family. Some time
> after the Religious Wars we left Norfolk, where we had lived since King
> John's time, and never seriously settled anywhere else. An eighteenth
> century great-uncle had been the Bishop of Ely, but from our ances-
> tors we had inherited, not land, but possessions and the love of them:
> china and silver, clocks, snuff-boxes, pictures, rings. A rather small,
> slow-breeding race, red-haired, with excellent bodies and trigger-set
> nerves. Persistent stock, touched with imagination, not too patient of
> convention, and very angry with fools. Undistinguished since Tudor
> days, when we made some show, East-country squires, rarely emerging,

often soldiers by profession. None too patient of our fellow men—that trait repeats itself—profoundly sure of ourselves, for reasons we ourselves know best.

For reasons of a secret common to our blood. A secret concerned with time and very little with death, with what perhaps medieval philosophers called *aevum*, the link between time and eternity.

It was on account of this blood-based secret that the stasis of those last Victorian years came to figure both redemption and destruction. In a remembered and retrospectively sanctified place like Salterns such stillness is proof of a pact with eternity and every little particular is touched by it; there can be no trivia, nothing of lesser significance within the walls of a paradise like this. But if fondness of childhood memory is partly responsible, Salterns also owes its stillness to the fact that its presence, like that of any other relic, stands as testimony to its survival. Salterns is *non-synchronous*, no longer fully contemporary with the society in which it is placed.[4] As a survival, it is a place to be understood in the enhanced terms of 'endurance' rather than in any more prosaic order of mere existence: there is a doubling of the attention in which the view thickens to form an aspic around its cherished object. No simply existing structure of mere stone or brick, Salterns becomes the kind of place in which one muses on what Mary Butts once identified as 'the brickness of a brick.'[5] As often happens, objects take on the aspect of heritage as they are endangered and the basic terms of their existence come into question.

Beyond the garden wall, stillness therefore tells a different story. Here, where the provincial middle-classes live, stasis does not testify to the endurance of timeless and essential continuities. Instead it is a mark of spreading stagnation, rot and degeneration which threatens, all too visibly, to engulf everything of value. Mary Butts calls this advancing growth 'The Tide.' She sees its embodiment in the advance of surburban housing, but there is also no limit to her horror at the pinched mentality which she considers to lie at the heart of these developments in mere brick and mortar—the meagre utilitarianism, the lack of style, the petty moralism, the only slightly disguised self-interest and, above all, the instrumentalist and 'materialist' science which is increasingly replacing religion as meaningful and legitimating worldview. As Butts puts it in the pamphlet *Warning To Hikers* (1932), something happened around 1830: 'for the first time, man began to manufacture every object in common use, from houses to boots, upon unvarying patterns of ugly vulgarity.'[6] No pact with eternity here.

It was from this lower stratum that Butts's upwardly mobile mother came. She entered this elevated family with its historical and cultural connections, but in her daughter's view at least she never learned to breathe easily in the more refined air of its home. Its freedom and openness apparently threatened her and she could never break with the stifling and anti-aesthetic puritanism of her own more provincial middle-class background. In a sense, then, she brought 'The Tide' with her into this gifted enclosure. But even if Mary hates her mother—which she seems at times to have done with real vehemence—she also recognises that the dead hand of middle-class Victorian culture falls with a particular heaviness on its women. As proof of this point, her childhood is disturbed by the ominous death of maternal Aunt Monica, found drowned in shallow water in a wood. A conveniently open verdict was returned on the death, but while the drawing room whispered about the reported presence of tramps in the area there were also rumours, nearer the kitchen, of suicide. These led Mary to see Aunt Monica as a victim not just of those ideas of the appropriate feminine station—the 'gentlewoman'—which had stood between herself and a much wanted education, but also, not entirely unrelated, of a widowed mother (Mary's grandmother) whose desire was 'to live, a mateless queen bee, surrounded by her workers, her mateless children.'[7]

So it is never a simple question of aristocratic culture as opposed to bourgeois or petty bourgeois philistinism, although this opposition is taken up and worked over repeatedly in Mary Butts's novels, stories and essays. Nor are we dealing with the straightforward emergence of a proto-feminist perspective, although this too forms part of the picture.[8] What we have instead is a far from logically consistent narrative complex in which family, a central theme in these writings, appears not as a problematic social institution, but as a transcendent value threatened by its own historicity. Thus a reverence for family and its deep (not to say imaginary—and by this I do not mean simply 'untrue') ancestral continuities comes to coexist with an equally profound suspicion of marriage and of the generational conflicts to which it leads. Marriage becomes the weakness of family—the moment at which it goes outside itself in search of renewal, and therefore also the moment at which 'The Tide' might find its way in. As the century turns, family seems only to speak of the past. The pact with eternity is increasingly threatened as the new century develops, and in the novels of the interwar years marriage has become an unequivocal fatality. Generations fall into cosmically defined opposition (Star Wars in the drawing room) as the money runs out, and marriage becomes identical with the contamination and destruction of the family. Family, in short, is a quality Butts had by birth and early childhood. Marriage is either a violation of family or merely a mediocre social arrangement, a stifling and corrupt domesticity for those who never had breeding in the first place.

With the death of Father (who was fifty-seven years older than Mary) the world itself withers. Mother (at least in the fable of *The Crystal Cabinet*) wastes little time and enlists Daughter's help in burning Father's disapproved books—morally dubious tomes by Burton, French memoirs and perhaps worse—on the tennis court. There are death duties to pay and Mother—financially as well as aesthetically inept— eventually sells the Blake watercolours and drawings along with other

treasures, and not at a good price. A year or so after Father's death, Mother remarries and Daughter starts to get in the way. Investigation reveals a suitably distant boarding school for girls up on the Scottish coast (in Saint Andrews) and off Mary is sent. Decline continues, until Salterns—this sacred home—is eventually sold, divided and (a point which, like others in this account, has been contested) part of it turned into a boarding house. Mary's subsequent life is informed by a feeling of blight and loss, one that is sharpened rather than tempered in the imagination of later years. As late as 1937, the year of her death, Butts was describing this loss in a language of melodramatic violence and contempt:[9]

> Place I shall never see again, that I can never bear to see. Now they have violated it, now that its body has been put to the uses men from cities do to such places as these. Now Salterns is no more than a white house pulled down and built onto, its back broken, split up. And in the fields are several little houses, like the house I am living in, little boxes of rough-cast; and beside them each another little box for the car to live in at night. The cars that allow these people to run about the earth, and wherever they go to impoverish it. Driving out and abusing or exploiting something that is not their own; that unconsciously they resent—and might do well to fear. . . .
>
> I shall never see it again. Except from a long way off. From Purbeck, from the top of Nine Barrow Down, it is still possible to stand, and see, on a clear day, the maggot-knot of dwellings that was once my home.

If family is a principal theme in Mary Butts's writings, it is typically articulated in connection with a place like Salterns—a threatened, if not already destroyed, habitation and lifeworld in which every particular is harmonious and meaningful: a place, as one might say bearing in mind Butts's involvement with Roger Fry and the Omega Workshop, of significant form. This is the England in her crystal cabinet, and it forms the enduring pre-occupation of the writing. As Mary Butts puts it in her first novel, *Ashe of Rings*, 'there is a tiny discomfort in seeing a surface spoiled'.[10]

Dérèglement

> What a party! What drink! What company! It will become a classic example—Christmas near Cannes, I hope. . .

Paris was a dream—we didn't go to bed for a week and spent *all* our
money on such binges! The last thing I remember was dancing solely
supporting myself by the lobes of Cedric Morris' ears...

(Mary Butts in letters written to Douglas Goldring during the
twenties.)

From school in Scotland Mary Butts moved to London where for a
time she attended Westfield College in Hampstead and also, apparently, the London School of Economics. There was some involvement
with a critical, presumably Fabian, politics; there were whispers of
IRA sympathies and during the First World War there was work of
some (probably voluntary and administrative) kind with the London
County Council in Hackney. For a time Butts was calling herself a
socialist, although by the thirties she describes this as only the for-
givable gesture of rebellious youth—a way of shocking instinctively
Conservative relatives and acquaintances which also, as she wrote,
gave her some practical knowledge of the urban working class: 'Taught
me to be friends with the common man (not the peasant but the town
workman), and to sit on a box or a pile of stones, try and talk Trade
Unionism and soon arrive at his family troubles and the way the fore-
man had behaved.' After a statement like this it scarcely needs adding
that Mary Butts never had much time for the 'Marxian apocalypse,' as
she called it: the revolution she wanted—at least by the thirties (a time
in which she still opposed the remembered Party Conservatism of her
county mother)—was to be 'of the mind not the body.'[11] While this
contempt for 'materialism' is something that Mary Butts may have
held in common with the more aristocratic wing of the Conservative
Party in those pre-war years, the first novel *Ashe of Rings* (written in
1919–20) is nevertheless peopled with characters who threaten, in
polite circles, to vote Labour, who support conscientious objection,
and who are strongly opposed in the narrative to the war-mongering
women who were handing out white feathers to un-uniformed men
on London streets. Likewise, Serge Sarantchoff, the Russian exile in
this novel, has fled the prisons of *pre*-revolutionary Russia. In the same
book, however, there is also ample sign of a shift from the nascent
political project of making a new world to the mystical and aesthetic
one of discovering and revaluing lost traces of the old. From 'cafes
and meetings of the revolution,' as it is for Serge, the narrative of
Ashe of Rings turns to a search for stolen property (jewelry, papyrus
fragments, Egyptian beads and other irreplaceable stuff of no mere

cash value) which is eventually found in the house of a 'Jew dealer.'[12] A noxious theme to which Butts will return.

In Mary Butts's life this seems quite literally to have involved a shift from politics to magic—conjurings (circles drawn on the floor in the house which she rented at 43 Belsize Park Gardens), an eventual (1921) visit to Aleister Crowley's 'Abbey' in Sicily, and an interest in myth and the ancient world.[13] This latter interest seems clearly to have taken in the neo-anthropological ideas of J.G. Frazer's *The Golden Bough* and also the writings which took this influential work as a point of departure: Jessie Weston's *From Ritual to Romance* and the work of the Cambridge School of classical scholarship, Jane Harrison, Gilbert Murray and F.M. Cornford. Such a heady blend of antiquity, myth and the occult informed much early twentieth century modernism (Yeats, Pound, Eliot, H.D. and also to an extent D.H. Lawrence), providing a basis, as has been argued, for various strategies of *dérèglement*—aesthetic or stylistic assault on the customs, habits and normative perspectives of the time.[14] Bombs may have fallen on London during the First World War, but one shouldn't entirely forget the translations of Meleager and Cavalcanti or the ruminations over Celtic myth, tarot and the 'meaning of meaning' which also went on.[15]

There was a short-lived marriage to John Rodker, a writer and publisher who was imprisoned during the war as a conscientious objector, and who had come into the literary world from Jewish Whitechapel (school and then, with Isaac Rosenberg among others, self-education in Whitechapel Library). There was a daughter who, as things turned out, would be brought up mostly by one of her mother's aunts, and generally a lot of style and glitter as Butts took up her relatively impoverished but nevertheless fast and flamboyant orbit in London's literary and artistic circles. Both interrupted and intensified by the War, the scene was reconvened in Paris, Villefranche and other continental locations shortly afterwards; its moveable festivities only decisively came to an end when some distant and unfortunate thing happened on Wall Street in 1929. 'Abroad' in this decade of high sterling, Mary Butts moved among the international Bohemian set of the time: the poseurs, the wealthy, the artists and writers, the displaced and war-damaged, people who were not so much poor as unaccountably without sufficient funds—White Russians for whom, like the prewar 'Poles' of Wyndham Lewis's contemporary description (and in part like Mary Butts herself), the past remained splendid even if the world had shrunk to a succession of cheap hotel rooms, bars, immigration problems and passing liaisons.[16] Butts spent nearly ten years in this world of stretched nerves—neurasthenia as she (together with the psychiatrists of her time) tended to call it—and raving, if not always desperate, good times. 'How,' as she put it in *Armed With Madness*, 'to be a grand seigneur on nothing a year.'[17]

But throughout the urbane turmoil and experimentation—literary, psychological, sexual and pharmaceutical—Mary had the 'green transparent world' of England in the back of her mind. When the time eventually came she returned, together with the opium habit she had developed in Paris and would never shake off. The last home was made in an impermanent and unsatisfactory marriage with a painter called Gabriel Atkin. A bungalow over-looking Sennen Cove, near Land's End in Cornwall, it was the speculatively built rough-cast box mentioned with such disdain in *The Crystal Cabinet*: a bunker from which regular indictments of contemporary society, with its creeping materialist 'Tide,' were fired in the approximate direction of a public which doesn't seem to have paid much attention. Death, following a haemorrhage which the Penzance General Hospital could not control, came early—in 1937. By this time Mary Butts was living on her own and finding increasing solace in Anglo-Catholicism. So much, then, for the life—a life of constant and dramatic self-creation.

It was somewhere between the Webbs and Aleister Crowley that Mary Butts began to write. There are three thematically interconnected novels, *Ashe of Rings* (1925), *Armed With Madness* (1928) and *Death of Felicity Taverner* (1932). There are three volumes of short stories, two historical novels (both of which take their themes from the ancient world), some uncollected poems and essays, two pamphlets *Warning to Hikers* and *Traps for Unbelievers* (both published in 1932). There is also a very interesting 'slim volume' called *Imaginary Letters*, illustrated with graphic hallucinations by Jean Cocteau (friend and perhaps also idol to Butts) and published in a small edition in Paris in 1928. These letters, signed from the Hotel Foyot in Paris, are written to the imagined mother—herself an exiled 'ghost' living in Yalta—of Boris, a dispossessed White Russian who has some sort of dependency on the writer (seems even to live with her, but not in any way to imply a generative relationship) while at the same time being given to disappear for days and nights into a wild carnival of drunken and polymorphous activity with young men—particularly, as it seems, young sailors ('the fashionable excitement just now'). Many of the characteristic themes of the early writings are worked out to their full in this thoroughly opiated text: cultural and economic dispossession, sexual and psychological extremity, male homosexuality considered in its possible relations with women (whose sexuality is also in question—although this is more discreetly expressed), pederasty, filiation, motherhood.

Butts's narratives are full of men who are driven, often war-damaged, and deeply uprooted. Some of them use cocaine, while others try to reintegrate themselves around a male mysticism which has both libidinal and aggressive elements—as if the force which drives the universe shone out of their own hungry eyes—and which isolates them even more.[18] These male characters are exacerbated mentalities, no more or less; scarred and sometimes crippled by war, they now face the larger task of reinventing the world-as-it-was from out of their own heads. Heads, let it be added, which are full of jangling and conflicting sensations—colours, sounds and above all memories which without warning strike them down from behind: 'He could not go back to the old life. It seemed to him that he would soil its loveliness. Its exotics would shrivel and tarnish as he limped by. "Light things, and winged, and holy" they fluttered past him, crepe velours, crepe de Chine, organdie, aerophane, georgette...'[19] Trapped by their own ghastly versions of a crystal cabinet, these men lack 'emotional focus' and are unable to escape their own fevered minds except through sudden acts of violence in which they take even themselves by surprise.[20] Full of desire for the women who flit before them (alluring images pulled from a Kirchner album), they are thwarted because for them desire can only be mental; a kaleidoscopic 'redecoration,' as Butts once put it, of their dislocated memories.[21] Flurries of activity alternate with moments of anomie, or of tense and melodramatically neurasthenic langour: 'Months passed. The fabric of his dream hardened into a shell for his spirit.'[22]

Such is the deracinated mentality which Mary Butts associates not just with the war-torn male, but more generally with that great undoing which for her was the modern city. It is a mentality which goes to the country for convalescence, causing the actual rural world to disappear into the merely retinal sensations of a pastoralism which Butts clearly associates with urban perceptions and not with any rural state of nature. 'Nothing came to trouble the continuity of his dream. The sheen on the new grass, the expanse of sky, now heavy as marble, now luminous; the embroidery that a bare tree makes against the sky, the irridescent scum on a village pond, these were his remembrancers, the assurance of his realities. Beside them a cow was an obscene vision of the night.'[23] For this mentality, with its sick pastoralism, getting up in the morning is quite enough work for one day. Thus does Pre-Raphaelite woman cut through the veils of inherited objectification to strike back at the onlooking, if no longer securely authoritative (or even entirely sane), figure of man.

Between Flight and Settlement:
England As Artificial Paradise

> Oh the days when we had some clothes. I am writing this from the
> heart of Paris, dressed for a shooting lodge. And our life is like that, of
> danger, sport and fatigue...
>
> *Imaginary Letters*

In this radically disordered modern experience the idea of a 'real' England takes on great value and importance for Mary Butts. Formed on the recoil from a modernity gone mad, this England is articulated against the lies of urban pastoralism with its cultural sources in Tennyson, its sentimental reading of Wordsworth and its deep ignorance of what Mary Butts knew to be the *really* authentic measure of the land. She, after all, had an earlier and genetically communicated access to older than pre-Romantic sources. As she wrote in an autobiographically resonant passage of her last novel: 'About 1700 our family took a turn; before Nature happened, Rousseau, Swedenborg, Blake.'[24] It is to the definition and defence of this authentic 'England' that Mary Butts herself turns in the later novels and essays. While there is a movement of *flight*—intoxication, destabilisation, disruption, an impulse towards new and transient forms of affiliation and urban society—in the earlier writings, the later narratives feature an increasingly dominant movement towards *settlement*, with its impulse of return to threatened family, inheritance and predominantly rural nation. These two impulses conflict to a considerable extent, the one tending to undercut and reveal the artifice and presupposition of the other. Thus while it is full of ancient and timeless continuities, the 'England' of the last two novels is also volatile and unstable—subject to sudden transformation of meaning and exposed to new forms of insecurity.[25] In one perspective, myth and magic are harnessed as stylistic artifice in a cultural critique of contemporary reality; in the other they become part of a theory of special people in special places—the gifted few. While Butts's England is formed in this tension, there are also wider aspects to its definition and two of these especially make the writing of far more than eccentric interest.

First, the sense of loss and decline which, for Mary Butts, came initially with the disintegration of family and only slightly sub-aristocratic home, is *generalised* by the experience of war and its aftermath. It is never just a particularistic question of personal history, the rancour of a dispossessed would-be aristocrat living on diminishing means. Instead, it starts to speak of the distresses of a whole epoch, of the loss of life and 'station,' of the disruption of political culture and tradition—the concert of old nations—throughout Europe. Closer to home, it also testifies to the decline of liberal England and the rise of mass democracy.

Far from being the merely personal foible of an unread writer, the return to 'England' is one of the fundamental tendencies within the established public culture of the interwar years. If this is a time when an upper-class idealisation of 'tramping' coexists uneasily with hunger marches, homelessness and unemployment, it is also the time of Baldwin's 'England': a kind of Conservative government by aspic which (as I have already mentioned) was clearly advocated in its 'historical' dimension by Arthur Bryant, the anti-'materialist' Tory who

made such a rousing case for the preservation of rural England and who spoke of 'the spirit of the past' as that 'sweet and lovely breath of Conservatism.'[26] Of course there was the General Strike, but there was also the BBC which obligingly kept both the Archbishop of Canterbury and the Leader of the Opposition (Ramsay MacDonald) off the air, and which (even more obligingly) played Blake's 'Jerusalem' on the heels of Baldwin's eventual announcement that the strike had collapsed.[27] There was Lutyens and more specifically his continuing work at Castle Drogo in Devon: a building which the National Trust would soon enough be cherishing as 'the last castle in England.' Butts's writing belongs to a time in which the 'country' was being brought to a newly abstract focus in Art (Nash, Sutherland…) with its spill over into the emerging and still experimental publicity of mass advertising (Shell's country campaigns, London Transport…); in music (Elgar still of immense patriotic fame, Delius, Grainger, Vaughan Williams) with its adoption of rural association and, in some cases, actual folk melodies; in much of the literature read and written at the time (Buchan, Henry Williamson, the Powys brothers, Dornford Yates, T.H. White, Belloc, Chesterton, Housman, Edward Thomas, the Sussex Kipling…).

This is also a time of new, sometimes Thoreau-esque, public schools in the country, and of a rather more genuinely public interest in the ways, landscapes, places and artefacts of rural Britain. The interwar period saw a substantial increase in motorised access to the countryside, and also the development and consolidation of voluntary associations promoting not just 'rambling,' but also appropriately regulated use and study of nature or 'natural history'—encouraging the public to accept that birds, say, should be watched (through field glasses or, after 1933, from new observatories), identified and perhaps counted in a census, rather than shot, stuffed, deprived of their eggs, kept in cages or worn as hats. In a curious but perhaps characteristic twist of the era, Tom Harrisson went from the national census of Great Crested Grebes to become the co-founder of Mass Observation.[28] As for Mary Butts, her writings define their 'England' within this very broad and more than single-voiced cultural tendency. That their relation with it can be conscious and critical is evident from their paradoxically pastoral anti-pastoralism and their eventual anger at the new mobility of urban 'hikers.'

The second point is that Mary Butts developed her literary style within the experimental ambience of European modernism. This has important consequences, and not just because it leads to a writing which foregrounds the operation of the text and its productivity over meaning. This is not a writing which exists only to testify to a mentalist 'textuality' supposedly underlying (or cutting across) all experience. To the contrary, it is a writing full of panic at the realisation that the world it craves can, for very good historical reasons, no longer exist anywhere *but* in texts; and in bizarrely Gothic, cranky and hallucinatory texts at that. In the modernist tradition, as may certainly be said, Mary Butts uses myth, ancient Greek religion, magic and an at times extraordinarily contrived literary style to attack what she sees as the mechanistic norms of the materialist 'Tide.' But there is another side to this too. For the writing is also 'modernist' in a less literary sense. In its pursuit of the measured 'England' which it would portray in a world of completely different social order and rationality, it has no choice but to go weird. From the literary-critical points of view which have been dominant this century such weirdness may be a mark of failure, but if so—and I doubt even this—it is certainly a failure which has its uses.

Mary Butts can't secure her transparent green world without going to extreme lengths of artifice. In doing so she not only reveals ploys and patterns of relationship implicit in the interwar return to 'England,' she also dramatises tendencies in this 'England' which are far from simply green or pleasant. Early in the 1920s J.B. Priestley reviewed the new 'impressionist' style which he found exemplified in Butts's first collection of stories, *Speed the Plough*.[29] He found this style at its best in portraying the urban psychosis of Butts's men back from the war, but he also judged it inadequate when it came to sustaining a narrative or peopling and dramatising a sufficient fictional world. These were not merely foolish comments. Priestley could not have anticipated the extent to which such a jangling 'impressionistic' style might go on to reveal the cultural and ideological presupposition lying at the heart of 'England,' that artificial paradise which it failed so significantly to realise. As for the lack of realisation, is this really just a matter of literary style or competence? Isn't it also a characteristic of the European world as it emerges from the First World War, with its massive destruction not just of humanity and its traditions but also of memory itself? How, as has been asked of Céline's writings, is there to be well realised character and realistic narrative development in a life which—at least until the redefinition of cultural identity in new national terms—is curiously empty of recognisable people? Only in legends of forgetfulness.[30]

Still-Life in the South

Dionysos was always of the people, of the 'working classes', just as the King and Queen of the May are now. The upper classes worshipped then, as now, not the Spirit of Spring but *their own ancestors*. But…Dionysos must be translated from the fields to the city. The country is always conservative, the natural stronghold of a landed aristocracy, with fixed traditions; the city with its closer contacts and consequent swifter changes and, above all, with its acquired, not inherited, wealth, tends towards democracy.

Jane Harrison (1913)

From Description to Myth and Invocation

Mary Butts's England is articulated in stylised and often rather florid terms, its nature and landscape no less than anything else. The resulting sense of strangeness, however, is not that of a writer seeking (or failing) to represent closely experienced changes in a prose world of description. It is utterly unlike the tense inventiveness which enters Thomas Hardy's novels as they strain to describe a landscape transformed and, indeed, abstracted by an increasingly mechanised and capitalised agriculture—the moment in *Jude the Obscure*, say, when a newly sown field in a geography stripped of customary hedgerows is likened to a stretch of brown corduroy.

In Mary Butts's fiction there is no longer any closely experienced country life to recount. Instead, if I may use a passage from Rimbaud, 'there are saints, veils, threads of harmony, and legendary chromatisms in the setting sun.'[31] Contemporary reality, at least as realist theories of representation would approach it, is of little interest to these writings, except to the extent that they are able to cast spells across it. Myth, celebration of immediacy, a galvanising mode of expression—the point of all this artifice is precisely to affront settled and habituated appearances, to break through the pseudoconcrete so as to shock the everyday world into a disclosure of deeper, more authentic meaning.

Like Kipling, many war poets, Stanley Baldwin (*On England*, 1926), H.V. Morton (*In Search of England*, 1927) and the John Cowper Powys of *Wolf Solent* (1929), Mary Butts sees her rural England most clearly from abroad, not (however rosily) from over the fence or across the aisle in Church. By the twenties and early thirties, at least as this writing suggests, it was all down to acts of remembrance and attempted reinvention. Back to the drawing board or, more accurately, to a nervous chalking of necromantic circles on the floor. In the earlier two novels especially, the textual methods which are used to conjure this authentic England into existence are identical with those which evoke the glamorous, stylish and emancipated women who pass so tantalisingly before the anxious eyes of Mary's returning soldiers. In both cases, ironically, the textual repertoire includes an abstracted and rather mindful sensationalism. Colours, smells (or rather 'scents'), sounds, brightness (which 'falls from the air' in one of Mary Butts's favourite literary quotations), reflections, felt textures (of luxurious fabrics like silk especially), darkness—these are among the basic terms of a writing which seems often to start with the language of refined sensation and alluring appearance, but which goes on to seek out a world in their evocation.

Use this language in unexpected connection and 'legendary chromatisms' may indeed start to shine from the surface of an exhausted reality. In *Ashe of Rings* especially, the world is imagined through startling and prismatic displays of colour, as if it were a sudden crystallisation within one of those bright glass paperweights which Butts liked to have around the place. It might indeed be thought that this is merely the repertoire of fashion, private beauty and the high-life put to new uses, but the point is more complex. Butts's style has as much about it of Baudelaire as of Harrods or the *Tatler*. It is an ambition of her writing that the ordinary and routine—not just the pseudoconcrete but also the 'vulgar' as it is so typically deplored in Butts—should be enlivened; just like the 'plainest middle-class' crockery—plates, cups, saucers—which Butts once saw in a Paris bazaar and described in her journal as glittering in a transfiguring display of colour and light which belied their domestic function.[32] A search for more authentic meaning, and a sustained assault on the routinised and increasingly devalued character of modern everyday life—these aspects of

Butts's writing lead in several directions, some of them far from easily acceptable.

In his novel *The Napoleon of Notting Hill* (1904), G.K. Chesterton describes an exiled President of Nicaragua as he wanders around forlorn in London. When this historically redundant figure is overcome with yearning for his homeland he tears a strip of yellow paper from a nearby Colman's Mustard advertisement and combines it with a rag reddened in his own blood. Red and yellow—these are the colours of a Nicaragua which has been trampled under 'the brute powers of modernity' and now only exists as an idea. As this perambulating throwback says: 'wherever there is a field of marigolds and the red cloak of an old woman, there is Nicaragua. Wherever there is a field of poppies and a yellow patch of sand, there is Nicaragua. Wherever there is a lemon and a red sunset, there is my country. Wherever I see a red pillar-box and a yellow sunset, there my heart beats. Blood and a splash of mustard can be my heraldry.'[33]

In the more recent but no less dislocated world of Mary Butts colours also seem to become substantial. 'Green,' for example, is suddenly a world in itself; people walk around and stand on it, just as they breathe and swim in 'blue.' Freed, if this is the word, from any simply referential relationship to a close experience, 'green' becomes the very ground of an England of the mind—well imagined (as it was also for Shell) close to the 'white' of chalk, the 'grey' of sarsen stones, and perhaps the bright stab of a wildflower which the prose will be careful to name accurately. It is the 'green' of imagined 'turf' rather than any literal grass; as an American character in *Armed With Madness* says, 'This is the England we think of. Hardy's country isn't it?'[34] The same abstract assertion of a 'green' which is 'thought of' is evident, although obviously in different forms, in other ruralist writers of the time: most noticeably, perhaps, in John Cowper Powys whose *Wolf Solent* is full of moments such as one in which a train plunges through an observed 'green pool of quietness that was older than life itself.' Housman once wrote of the 'coloured counties,' and in the interwar years these increasingly abstract colours were well viewed from a train. As the unambitious Wolf Solent himself says: 'All I want is certain sensations!'[35]

Then there are names—of villages, plants, landmarks, birds, stones and the accoutrements of rural life ('ashplants' rather than walking sticks)—which aren't used to describe a world so much as anxiously to conjure one up. Things are *invoked* into being through a process of naming which is enacted in a deliberate and conscious assertion of itself. To get the name right is everything. It is as if the answer to urban modernity was for everyone to learn the names of the plants and places again—an anticipation, perhaps of those recognition games like 'I Spy' or of the Shell country calendars which were to achieve prominence in the childhood of 1950s Britain. If this is a landscape of names, moreover, it is also one of literary quotation ('something far more deeply interfused'...) and repeated references to Celtic (sometimes spelt with a 'k') and Grail mythology. Birds and plants serve to echo older, threatened and partly occult meanings. While the pastures—or rather the 'meads'—of this landscape bear no connection with modern agriculture, they have nevertheless been heavily seeded. They occur in a geography which craves the understanding of those rare and imperilled people who *really* belong to it. With its secret sense of measure, it is laden with myths which both await completion and also theaten to fade away for ever: 'Like the mass of Keltic art. Like, now she considered it, the whole grail story, the saga story par excellence that has never come off, or found its form or its poet.'[36] And this, in a sense, is the challenge which pre-occupies the writing—who is to complete the suspended fable, bring meaning back, and give security to all these threatened and violated prospects? As for its nomenclature, Butts's land seems to demand a vocabulary which might well have been inventorised in a dictionary comparable with the one which Percy Grainger, pianist and composer, was in the same years planning to compile of 'blue-eyed' or 'Nordic' English.[37]

Within this world there is, repeatedly, a house. It usually overlooks the sea; there are cliffs, a wood full of lingering pagan vibrations, a nearby village and a vicar or priest who still has adequate things to say. There is 'green' spilled everywhere. There may be ancient herms— stones which, at least in the secret wisdom of local understanding, were being dragged to Stonehenge but had to be abandoned because they bore an uncomfortable resonance and charge. There are green roads (an increasingly popular theme as interwar ruralism lines itself up against the encroaching motorcar), set off against flint and chalk.[38] There are dew ponds and timeless wells which, reflecting the crisis of modernity, sometimes dry up, leaving the people of the house to make their tea out of soda water. There is a set of green rings—like Badbury, Cissbury or Flowers Barrow—near the house, and through them the narratives indicate immemorial connections linking family and place: a blood-based understanding of the soil, secret memories, sites of special association...In *Ashe of Rings*, there is even a book of the family—a sort of genetic journal—which goes back, in secret script, to disappear into the primordial mists of time.

History as Secret Meaning

Life pushes itself up out of the ground, and the whole of human history can be traced out in the personalities of this England. Thus Carston, the American in *Armed with Madness*, recognises an embodiment of history when he comes up against the father of an old English family: 'The impression was that he was opposite someone very old—not particularly in years but in something built by centuries of experience, and now no longer in flower.' Carston's American thoughts continue:[39]

> The eighteenth century had produced this type, had set him in culture and conviction that nature had appointed certain old men to approve and modestly direct her arrangements of fire and air. The renaissance had kicked off that ball, now frozen into the marble and stucco that he was sure adorned his park somewhere. Behind that there was the matrix; the middle ages, feudalism, Christendom. Faith in a childishly planned universe as one thing. *The earth one great city of gods and men.* His history lessons were taking life at last.

There is indeed likely to be a county history or two lying around in the house, although one senses that these books are there only to have their errors corrected by people whose knowledge of the locality is superior to that which can be derived from any normal archive.[40] Thus in *Death of Felicity Taverner* there is a character called Scylla Taverner who, like Mr Urquhart in Powys's *Wolf Solent*, has designs on the history of the county:

> Scylla's passion, shared with the innocent man in the *Adventure of Miss Annie Spragg*, was—spending if necessary her life over it—to leave behind her the full chronicle of their part of England, tell its 'historie' with the candour and curiosity, the research and imagination and what today might pass for credulity of a parish Herodotus. There was material there, for ten miles around about them, which had not been touched; not only manor rolls and church registers or the traditions which get

themselves tourist-books. She had access to sources, histories of families, to memories that were like visions, to visions which seemed to have to do with memory. To her the people talked, the young as well as the old; and there were times when the trees and stones and turf were not dumb, and she had their speech, and the ruins rose again and the sunk foundations, and copse and clearing and forest changed places, and went in and out and set to partners in their century-in, century-out dance. There were times, out on the high turf at sun-rise and set, when in the slanted light she saw their land as an exfoliation, not happening in our kind of time, a becoming of the perfected. She did not know how she knew, Kilmeny's daughter, only what it looked like—the speechless sight of it—her thread to the use of the historic imagination, Ariadne to no Minataur in the country of the Sanc Grail.

In this curious historiography the family home becomes an embodiment of the true and essential past. It may not be crudely wealthy—indeed the atmosphere is usually one of elegant and measured poverty (the frayed carpets of bygone grandeur)—but the house is still a realm of charmed and irreplaceable particularity, to be understood in terms of style and priceless authenticity, not financial value. Such secret anti-financial value emanates from everything that can claim association with this threatened Albion. As participants in this transcendent valuation, disparate and normally insignificant things are combined along the plane of a special and increasingly occult significance ('all flowering things together,' as a contemporary poet would write of her different *logos*, while the bombs fell on London during the Second World War).[41] Like the objects Mary Butts saw in the elegance of Gertrude Stein's Paris flat in 1927 and catalogued in her journal, the dead Felicity Taverner's possessions need only to be listed as they are turned up in a search—their participation in the 'gloire' of this gifted personality is apparently all that is needed to combine them:[42]

The jay-feather posy, a handful of red rose leaves, paper dry; a ring of grey jade, two anonymous keys, a bundle of orange sticks, a rouge pot, a box of nibs, four french stamps, a bar of green sealing-wax, a bar of black; one drawing pin; a sock of the gayest pattern and the softest wool trodden into huge holes. Three curtain rings, an amber cigarette-holder, once a thin gold trumpet, now in half, with a tooth-bitten hole at its mouth. Half a french card-pack, a domino, a cribbage-peg, a spellican, a draught piece, two chess men and a halfpenny to play shove ha'penny. A pin, a safety pin, a needle, a darning needle. A ball, a reel,

a card, a skein, of wool, of silk, of cotton. A coat button, a trouser button, a shirt button, a boot button; made of bone, of brass, of shell, of
wood. Pinned together in a colour-sequence, a green rag of cloth, of
linen, of velvet, of muslin, of canvas, of lawn.

Several dimensions of meaning must be grasped here. For a start, this
is the idealised particularity of a violated intimate world: a home perhaps, but more pointedly the aestheticised 'household' of a woman.
The movement into a predominantly occult sense of value and significance is therefore in a sense directly realistic: a point about women and
their 'hidden' position in the social order finds some expression here.
It should also be remarked that these treasured and auratic objects,
defined in terms of beauty and charismatic association, are of the kind
that Butts herself kept around the place (even in the financial chaos of
her rather seedy flat at No. 14 Rue de Montessuy in Paris there were
apparently such objects—glass paperweights, a cherished malachite
box...). In several of her writings Butts projects such objects far out
into the world. Thus a jade cup (an ashtray but also the Holy Grail) is
carried through the pages of *Armed With Madness*; indeed, its sudden
appearances and disappearances, together with the interpretations to
which they give rise, are basic to the progression of this narrative. In
part of course, this is the artifice of mythical allusion—something one
could look up in a book on Grail mythology. However, it seems more
important to grasp that this cup is also a resonant fragment projected
outwards from the small and cell-like space (the crystal cabinet again)
of an intimate and personal realm in which aesthetic value, together
with a certain understanding of culture and even of civility, can still
act as fundamental principles in constellating the world.

Implicit in this revaluation of particular objects as they appear
together in the charisma of threatened association, there is also an
emergent tendency in the three novels for the home to become more
and more like a *museum*: more and more something that is viewed not
just aesthetically, but as a world that is separate and under threat.
In this perspective, the jade cup is no longer capable of animat-
ing or subverting the wider reality; instead it needs protection, and
the crystal cabinet must therefore be traded for the glass case. This
impulse, leading as it does towards guide-books of the very sort that
Mary Butts elsewhere tends to disparage, is a clear index of threat. It
comes to its peak in *Death of Felicity Taverner* where the house is about

to be put to commercial uses and the sacred geography destroyed. In this last novel the threatened home becomes an irreplaceable 'period piece': 'rather too perfect: a museum-piece…you see it as an *objet d'art*. Round quicksilver mirrors set in ebony on the panels of an octagonal room. Some painted with birds, or with diminishing glasses in their glass. Curtains and coverings of old *toile de Jouy*, and some royal brocades. Cupboards with glass doors sunk in the walls. And a small shallow stair that mounts as delicately as an empire train.'[43] There is a different determination in play here. As the financial security of this post-aristocratic family and world is threatened, the urge for its preservation appears abstracted in the anti-financial and aesthetic terms of threatened architecture and artefacts. The language is no longer that of a semi-mystical and threatened animism, or for that matter of a constrained femininity; it has shifted to include the preservationist vocabulary of the National Trust, an organisation which flourished in the interwar years (even if it didn't start picking up stately 'homes' in any quantity until after the Second World War).

The Reduction of Personality to Given Essences

Then, of course, there is the question of people and their characterisation. While this green world of the novels is said to be where one finds that 'deep life of personalities' which Butts opposes to both the uprooted subjectivity and also the political reality of urban society, the characterisation which goes with this landscape is actually about as minimal as can be imagined.[44] Characters have names (precious or mythically resonant ones like Picus, Felix, Scylla, Clarence or Dudley); they may suffer from war-wounds and have family connections, but mostly they are ciphers and without substantial interiority: figures rather than characters, they form part of a post-Parisian international set, and nationality is to a considerable extent the key to their affiliation and identity. Thus there is Boris—the White Russian who is an epitome of dispossession in the Butts style. For him everything is either in the past, in memory or in the blood: a betrayed nation and racial ('Slav') character stacked up behind a name. Mary Butts seems to identify with Boris; she too has lost her world (Salterns), although she lacks the indisputable clarity of the Revolution which swept Boris's remembered legacy away.

If Boris stands there as White Russia on legs, there are also Americans who, coming from a young rather than old country, have 'no memories'[45] to nourish them. In these terms of nationality, to have character is to be possessed above all of an acceptable past and history. Based on remembrance, nationality is not necessarily a comfortable experience; indeed, for Boris memory is 'no mother of the muses, but a machine gun for which he was target.'[46] The disturbances of 'the war that confounded all shores' are not reversible; '*For ever* written in steel on the walls of the Third International.'[47] As for the Americans, with Mary Butts returning more and more to her familial and national roots these people from a young country appear more and more to lack recognisable identity; rough and impetuous, they are characterised as absences compelled towards some future in which a presently obscure national identity might form. In their search for cultural meaning these Americans are already offering to buy up all the objects of historical or aesthetic interest. A foreshadowing doubtless, of the present-day Getty Museum in Malibu, and of the transatlantic cultural market which is now even able to dispose of Mary Butts's almost entirely unread books for hundreds of almighty dollars apiece.

The most significant feature of this minimalism lies in the way it defines personalities in terms of *being* rather than action. Nobody *does* much at all; indeed, to act is to reveal oneself evil, mad, or at best the helpless victim of desperate circumstances. In this frail and destabilised world, action is by definition disturbing. Characters relate to their environment in a contemplative fashion—through reveries of belonging or the mysteries of animistic understanding. Like Jane Harrison's 'moderns,' they don't approach the world with purpose or active desire to make sense of it; they merely attune their ears and 'trust the background to tell its own tale.'[48] Or, as Butts puts it in *Death of Felicity Taverner*: 'Like others of our age, they had re-discovered also the still life that, however it might get itself painted, it is not "nature morte,"' ... They knew that the twenty four hours of the day and night are a cinema, an *actualité*, a continuous programme, whose hero is the sun and whose heroine the moon.'[49] Mostly frozen in contemplative inaction, Butts's characters may indeed raise themselves to paint a little, to do a bit of sculpting, to watch birds or dig the garden in a desultory sort of way. One of them is even rather good at whistling. When it is absolutely necessary they may go away to 'turn an equivocal penny' by leading, say, a party of American 'art-lechers' (but who is the huckster?) on a search for culture in North Africa; but there is a more representative moment in the earlier *Ashe of Rings* when a distant figure is watched, moving across a landscape. Is it a shepherd? No, he's wearing grey flannels. 'It's someone with nothing to do.'[50]

Mary Butts's artificial England won't bear action and any further characterisation would tear this green world apart. Characters are defined by the fact that they 'know' their place, being attuned to its vibrations. They have the wisdom of the stones, knowing precisely when to go to which corner of what 'mead' to pick the sudden field mushrooms. Without practical activity there can be no history here; only ancestral memories of genesis. But then that is exactly the point: when history has gone bad, there are struggles to root it out altogether. Similarly, society (with its stink of the city) disappears into a deeper national mystery which Mary Butts once named 'the magic of person and place.'[51] People are simplified; they are purified into harmonious figures who move in poetic relation to an appropriate landscape. If this world is considered in terms of the nineteenth-century novel, then there can only be an overwhelming sense of impoverishment. In a genre which has been used so fully to open up questions of action, motivation, belief, determination—the experience of a tormented modern society—we now come to this quiet and airless vacuum in which everything is reduced to a contemplative version of 'being.'

In a sense what we see here is the price of a return to myth—that characters become the marionettes of deeper meaning. While this may be a sufficient way of defining the figures of mythical drama—figures through which startling patterns of interconnection and significance can be made visible—other troubles start when, as seems clearly to

happen in Butts's work, myth comes also to provide the basis for an understanding of real people in the actual world. For then nothing is necessary except this primordial pact of blood, consciousness and the soil—a pact which is irreconcilable with any practical or even fully intersubjective conception of meaning, but which doesn't forebear, nevertheless, from whispering endlessly of the 'meaning of meaning.' In this world meaning is always deep and it can only be 'lost' or 'found': there is no possibility of actively making it anew in the present. As for the abolition of society, this even extends to customs and immigration officials. Thus Boris lacks requisite travel papers for the modern world, but this doesn't stop him travelling from Paris in a secret boat which delivers him to a cove beneath the house. There is little more to it than of 'being' in one place and then, simply enough, of 'being' in another. The bearer of sufficient blood, bone and memory may have nationality, but he stands in no need of a passport. It is consistent too that when Mary Butts looked for the best of contemporary English prose she should have found some of it in the supernatural stories—those studies in national resonance—of Montague James.[52]

From Politics to Magic

Just as society is replaced by the 'magic of person and place,' so the political rationality of modern social organisation—of industrial capitalism and the liberal consensus of mass democracy—is also replaced by a different type of causality and relation. It is replaced, in no hesitant way, by a *magic* which is presented as the deeper reality underlying the mechanistic materialism of modernity. This magic is, of course, a secret rationality which discloses itself on occasion to the initiate, proving that for all the disasters of modern history the stars don't actually run blind—and that Albion has not been completely destroyed.

It demands, as Mary Butts put it in *Traps for Unbelievers*: 'a very particular kind of awareness, an awareness modified and sometimes lost by people whose life has been passed in towns. It is most difficult to describe. It has something to do with a sense of the invisible, the non-existent in a scientific sense, relations between things of a different order: the moon and a stone, the sea and a piece of wood, women and fish.'[53] Elsewhere Mary Butts talks of the knight's move in chess, a move that works in a curious dimensionality of its own. She talks (courtesy of contemporary anthropology and classical scholarship) of 'mana,' of a place which is to the right and left of where we are. Her characters are likely all of a sudden to 'pass through' in Svengali style to this other realm. They are also likely to step on to a London bus, arrive at their destination (not prosaic Camden Town but a place where five roads meet) and declare that 'this place is not here.'[54] And of course, there are sites which carry the charge more than others— the usual assortment of herms and neolithic rings but, as Mary Butts claims quite seriously in an essay on 'The Uses of the Supernatural in English Fiction,' even the city unbends in places. There is, she says, a part of Lincoln's Inn which does not 'stay put. Also Great Russell Street. But that, whatever it is, is something projected out of the British Museum.'[55] Generally then this is the different logic and rationality of another reality which keeps looming into view in the prosaic world of the modern industrial state: 'We are spectators of a situation which is the mask for another situation that existed perhaps in some remote age, or a world that is outside time.'[56] Back to the still-life.

Access and Threat from the Outside

How does a person enter this strange and gifted England which lies at the heart of Mary Butts's writings? Access is at best distinctly problematic. Indeed, there is no access for those who are not already included by nature or history. Either a person is 'there' or not. Since it all comes down to the sympathies of an animistic consciousness and a quasi-genetic notion of 'being'—of what one is before starting in the world—a person can only be a pregiven participant in 'the magic of person and place' or a threat to it. Like the fashionable women's clothes in some of the earlier short stories—clothes of an extravagant and bewitching beauty which can't be bought in shops (a mystifica-tion/sublimation of war shortages)—this England lies beyond the formally democratic rationality of the liberal market. Either it lies in your bones or you're a hustler trying to break in. Like the visiting American in *Armed With Madness*, you may try to buy the antiques but it will doubtless only be to find that once reduced to cash value such objects lose their aura, thus proving that their pricelessness lies in the charismatic associations linking them with, once again, special people and special places. And even if, as with the spouses (both male and female) who marry into the family, it is possible to become legal owner of the ancestral home, the memories which cling to its hallowed hallways will somehow always single out those who don't really belong.

But if this England is inaccessible, except via the deep and long-completed attachments of a past 'history,' it is certainly not free from threat. As a world it is radically unstable; its meaning is increasingly occult and inclined towards dramatic and unpredictable shift and change. Most fundamentally, however, and as the first sentence of *Armed With Madness* indicates, the economic power through which this England has previously been secured is dwindling: 'In the house in which they could no longer afford to live, it was unpleasantly quiet.' And as the sound of a wider more contemporary outside world becomes louder and louder a defensive demonisation also begins. This demonisation plays an active part in defining Mary Butts's England and, unsavoury as it may be, it cannot conveniently be detached to turn the seeming tranquillity of the 'magic of person and place' into the acceptably pastoral mode of a mere anti-industrialism. Exclusion and anathema are principles active at the foundation of Mary Butts's sacred geography, and in the writings they take two primary forms: one political, the other racial.[57]

Exclusion: The Urban Proletariat as 'Hiker'

Mary Butts associates her world with an aristocratic order of society which has been superseded. As is evident in her late meditation on Salterns (*The Crystal Cabinet*), the problem is seen to stem from the consolidation of the English bourgeoisie with its 'materialist' industrial capitalism, self-interest and urban culture—even if it doesn't remain there. As she puts it in 1932: 'The residential parts of such industrial towns as I have seen, the homes of their chief citizens, were masterpieces of graceless comfort and self-satisfaction.'[58] The class which produced Mary Butts's narrow-minded mother also throws up 'huge, greasy entrepreneurs' such as one whose anti-aesthetic philistinism grates on more sensitive ears in a story called 'The Dinner-Party'; but if this is where the problem begins, its really disastrous manifestation comes later with the mass enfranchisement of a deracinated urban working-class.[59]

Here are the creeping hordes, and they have an increasing visibility as the writing progresses. At first the reader is only given glimpses of their more feudally situated forebears—much loved nannies, especially,

but also butlers who don't just stagger under a combined burden of
deference and the dinner service, being additionally weighed down
by the exotic figures of speech through which the narratives stylise
them—as scarabs, black beetles . . . . The fate of these people, modelled
as seems likely on the clearly stationed domestic staff of a remembered
Salterns, is to be uprooted and to fall eventually into the disorder of
town and encroaching suburb: that 'monstrous area of unplanned
streets and impure grass between the country and the town' in which
the intrepid explorer John Betjeman (fuelled, of course, by Shell) had
yet to discover England.[60] On one occasion such urban proletariats
are found on a train which is bearing some members of Mary Butts's
charmed circle out into the country. They are there simply enough, to
look up from the depths of their own spiritual and aesthetic perdition
and to ogle the beauty of these evidently superior beings. At other
times their existence is registered only as a temporary absence: during
the First World War, for example, it is hard to find a porter at Charing
Cross Station.

The urban working class certainly isn't invited into Butts's green
world: it breaks its way in progressively as the century advances, and
it is not until the 1930s (decade of the mass trespass and 'rambling'
as well as of an escalating domestic tourism) that its unwitting members are met with a full scale anathematisation fired from that concrete bunker overlooking Sennen Cove in Cornwall. This is *Warning
to Hikers* (published by Wishart), a pamphlet which goes to the point
of craving the destruction of all human society before it would see
the ordinary town-dweller out for a hike or Sunday stroll. In a representative passage Mary Butts recalls a day spent up on the hills of
north-east England:[61]

clouds began to stream over from the north, from the Cheviot Hills,
and the rain began. I fitted myself in between two boulders, into a
stone chair, and began to eat sandwiches and ginger nuts. Then round
somewhere to the left of me, invisible, I heard voices; harsh Tyneside
voices, whose every other sentence ends with the word 'bugger', a
wholly non-commital endearment. A few moments later, about fifty
yards beneath me, through the mist travelling in ten veils, there trailed
across a 'hiking' party. Youths and their girls from Newcastle or South
Shields or Gateshead. I had seen such parties before, going out noisy
or returning drenched and sullen, but not before on the high moors.
They were not noisy or indefatigable or resolute or at ease. Or even

happy or unhappy. They were there. And from their movements they did not seem to know where they were or how they had got there; what they meant to do or what there was to do; how to stay or how to get back. They were a very long way from anywhere. Two thousand feet below were the enormous trees, the flowering grasses, the quick bright rivers of the valleys of the north and south Tyne. We were above them, sitting on top of the world. They drifted past, less articulate than the curlews, the girls treading over in their ridiculous shoes. An arm of the sun wheeled like a searchlight over the moor. A scarf of mist spun in and extinguished it. They seemed to take no notice.

'They were there...' Yet despite the 'warning' from Butts Nature doesn't always strike down those without sensible shoes, and the real destruction goes on elsewhere. The mere presence of these people, with their ignorance of 'the magic of person and place,' testifies to the shattering of Mary Butts's artificial green world. If this the 'inmost form,' then indeed the crystal cabinet is burst.

Never a mention of general strike, mass unemployment, hunger marches, or even of the political rather than aesthetic ideas of *access* to the countryside which motivated the mass trespasses of the time; but if hard political reality is always elsewhere, there is nevertheless fragmentary evidence of a more sufficient understanding in Mary Butts's writings. There are occasional hints at the importance of an emerging urban and popular culture (which Butts indicates in *Warning to Hikers* but makes little attempt to define or understand) and at times Mary Butts's concern with the 'uprootedness' of modernity indicates the possibility of a humanitarian care like that of Simone Weil.[62] Her analysis of the collapse of religion as meaningful and legitimating world-view (together with its only partial replacement by science) is precise and could stand as point of departure for a very different cultural and critical project. Likewise, there is an identification of potential in the Stoic-Epicurean perspective ('Good can be attained; evil can be endured,' as she puts it in *Ashe of Rings*) with its suggestion that even in the most awful of worlds total defeat may be resisted by those who, in whatever space they are able to make, continue to live in an ethically principled and also pleasurable way. This suggests a response to modernity of the sort which, over the same years, motivated the Catholic anticapitalist Eric Gill and which has more recently concerned thinkers from a Soviet–European background like Agnes Heller.[63] Possibilities such as these are identified and in some cases examined more fully but in the final analysis they can only be listed to name routes left untaken, at least in the published writing.

What the reader meets instead is a vilification of the downtrodden in which victims are blamed for what is considered (inaccurately, as may certainly be argued) to be their condition. Ignorant, uncultured, motivated by a 'cult of nature' from which Mary Butts struggles to differentiate the deeper authenticity of her own green world, these are the bereft and, as *Warning To Hikers* suggests, too much has been granted them already: 'The enemy is the democratic enemy, in a country where people have lost their stations and like badly-trained children can neither keep to their own places nor respect other peoples'. It is not the better-bred or even the better-off who are most at fault. In this case the more a man belongs to that minority, the less guilty he is likely to be.'[64] Or again, as Butts puts it, in terms which certainly don't lack a contemporary echo: 'What is to be done about this error, which may threaten our whole civilisation? Nothing, it seems, but to correct our enthusiasms, unchristen our barbarians and return to the facts of the case—the unequal nature of man as he is—with as little brutality and as little panic as possible.'[65]

Exclusion: The Jew

If the urban proletariat is demonised at one end of Mary Butts's England, a classically anti-Semitic identification of the Jew as despoiler goes on at the other. The odd 'Jew-dealer' appears in the early writings, embodying a 'usurious' reduction of cultural value to purely economic terms; and it could conceivably be argued that this definition of the Jew, together with much of the anti-Semitism which was prevalent in the Edwardian era, is merely a regrettable response to the success of some German-Jewish capitalists operating in the basically stagnant economy of early twentieth century Britain.[66] Yet it seems far more important to acknowledge that in this anti-Semitism the Jew is actively given a meaning which is culturally *necessary* to the valued England which he contaminates. Such an attribution of meaning is made explicit in Butts's last novel, *Death of Felicity Taverner*. In this book the genetic heroine is dead before the narrative opens. Felicity Taverner is, as we have already seen, another passionate and beautiful embodiment of 'the magic of person and place.' Here again, an autobiographical aspect permeates the story. Felicity Taverner fell on hard times: her mother failed to underwrite her sufficiently, and economic insecurity left her prey to the solicitations of Nick Kralin, who won her hand in what is clearly presented as an unnatural marriage. Felicity Taverner eventually flees to the continent, escaping from the 'grey thing' she recognises Kralin to be, and dying in obscure circumstances.

It is certainly likely that in the deeply autobiographical (and psychoanalytically resonant) texture of this novel the figure of Kralin is to an extent formed after the image of John Rodker, the Jewish writer and leftist publisher who had been Butts's first husband and who was also the father of her daughter.[67] In a comparable sense and as the imagery of the novel suggests very strongly, the sacred landscape and house in this novel are probably expressive of Butts's own being. Yet even if Butts was using the prevalent culture of anti-Semitism to strike at Rodker (this man who built a bungalow on her unspoilt beauty), the almost physical sense of violation which forms the main compositional principle of *Death of Felicity Taverner* is not in any adequate way to be accounted for by a biographical reference of this sort. Whatever its starting point, this sense of threat and violation takes on a multiple meaning as it is projected through the gathering narrative in which Butts defines it.

The novel opens with the family house at stake. Kralin, who has taken up with loose lower-class women ('out-of-a-town by rapid transit from its slums; heavy haunched and over breasted, wearing a terrible parody of country clothes') has plans to buy up surrounding land and, benefitting from the speculative freedom which existed before Attlee's Town and Country Planning Act (1947), to commercialise the sacred geography.[68] There will be plotland development (like that which produced Butts's own despised Sennen residence) and there will be 'snowstorms' of litter like those which C.E.M. Joad reported having seen all over Sennen Cove in an article published the year after Butts's death.[69] Kralin has plans to put a golf-course and holiday bungalows into the crystal cabinet, and he tries to blackmail the Taverner family into compliance by threatening to publish Felicity's erotically revealing and scandalous (doubts—and here again perhaps there is an autobiographical connection—about the paternity of Felicity's brother) personal papers.

Kralin is not just a man who is Jewish. Nor is he a merely resented image of existing financial power. He is a personification of evil and destruction. Not 'officially' Jewish, whatever this may mean, he is nevertheless described as the 'Jew-about-town,' and even the landscape seems to shrink from him. While Felicity Taverner is evoked in terms that make her seem to emanate from the soil ('the hills were her body laid down') Kralin is characterised as unnatural and repulsive: his eyes, for example, are 'two almonds of grey jelly.'[70] As a Jew in this anti-Semitic definition Kralin is the embodiment of everything Mary Butts opposes to her precious and threatened world. He represents the triumphant uprootedness of the city (the urban underworld in which Bolshevism and revolution were schemed) and a post-war Europe in which traditional nationality and culture have been confused. He embodies the naked and uncultured power of capital and the mechanistic science which facilitates its industrial expansion. His consciousness is a development of the anxious and sensationalist mentality which in the earlier narratives is associated with the war: his properties being those of 'a man whose interests were all cerebral, in the abstractions we have made for our convenience out of life,' and who has nothing but contempt for 'the meaning of meaning.'[71]

Finally, as his name with its echo of Stalin suggests, Kralin is an embodiment of the same 'materialist' and by now 'mass democratic' Tide which Butts also, and without much heed to questions of historiographical accuracy (although there is an attack on Soviet Taylorism in *Imaginary Letters*), portrays as the winner of the Russian Revolution. Kralin is son of a Tolstoyan proletarian-idealist who fled pre-Revolutionary Russia and, as Boris concludes, 'his greyness is the same power that made our revolution distinct from other revolutions.'[72] As a defining principle at the edge of Mary Butts's England, therefore, the Jew Kralin embodies everything that threatens the security of this green world. White Russia and Salterns, both were lost to this primitive figure of the Jew. The outcome is brutally simple, for 'the Tide' must evidently be rolled back and as a personification of all that is evil the Jew makes such a purification of history imaginable. Kralin must be killed if the measures of this England are to be sustained, and the murder, naturally as the narrative suggests, falls to Boris the White Russian. It is a murder which stands justified—the world of the book demands it—and everything suggests that it will go undetected. Within a decade of the Yellow Star of David, such a murder can be imagined only to violate urban, liberal-democratic and therefore by this anti-Semitic definition, *Jewish* law. What price this when the precious soil of ages demands blood?

The political and racial aspects of this England are not simply detachable as bad but discrete moments or elements. Neither are they merely 'responses' to a contextual reality. There is no innocent pastoral here, drifting into unfortunate but occasional contact with unsavoury attitudes. In both cases Mary Butts follows her stripped down and animistic 'England' through to conclusions which are far from arbitrary or whimsical. She may take tendencies through to a demonstration of their extremes, but because these tendencies are intrinsic to her England such enactments are also moments of real clarification. Thus anti-Semitism is a precipitate of the basic perspectives of the sacred geography itself, and not a separate addition or a passing comment on Jewish capitalists. The 'England' of *Death of Felicity Taverner* is like the France which Sartre found at the heart of the anti-Semitism which he investigated in the 1940s.[73] It is a particularistic 'England' in which belonging is mystical and intuitive, in which a form of proprietorship which is merely formal or legal is challenged by another which is based on timeless participation, and in which true subjects crave impenetrability in the face of threatening or incomprehensible social change. It is an England in which to be English is to be *against* necessary outsiders, a member of an occult secret society diffused throughout the merely legal collectivity of liberal democracy. In this England, as in Sartre's anti-Semitic France, 'there are people who are attracted by the durability of a stone.'[74]

Nation Against Society

Contrary to much contemporary literary theory, I see no need to abolish the author in order to read these writings against what they may seem actually to say. 'I strove to seize the inmost form,' as it is put in the highly appropriate quotation from Blake's poem which is now on Mary Butts's grave in Sennen, and if anything fails to exist it is of course the text itself.

Mary Butts may well have found it difficult to accept the poison which was concentrated at the heart of this 'inmost form,' but even if her personal sense of desolation can only be guessed at (and the last years sound fairly terrible), credit of a kind should still be granted to this author for taking her unstable England through to the murderous settlement which she discovers at its implicit extremes. The honesty involved in this breaking of the crystal cabinet is surely not that of any straight-forward advocate of violence but rather of a writer who has explored and dramatised potentials within a culture and organic self-understanding which is not simply her own—a writer who has staged the whole show, rather than merely excerpting the acceptably pastoral passages which could have (as indeed they did) achieved a much broader and apparently unproblematic circulation as fragments. Mary Butts was in no sense the author of English anti-Semitism, but she can certainly be read as the writer of texts which usefully expose some of its presuppositions. These were the bricks that Butts had to build with, and if Kralin was modelled to any extent on Rodker, then the heaviest of all was the one she picked up when she designated her former husband a 'Jew.'

I make this return to Mary Butts's writings in a decade which grows increasingly accustomed to the dreaming prefects of the New Right, with their political and cultural fantasies on the themes of authority, race, monarchy and nation.[75] Another time it may well be, but if this right-wing mysticism is to be believed we remain in the same place after all. There are still those for whom a name cut into the grey stone of a national war-memorial is infinitely more moving and meaningful than the messy social contingency of any person's actual life. As for the left, we've already heard Priestley on Butts, and it remains to George Orwell, that other genuinely moving analyst of England, to give the last word on Sartre. Ailing as he was when he received it in 1948, Orwell dismissed Sartre's book on anti-Semitism as the work of a 'bag of wind.' He set out to give the book a 'good boot,' writing a review (published in the *Observer* on November 7th, 1948) which reduced Sartre's analysis to a crude and abusive theory of types, before concluding that Sartre's book would if anything 'make anti-Semitism slightly more prevalent than it was before.'

Sartre may indeed seem to hate the very existence of particularity, but Orwell's assertion of people and ordinary 'human beings' against these immobile and merciless 'types' still leaves all of Sartre's questions about the systematic character of anti-Semitism evaded rather than merely unanswered.[76] I do not say this with any intention of belittling either the better possibilities in people or the popular anti-fascism which accompanied the British entry into the Second World War. But the Lion and the Unicorn as Orwell told it was not necessarily the only story even at the time, and there are surely no grounds for treating it as adequate to the 1980s. The books of Mary Butts did not find a public in their own time, and if this is the place to acknowledge the possibility of a positive and perhaps even laudable form of neglect, it should also be recognised—and I think this is a much stronger case— that the writing continues nevertheless to testify to political and racial perspectives within an 'England' which is still with us. *Death of Felicity Taverner* finds the racial enemy *within* its valued England, not at the far-flung peripheries of empire. It is possible, at the very least, that since passing through this novel the culture of pre-war anti-Semitism has gone on to serve as a resource for the racisms which in the post-war years have accompanied immigration from the fragments of disintegrating empire. I say 'racisms' in the plural because there is a more 'civilised' and assertively cultured racism which needs to be understood as it differentiates itself from actual brutality. This is an aloof racism which, although capable of the most stirring demagoguery, never stoops to 'contact,' never enters explicitly into the more violent forms of expression with which it colludes. This is the 'higher' racism of a Conservative figure like Enoch Powell, and it stands close to pre-war anti-Semitism in its assertion of threatened tradition, valued geography and other incommunicable 'great simplicities' (Powell's phrase) of nationhood. Indeed, this connection with an earlier and not always explicitly recognised anti-Semitism may be a major principle of its elevation.

More generally, Mary Butts's writings suggest that the quasi-mystical assertion of nationhood in which they participate is in no simple respect a bid for dominance or cultural hegemony within the public sphere. Butts is not attempting to *establish* her post-aristocratic definition of England over others in public understanding. Quite the opposite, the nationalist and organic mode of self-understanding, which Butts finds in her 'England,' is identical with a *refusal* of publicity and a flight into *secrecy*. Butts is aggressively opposed to the pastoral ideas of nature which have filtered into the mass public consciousness of the cities. Hence her apparently self-contradictory anti-pastoralism: her criticism of Tennyson, of nature as cult or a Shell advertising image, and also the ridicule she reserves for those who think the country is epitomised by the semi-suburban remnants of Epping Forest.[77] When nature enters mass consciousness, in this view, it is automatically falsified. Butts's 'England' is found in flight from the communicative rationality of public discussion and understanding: a flight, indeed, which leads from sociality in all its forms to the stripped down, particularistic and immediate world of an imagined genetic nation. As with the France of Sartre's anti-Semitism, this secret 'England' never attempts to explain or justify itself. It is not up for discussion. When questioned it simply slips away into an occult and ineffable realm 'beyond words.'

Mary Butts's books are secret writings. Like the books which she claimed to have helped her mother burn after her father's death, even more like the Book of Ashe with its occult script or the erotic and esoteric papers of Felicity Taverner, they seem to crave obscurity, demanding the devotion of a few select initiates rather than the attention of a public.[78] They are documents of defeat, of a world lost, reimagined and still passed by, but they also show that the flight from all forms of social rationality which they trace can be neither successful nor innocent. Indeed, although the writings are often explicit in their retreat from politics they continue to make their hermetic definitions within a notion of nationhood which takes a whole political disposition for granted and, as they reveal, can also work to set it beyond discussion.

I would draw three basic conclusions from these writings. First, they stand as testimony to a type of English national consciousness which is above all *particularistic*. It is not guided by potentially universalistic political ideas or values such as 'freedom' or 'equality' (the ideas of earlier bourgeois nationalism), but instead it makes an exclusive principle of a well-rehearsed imagination of history, race, place and belonging. Secondly, there is evidence in these writings to suggest that cultural domination is no simple matter of implanting certain contents

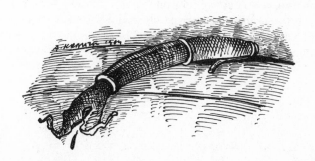

or emphases—a dominant ideology, perhaps—into public conscious-ness. As Butts's writings show, there is also a nationalist mode of self-understanding which refuses the rationality of public communication, but which is all the more powerful and normative for the fact that it continues, nevertheless, to go without saying.

The third point is that the oppositions riddling the bourgeois cul-ture of interwar England are not adequately defined only in terms of dichotomy between ruralism and industry, or between 'culture' and 'economy.' Mary Butts's writings testify not just to the existence of a more complex and inclusive polarity in which *nation* stands opposed to *society*, but also to the relentlessly political matrix in which this opposition itself is elaborated. If this political matrix is not drawn sufficiently into consideration we may well end up, as Martin Wiener does at the end of his recent book, concluding that English 'culture' is disastrously opposed to 'industry' (whatever unities these may be) and then, with this taken as the whole truth, wondering whether perhaps Margaret Thatcher will be adequate to the challenge.[79]

Mary Butts's writings point in a different direction. They suggest, negatively as it may often be, that a liberating sense of human and cul-tural value can only exist beyond the threshold at which Butts herself seems finally to have balked. It will only be when we have moved from a quasi-genetic definition of the *nation* and accepted that the question properly belongs within mass democratic *society*. And accepting the existence of society (an aim that is very modest in one sense but vastly ambitious in others) implies at the very least an acceptance of people in their cultures rather than sacred stones, of public rather than secret meaning, and of an open-ended multiplicity of traditions and histories rather than the artificial severity of a single and already completed national lineage which can only be witnessed in exclusive (if not always murderous) ceremonies of remembrance. Irreducible, impatient in its struggle for meaning, given to persistent transformation of the settled world—the imagination (as aspects of Butts's own writing testify so clearly) can be full of possibilities in this direction as well.

4

A Blue Plaque for the
Labour Movement?
Some Political Meanings
of the National Past

Remembrance Day 1981

> It was interesting to note how in the early, wild and enthusiastic days
> of the Revolution the characteristic costume was a great-coat flung
> over, a hat askew, a hand spread outwards; later the representations of
> leaders became identified with neatly buttoned uniforms, well set caps
> and firm salutes, and only the Cossacks, as in tsarist times, had been
> allowed to display a certain freedom...
>
> Michael Moorcock, *The Entropy Tango* (1981)

Irritated commentators don't seem to have been sure whether it was
actually a dufflecoat, with its early CND connotations, or a donkey
jacket, resonant of sullen proletarianism, but it was certainly green
rather than black, untailored and—as many people will doubtless
still remember—distinctly out of place on the back of the Leader
of the Labour Party during the solemnities at the Cenotaph on
Remembrance Day 1981. Among those black columns of uniformed
men, Michael Foot's garb was taken as giving his appearance over to
the ordinary, the casual and even, in an intellectual CND sort of way,
to the popular.

Walter Johnson, Labour MP for Derby, started the fuss by accusing
Mr Foot of looking like an out-of-work navvy on the way to a demo.
The following morning, on 9 November, a *Daily Telegraph* leader
described Foot as 'an old man'; he looked like 'a bored tourist at a bus
stop' and he laid his wreath 'with all the reverent dignity of a tramp
bending down to inspect a cigarette end.' The effect of these objec-
tions was to sharpen debate on Foot's efficacy as Leader of the Labour
Party; the coat was taken up as another of those 'last straws' which
assume such powerful metaphorical presence in public debate. Here

I am not concerned with Michael Foot himself or his private sincerities and intentions, but with the public image which was articulated around him on Remembrance Day. As he was drawn into the public eye on that day Foot was taken to be 'demonstrating' in a mild way against the customary proprieties of what the offended Labour MP thought should be 'a solemn act of respect and remembrance.' Foot was to comment afterwards that 'respect for the dead isn't a matter of the clothes you wear.' His defenders also showed little concern for appearance, invoking the invisible authenticity of what is felt at heart, and opposing this not just to the relative triviality of dress but also, in some cases, to the military rigidities of the Establishment on parade.

Some sections of the press staged this as a matter of informality versus formality—as if Foot were merely a slob who needed to 'pull his socks up' (the *Standard*'s phrase)—but the real significance of the incongruity of his appearance was that it represented a clash between opposed modes of public remembrance.

The Establishment mode of remembrance is both militarist and nationalist. Remembrance is a state occasion structured through regimental history and parade; retired generals and admirals speak in grave tones on the BBC World Service. The interest of this mode does not lie primarily in any selectivity it may bring to bear on previous events—its concern, as might be imagined, with glory rather than gore. Remembrance of this kind does not merely obliterate the 'realities' of war. Its essence lies instead in the *transfiguration* which its ceremonies bring to bear on past war, introducing order, solemnity and meaning where there was chaos, disorder and loss. Acts of commemoration *re-present* the glory of war, its transmutation of destruction into heroism and, above all, that precious sense of nationhood. In its contempt for society at peace, establishment remembrance tends to accuse the post-war present of mediocre survival, of ending up spineless and bent over a stick. These attitudes were implicit in the way the *Daily Telegraph* derided Foot as 'an old man.'

In his green coat, brown shoes and plaid tie Michael Foot stood out from all this. Instead of transfiguration, Foot's image presented a spectacle of *peaceful* solidarity. Not the uniforms, the ranks, the regiments, nor the specious ceremoniousness: all this was antithetical to

Foot who appeared—in public image if not conscious intention—to stand in homage to the ordinary, to the civilians of no particular distinction who were caught up into war, militarised and destroyed, to people whose drive generally was towards justice, socialisation and democracy. The people of the United Kingdom, perhaps, but especially, as some of the press implied, the people of the labour movement—people who might also have lived to find very mixed feelings at heart on Remembrance Day. The sentimentality tends to be part of the image.

Both these opposed modes of remembrance invoke the authenticity of history and tradition. In the establishment mode history *is* tradition. That is what redeems it. As for authenticity, this is something to be made: it is the sacramental effect or goal of traditional ceremonies, what the public act of remembrance is meant to bring about. Traditional authenticity exists in the present: it is bestowed upon the dead in ceremonies through which the present also reaffirms its continuity with the past. The dead are authenticated through measures which link them to the traditional rituals of church, army and state. Establishment remembrance raises the dead ritualistically in order to reposition them at the heart of what it simultaneously reaffirms as the 'nation.' In this way it calms the contradiction between their historical diversity and the single unity of the nation to which they are assimilated.

As it was presented in Foot's image, however, authenticity is not merely a necromantic and ideological effect of public ceremony, but involves a more direct and partisan *identification* with some especially among 'those who have fallen.' In these terms it is a question of *where* one stands rather than of the ceremonial steps one might go through. Foot stood there as bearer and manifestation of the history of the common people, of the aspirations, consciousness and courage which have produced and sustained the labour movement. It was the appearance of this oppositional history that discomforted the traditions of Church, Army and State. The two different articulations of history and tradition share no neutral ground on which they can achieve equal public visibility in order to compete. Remembrance Day 1981 indicated the extent to which the public field of meaning is already occupied and structured by some traditions to the exclusion and mockery of others (and by some ways of understanding those same traditions as opposed to others). Faced with the ritualised and spectacular ceremonies through which the Establishment lays claim to the traditions of nationhood, the history with which Foot stands associated was open to lampoon. On 10 November, both the *Sun* and the *Daily Telegraph* caricatured Foot as Worzel Gummidge, the scarecrow hero of a popular children's book and television programme. The *Daily Mail* presented a centrefold of Foot as a cut-out doll and offered the reader costume options (including cloth caps and CND badges): 'Dress Your Own Michael Foot,' read the caption. As for the *Daily Express*, it showed what Ronald Reagan's British born 'groomer' would have done for Foot: a composite picture showed 'Rt Hon Scruff' looking no longer like a 'lecturer' but smooth with haircut, streamlined glasses and a business suit.

Foot was open to being taken as a personification of a history and traditions which have only the most inadequate if not simply subordinate public status. Everything he might have invoked as support could thus be articulated back into identity with the frail and scruffy appearance of this 'old man.' By identification with Foot the labour movement was staged as a worn out relic. It was mocked as having only an archival existence: something that most working-class people have long since forgotten or disowned, and which Foot, known to be a historian of the labour movement, will therefore be among the last to know about. The Conservative press was able to flaunt the difference between spectacular public tradition and that mere history which it identified with the esoteric antiquarianism of a 'decrepit' intellectual nonconformist. Foot's coat left him open to a critical attention; his supporters, both in Parliament and Fleet Street, continued the personalisation by talking about authentic feelings felt sincerely at heart. The Conservative press did the rest: it used the image of Foot to blow the history of the labour movement off the stage, and it did this in the name of national tradition.

Thus (and without any elections) was Worzel Gummidge installed as Leader of the Labour Party, and let anyone who would consider this to have been of merely anecdotal significance remember that, for large sections of the Press at least, it was also Worzel Gummidge who led the Labour Party into its resounding defeat in the 1983 General Election. What, meanwhile, has happened to Remembrance Day itself? The show has gone on. In 1982 Foot was still there, this time standing rigidly (if rather uncomfortably) to attention, and since then it has been Neil Kinnock—dapper, but carefully undeclared and admitting nothing. In 1984 David Owen joined the line, standing there with that lean and hungry look of his, for the newly admitted Social Democrats. Meanwhile the 'Old Contemptibles,' those slow but also moving figures of a directly experienced and passionately remembered First World War, wander their untidy way through the spectacle in ever-diminishing numbers: curiously out of place, these are the 'old men' who remind us that all our just wars have not been waged against Communist Russia or what Thatcher is pleased to call 'the enemy within.'

Is it surprising that a certain nostalgia should be haunting Labour circles—one that can achieve truly Gnostic dimensions as it surges back towards that distant realm of light ('home') from within the killing clay of these dark modern times? What is wrong, say, with reimagining the splendours of Armistice Day 1922, when twenty-five thousand unemployed ex-servicemen marched past the Cenotaph with their medals dangling from red marching banners and with pawn tickets pinned to their lapels? Wal Hannington was there and he reported hearing from the women who were gathered in their usual place along the margins of history:[1]

'Who are these people?' asked one young woman to another on the sidewalk? 'Why—they're the unemployed'. 'Then good luck to them', said the first girl bitterly, almost savagely. 'Disgraceful', snorted a red-faced old man, with a fur clad young creature on his arm. 'Those men are Bolsheviks', he said. 'But look at their medals', said the girl. A woman in a black shawl turned on the old man. 'Shut up your bloody gap! If you'd been out of work as long as my old man, you'd be a Bolshevik.' A murmur of approval went through the crowd.

But this was before Bolshevism culminated in its own style of dictatorship, and anyway temporality doesn't allow for going back. Doubtless Michael Foot sometimes thinks on these matters as he paces around Hampstead Heath. The important question, however, is different: would he agree that we shouldn't really want to go back either? Labour history aside (if only for a minute), wasn't Nietszche right in saying that we must have the strength to break up the past—and not just the dominant stately one either?[2] Rather than yearning for the reimagined splendour of old defeat, shouldn't we be dismantling the past to make a theory (rather than a philosophical romance) of history—one which can inform a political project which is capable of winning ground in the future and which therefore stands on an adequate analysis of the present rather than on wistful solidarity with marchers of old? It can surely only be a Nietszchean form of remembrance which shows sufficient respect for those marchers and onlooking women—people who wanted to see some change in the world, after all, not to get frozen as fond figures in the historical memory of a failing labour movement fifty years on.

The National Past

In times when history still moved slowly, events were few and far between and easily committed to memory. They formed a commonly accepted backdrop for thrilling scenes of adventure in private life. Nowadays history moves at a brisk clip. A historical event, though soon forgotten, sparkles the morning after with the dew of novelty. No longer a backdrop, it is now the adventure itself, an adventure enacted before the backdrop of the commonly accepted banality of private life.

Milan Kundera, *The Book of Laughter and Forgetting* (1982)

Other events besides Remembrance Day 1981 could open discussion of national tradition and its place in current strategies of legitimation—most obviously the efflorescence of confused nationalism, vindicated nostalgia, aggression, incredulity and make-belief that accompanied the killing, maiming and official secrecy of the Falklands war, but also the momentary ruffling of relations between the Tory government and the Church of England or the continuing popular obsession with the public rituals and domestic tittle-tattle around the Royal Family.

Major events and ephemeral incidents follow hard and fast on each other, but perhaps more significant have been the developments, and also the fundamental continuities, in the way such occurrences are articulated and assimilated within public opinion. We hear news of this or that particular event through an interpretation that encourages us to understand occurrences (and our relation to them) in the accumulating terms of national identity, culture, history and tradition. The address varies, mobilising hopes, fears, memories, rationality, prejudices, confusions and just plain ignorance as it will. Sometimes it explicitly opposes its 'British' sense of balance to the emotionalism, deviance, bigotry or aggression of others ('Foolish Europe' has recently been modulated to 'Bloody Argies'); at other times it moves in the safe assumption that we—the public—already share the values of the presentation, and at still other times it marshalls 'us' more manipulatively (during the Falklands adventure the *Sun* was spewing out a rhetoric of 'reason') to what it hails as the consensual measures of public opinion. It is within this public framing of events that the 'nation' has been posed so thoroughly of late. Indeed, during 1982 this nationalising interpretation of British life seemed to enter the news not just as a formal characteristic of its presentation but increasingly at the level of content itself: it seemed to become so strong that it was actually capable of generating events.

So the 'nation' has become a key figure in British politics, one that must be understood and carefully negotiated if we are to move beyond the passive experience of deadlock to an active public engagement with the issues determining our situation. To a considerable extent this upsurge of public nationalism reflects the crisis of a social system which, while its development is leading directly to the destruction of traditions and customs (many of them locally based), at the same time demands an ever deepening source of cultural meaning to legitimate itself.[3] In this situation tradition appears as artifice, articulated not in particular or essential connection to people's experience, but at the generalised and diffuse level of an overriding 'national' identity. The 'nation' of this concern therefore has no easy relation to the existence and historical development of the nation-state; it is instead a structuring of consciousness, a publicly instituted sense of identity which finds its support in a variety of experiences, and which is capable of colonising and making sense of others. Among its most fundamental elements is a historically produced sense of the past which acts as ground for a proliferation of other definitions of what is normal, appropriate or possible. This mutual construction of a sense of the past and of a national identity was invoked in press caricatures of Foot at the Cenotaph on Remembrance Day 1981: Foot was not lampooned just for being slipshod and scruffy, but also for representing a recalcitrant and perhaps even oppositional sense of history. What is this national past, and how does it bear on the critical expressions of history which come from within the labour movement?

Far from being somehow 'behind' the present, the past exists as an accomplished presence in public understanding. In this sense it is written into present social reality, not just implicitly as residue, precedent or custom and practice, but explicitly as itself—as History, National Heritage and Tradition. Any attempt to develop and assert a critical historical consciousness will find itself in negotiation if not open conflict with this established public understanding of the 'past.' It is therefore important to understand what it is that functions as the 'past' and to distinguish it from history. J.H. Plumb provides a starting point by describing 'History' as an intellectual process—the endeavour to establish the truth of earlier events—which is pitched against the 'past,' conceived as a more mythical complex inherent in the present as a 'created ideology with a purpose.'[4]

Many socialist (as well as liberal and social-democratic) historians have worked along comparable lines, holding that a developed historical understanding will help cut through the ideological mists of the 'past' and in this way contribute to changing the political agenda in the present. While much has been achieved in this way over the last fifty years or so—indeed, the 'past' has been substantially rearranged so that it now contains a wider acknowledgement of, for instance, women and the working-class—this achievement has been won against considerable and undiminishing resistance. Plumb's 'History' is not a corrosive sublimate capable of burning the 'past' away, for the 'past' is neither free-floating ideology nor illusion; it is an established public institution, with all the historical materiality which that word implies. I don't necessarily dispute the ambition of Plumb's 'history' to achieve a higher order of truth, but it would certainly be a mistake to carry forward his implied denigration of 'the past.' This, after all, is the area not just of publicly installed illusion and ideology but also of everyday historical consciousness—of stories, memory and vernacular interpretations which differ (sometimes in fully conscious opposition) from that superior 'History' which, while it has always spoken with easily assumed authority, is distinguished not just by its laurels but also by the difficulty it experiences in achieving its gloriously neutral 'truth.'

The inertia of the past—its ability to withstand the corrections of 'History,' for example—reflects its entrenchment in the public field of meaning. The past is not just implicit in the present as the kind of historical continuity—paradigmatic or otherwise—which might more accurately be called tradition. Beyond tradition is a cultivated sense of the past which is reproduced through a variety of public agencies (schools, television, political debate, historical fiction...), and which stages the past explicitly as itself. This public staging of the past—I call it the 'national past'—remains relatively heterodox (even though it features heavily dominant tendencies) and it works in close and intricate connection with what Agnes Heller calls 'the sense of historical existence' and attributes not to any special knowledge of history but to the everyday consciousness of 'practically everyone who reflects upon his/her life experience in our world.'[5] So while there are problems of representation to be addressed at the first level there are other issues concerned more directly with lived experience (memory, disappointment, the persistence of childhood into adult experience and so forth) at the second. The national past works powerfully in the context of everyday consciousness and for this reason the related set of problems concerning the 'sense of historical existence' cannot simply be bracketed out of discussion.

The Past as Interpretation

The national past owes much of its public status to the work of nineteenth-century historiography which, as the Conservative Edward

Shils has recently argued, sought to order 'antiquities' and also to develop records which would provide a basis for systematic study of national institutions. This historiographical activity was accompanied by developments in the schools as the study of history gained prominence. The national past was recognised as possessing a legitimising capacity and, as Shils has written with perhaps more specific regard to the US than to Britain, 'the promotion of a belief in continuity and identity with the national past, reverence for national heroes, the commemoration of great national events ... were among the tasks laid on the teaching of "national history".'[6]

There is little existing analysis of the educational uses to which history has been put in Britain, and many of the important questions presumably remain unasked, to say nothing of any answers. Valerie Chancellor's *History for their Masters* shows some of the possibilities open to a reading of school history texts, even though her study, which confines itself to nineteenth-century texts (all of which were published before the study of history was exactly mandatory on any school curriculum), also indicates the difficulty of differentiating what is written from what is read and taken to mind.[7] To my knowledge the most useful analysis of school history is Frances Fitzgerald's *America Revised*, a study which tells a quite fascinating story of books which are 'managed' and 'developed' rather than written, of publishing houses which function as 'Ministries of Truth for children,' and of a miraculous text-book industry which enables famous US historians to revise books they have 'authored,' even including discussion of events which have occurred after their own deaths.

Things also happen at the more thematic level of the 'content' of school history. When 'conflicts' become too embarrassing, the day of the 'problem' dawns: Imperialism, for example, can be staged as a world literacy campaign. Similarly, and in terms traditional to portraiture, the dramatisation of history around character can reduce a multiple society as complex as India to a 'country,' and then to a measure of ground under the hooves of Clive's horse. If character is not the principal organiser of a historical account then institutions are likely to play that role: thus Parliament can appear as the institution through which democracy was accomplished (which puts a date and an end to that particular struggle). While the fact that these are easy points to make does not discredit them, it is important to remember not just that the problems of devising a more adequate school history are complex (it is no good just trading one bias for another, for example), but also that people play a very active part in making, or failing to make, their own sense of the information and analysis presented to them. As Frances Fitzgerald puts it: 'Rabbits, it is said, cannot remember pain or fear for more than sixty seconds. Perhaps human beings cannot remember things that bored them. Memory has its own antidotes.'[8]

While it is essential, therefore, to acknowledge that the education system certainly does not implant any single, or even particularly coherent interpretation of the past into public consciousness, one must, I think, acknowledge that its interpretative influence remains large. People may not remember whatever detailed analysis was developed for them as schoolchildren, but certain models, stories and 'general sketches' (to use Agnes Heller's phrase) do remain, and they inform everyday thinking closely, especially as they are exercised over and again by politicians and the media seeking to make public sense of current events.[9] If an example is needed to make this clearer one can be found in the special place occupied by the Second World War in public consciousness in Britain and, more particularly, in Margaret Thatcher's increasingly deliberate manipulation of Churchillian sketches over the period of the Falklands crisis. The educational apparatus, therefore, contributes largely to the formation of the national past, but it works not only in loose connection with other agencies of public meaning (the press, television, historical fiction, advertising, the conventions of political rhetoric and the culture of national tourism) but also in close relation to living memory and, once again, to the 'sense of historical existence.'

The Past as Presence

To say that the national past has an achieved public presence is not just to speak figuratively: recent decades have seen an increasing stress on the past as something that is actually present. National ceremonies such as Remembrance Day are certainly involved here, but so are those other phenomena which together make up the National Heritage: landscapes, old buildings, monuments, folkways, skills and exhibitable objects. If the various agencies of public meaning tend to reproduce a 'national' understanding of the past which includes 'reverence for national heroes' and 'the commemoration of great national

events,' they also ground this understanding in the concrete, unargu-
able existence of a National Heritage which stands in need of preservation, deference and respect. While this National Heritage may
initially have been assembled under the bourgeois academic signs of
'Beauty' and 'Culture,' the post-war years have also seen a significant
expansion in its repertoire. While it maintains its attention to unique
phenomena of overriding 'national' significance (and also especially
still to Art and Architecture), Britain's National Heritage is now also
organised in relation to an industrial archaeology, traditional working-class culture and skills, local forms of conviviality, the countryside
(increasingly projected as an image of nationhood) and the family.

As a public presence, therefore, the 'national past' tends to institute as fact its thematic generalisation of history, and it presents this
interpretative work in the concrete terms of what at the same time it
stresses as the National Heritage. The dovetailing of these two aspects
means that the urgently preservationist emphasis characteristic of
National Heritage can slide over to provide cover and substantiation
for the interpretative account forming the other part of the 'national
past.' This dovetailing is evident at a structural level between the two
main foci of television history, where a 'documentary' treatment of
the sites and objects of National Heritage tends to corroborate, and
in some cases is deliberately used to authenticate, fictional dramatisa-
tions of the past.

Public Philosophies of History

In its primary perspective the national past postulates a collective
subject: it presents the 'nation' as the place and state in which 'we'
live. In this sense the national past can be thought of as a controlling
attribute of citizenship: something that at a generalised level enables
citizens (and in Britain, of course, there are legally only subjects of the
Crown) to find a unity (as contemporary racism shows all too clearly,
out-groups are produced in this process) between themselves and to
override unresolved socio-political contradictions and differences.
While its definition is certainly not genuinely open to all, the nation
nevertheless occupies the public stage as 'ours,' not just the possession
and right of a few. Within this overrriding 'national' perspective there
is accommodation for both interpretative representations of history
and the concrete presence of the National Heritage.

The national past seems also to institute several distinct ways of conceiving the past *in relation to* the present. These past–present alignments have histories of their own which show that while such alignments have specific origins they do not continue to exist in simple identity with particular social or political interests. Indeed, they have a significant degree of autonomy and can be variously overdetermined and used by very different and even opposed interest groups.

These alignments are not dependent on any great understanding either of past or present, but they do give expression to the everyday 'sense of historical existence.' As public philosophies of history, they deal in a rather vague and invocatory sense of 'pastness,' and their abstract generality appears to contribute to the strength of their operation.[10] Unlike school history and the National Heritage, these past–present alignments do not work to secure and stabilise a national account or representation of the past, but rather to mobilise a legitimising but abstract sense of 'pastness' around present social and political events or issues. At this stage it seems worth trying to

differentiate three such alignments, each of which has made its entry into the 'national past' through bourgeois culture, and all three of which were evidently in play during the public response to Remembrance Day 1981. I shall call the first one *the complacent bourgeois alignment*. This alignment makes it possible to think of historical development as complete, a process which finds its accomplishment in the present. Historical development is here conceived as a cumulative process which has delivered the nation into the present as its manifest accomplishment. Both celebratory and complacent, it produces a sense that 'we' are the achievement of history and that while the past is thus present as our right it is also something that our collective narcissism will encourage us to visit, exhibit, write up and discuss.

But in contemporary political terms the nation is frail and far from being fully achieved, and there is consequently a darker sense that historical development, far from finding its completion in the present, might actually be 'over'—that its hold on the present is increasingly weak and likely to be lost as society becomes more fractured and discontinuous with the past. This introduces a second past–present alignment. *The anxious aristocrat alignment* is organised above all around a sense of betrayal—a sense that history has somehow been sold short or cut down in its prime, so that the national unity which it bears as its goal or promise may never be fully realised. According to this second alignment, citizens are always on the brink of collapsing into barbarism again (reverting to fragmented class cultures perhaps, or to inappropriate coats) and historical development of becoming entropic, its unfulfilled promises now lying as fragile traces which threaten to slip away 'behind' the present rather than finding secure realisation within it. In this second alignment 'we,' like the monks of Lindisfarne during the Dark Ages, are the 'trustees' or custodians of the past.

These two past–present alignments have served different political interests at different times, and in their public existence they are often now found in combination with one another. This combination is clearly evident in the connections which the national past makes between elements of interpretation and the celebration and display of the concrete landscapes, buildings and monuments constituting the National Heritage. There is, for example, an interesting coalescence between the complacent bourgeois alignment, in which historical development is seen to find its culmination in the present, and the physical existence of those buildings, artefacts and traditions comprising the National Heritage. Through this coalescence the past becomes physically present in the sense that it is 'there' to be venerated as tradition, monument, pageantry, spectacle and display. But because the National Heritage is in danger and therefore dependent on measures of preservation it also makes connection with the anxious aristocrat alignment. In this second connection the very precariousness of the National Heritage comes to witness the precariousness of historical continuity. 'Preservation' thus arrives at its ambivalent and complex meaning: it applies to the maintenance of old buildings and the like, but at the same time it can be implicitly and in a displaced way about preserving those social relations which are taken for granted and legitimised by the public rendition of history as the national past.

Over recent years this combination of a high bourgeois interpretation and philosophy of history with the concrete phenomena of National Heritage has been apparent in the public statements of so-called 'wet' Tories like Patrick Cormack and Norman St John Stevas who have campaigned heavily for the National Heritage. Towards the end of 1981, however, a different formation began to emerge. A fissure in the government saw St John Stevas, main proponent of the National Heritage Act (1980), moved out from the inner circle of power. With the marginalisation of Stevas and the constitutionalist Ian Gilmour, a

more traditionalist and even 'cultural' one-nation Conservatism lost out to a hard-nosed and extremist monetarism. In the particular terms of National Heritage this led to some fairly immediate developments; the National Heritage Memorial Fund, established by Stevas's Act, had its annual allocation of funds somewhat reduced, and Michael Heseltine through the Department of the Environment even went on to float plans for getting shot of the National Heritage altogether by the familiar process of 'commercialisation.'

These culminated in the National Heritage Act (1983) which established English Heritage (The Historic Buildings and Ancient Monuments Commission). Under the Chairmanship of Lord Montague of Beaulieu (who has already made his own stately home into a highly successful tourist attraction) and with a membership system which seems to be modelled on that of the National Trust, English Heritage is setting out to go beyond the gauntly authentic stone and the baize-like lawns ('Keep off the Grass') traditional to the Department of the Environment's semi-academic stewardship of the nation's ruins.

Respectful but commercially-minded *reanimation* is to be the way forward in this new world of theme-parks and mass tourism. Rather than the bare and merely Roman or Saxon stones of Dover Castle, for example, let us bring back real and living history by commemorating the Dunkirk evacuation (an early but splendidly victorious engagement in the battle against socialism) which was 'controlled' from this national heritage site.[11] More generally, however, this turning of the screw within the Conservative government also included an abandoning of the idea of historical and traditional continuity—which Stevas and Gilmour, among others, had been promoting quite assiduously. In this respect the change was informed by a third past–present alignment which, although itself vehemently anti-traditional, forms a key tradition in present Conservative thought. In this third alignment, which I shall call the *anti-traditional technicist alignment*, the past continues to exist in the present, but it does so in discontinuity with modern social reality. Disjunction is the crucial term here; the past exists, but it is 'other,' not as something which has been betrayed but as a true swamp of backward traditionality with which 'we,' the bearers of modern rationality, want nothing to do.

All three of these alignments depend upon a sense of the past as present, and they consequently need material supports in the world. In the case of both complacent bourgeois and anxious aristocrat alignments, the National Heritage provides such material support. In the case of the *anti-traditional technicist alignment*, however, the presence of the past is somewhat different. As an 'other' the past may indeed be exoticised as a place for tourists and school children to visit, or as a site of lost romance and betrayed glory, but it can also serve a rather more rhetorical purpose, as it did over Remembrance Day 1981, as a kind of dump into which the supposed causes of present social disorder may be thrown.

In this latter and far less romantic use, the past becomes an accusation and to be identified with it is to be consigned to a junkyard cluttered with antiquated apparatuses which persist in the present either as pathetic relics or as more demonic engines of social inertia and stress. In the anti-traditional technicist alignment, therefore, the past is characterised not by castles and customs but instead by such things as the trade unions which, under the Thatcher government and also in SDP thinking, are prime targets of this kind of attack (the onslaught against the closed shop and picketing which formed the background to Tebbit's 1980 Employment Act made much of their claimed antiquatedness, just as Thatcher responded to the 1984/5 miners' strike by accusing Scargill of wanting to plunge Britain into a 'museum society'). This sort of accusation is simple enough: to be 'historical' is not to be part of the national glory so much as it is to be 'old-fashioned,' and to be 'old-fashioned' is to be an impediment to social recovery. In the Conservative government of triumphant monetarism, therefore, the past is not just a heritage or trust in need of reluctant, because costly, protection. Neither is it just a convenient camouflage for preserving relations of domination under the guise of national identity and interest. It is also the oblivion which stands there as the rightful abode of all those anachronistic forces which resist the 'rationalisation' of social relations around market forces and new technology.

As for the connection with everyday historical consciousness, this too is beyond doubt. Heller has argued that 'the historical present is identical with the *new*: new social structures, cultural structures, structures of belief' and that in this respect 'all historical presents are *discontinuities*.'[12] The idea of a discontinuous past does not need reinvention—even if considerable reinterpretation is necessary to identify it with everything except present Conservative ambition.

The anti-traditional technicist alignment brings us firmly back to Remembrance Day 1981. The pillorying of Foot certainly provided

a reminder, if one were needed, that the public field of meaning is loaded against assertions of class to the same measure that it promotes feelings of nationhood. Foot's appearance was presented as if it marked a deliberate identification, and therefore also an intended historical solidarity, with the working-class movement. The *Daily Telegraph* mocked this solidarity as spurious and imaginary, implying that in his sentimental concern with 'history,' Foot had fallen out of line with the present-day working class—people who are now fully qualified as citizens and capable of honouring the 'national past' as well as of paying their respects to the dead. As a leading article put it on 9 November, 'No member of the working class, which Mr Foot believes he represents, would have worn his working clothes for such a solemn occasion, quite out of the run of ordinary life.' This criticism was made not just in the knowledge of Foot's standing as a historian but also in smug awareness of the crisis besetting the Labour Party and of the difficulties facing attempts to express and develop working-class solidarity, especially those which make any sort of appeal to an historical dimension. In a nation of subject-citizens, working-class forms are not just unfashionable, they are presented as being positively archaic—and never more so, of course, than in their appeal to historical consciousness. Hence the blue-plaque operation in which Foot was credited with 'history' so that he, and by implication the entire labour movement, could be all the more easily consigned to the scrap-heap of a very different public rendition of the past.

The Labour Movement and the 'National Past'

While the labour movement faces problems negotiating the loaded interpretation of the past which is instituted within the public field of meaning, there are also serious difficulties of a different sort bearing on the apparently unequivocal presence of the 'national past.' In order to clarify this second area it will help to introduce a fourth past–present alignment, and this one might as well be called *the marching proletariat alignment*. This axis, according to which historical development is imagined as a slow but continuous process of struggle through which the working class 'wins' the present, has played a key part in organising the understanding and use (both analytical and also gestural in the use of slogans) that the labour movement has made of history.

This, of course, is the Forward March of Labour, and as we know it is a procession which has been experiencing some difficulties lately. Many of the marchers seem to have scattered from the road, some of them have definitely defected to the other side, and there have also been serious problems with what limited 'winning' of the present has taken place. While the post-war years have indeed seen some realisation of egalitarian and democratic ideas, an overwhelming greyness has also crept over the picture—the bureaucracy, the waiting lists, the destruction of communities and traditional forms of self-understanding, the reduction of ideas of change, social responsibility, emancipation and development to the pallid state practices of 'nationalisation' and 'planning,' the political principles of democracy caricatured in the pragmatic bargaining which has gone on between the most powerful partners in the corporatist arrangement. If an earlier time saw the making of the working class, the events of the post-war years have lent great strength to those interests which now benefit from its unmaking.

Recent Labour governments have indeed been greatly disappointing, but it still seems to me that socialist claims in relation to the 'national past' or to historical development face a prior problem which is of a fairly formal kind. Because socialism does not conceive of historical development as a process which is in any full sense achieved or accomplished in the present as we know it, it cannot work up an easy public presence for its sense of history. Socialism is so evidently not present (except through its mistakes or by negative ascription from its opponents as bureaucracy, union intransigence, East Europe and so forth) and its relation to the present remains one of critical chal-

lenge. It still exists, in other words, as an idea, and as one which is increasingly difficult to define in traditional class terms. Recent events (including Remembrance Day 1981) suggest that socialism cannot match Conservative claims to the 'national past' and tradition. The Conservative interests have an easy time in this area, resting their case not so much on any idea as on the overwhelming presence of the 'national past'—its traditions, monuments and institutions. It is a relation of identity rather than critical challenge that is assumed here; manipulative, certainly, but it has been remarkably successful in making even an extreme monetarist Conservatism seem like an emanation from the national interest, and therefore a 'natural' guardian of the national identity.

The labour movement has often responded to this difficulty in ways that appear only to reinforce the accusations which are made against it. It is worth giving two examples of this kind of response. The first consists of simply laying claim to those public presences—institutions, ceremonies and customs—which exist in such apparently easy allegiance to the dominant interests. A strategy of this sort was evident in Michael Foot's initial and outraged response not to any Tory but to the appearance of the ill-starred Peter Tatchell as Labour candidate in the previously rotten borough of Bermondsey.

Ostensibly this argument concerned Tatchell's supposed allegiance to 'extra-Parliamentary' activity. It was also significant, however, for what it revealed about Foot's relation to the institutions of Parliament. In true constitutionalist style, Foot laid claim to Parliament as the institution through which democracy had been accomplished and through which further political change should be secured. He identified the Labour Party's historical development and mission with Parliament. The problem is that it is not possible just to 'lay claim' to national institutions such as Parliament unless one is prepared to accept on the recoil their overwhelmingly powerful definition of one's own cause. It may indeed be historically inaccurate to identify the development of Parliament with the struggle for democracy, but additional difficulties follow from the fact that the institutions of Parliament are indubitably present. More than this, their physical presence in Westminster is encrusted with a powerful national symbolism which establishes them as fetish-objects rather than institutions of political change. If the presence of the House of Commons is claimed as witnessing the achieved presence of the labour movement, then the way is also opened for the conclusion that the struggle for democracy is over—a thing of the past, perhaps even part of the national heritage. The reality, of course, is different. Evidently, then, it is not possible to treat national traditions and institutions as if they were merely contested items in a claim over inheritance. They have no such singularity and come with entire philosophies of history attached.

The second problematic response to the crisis in the labour movement's public image has been a tendency to fall back onto the historical style—the gestures and vocabulary—of a time when solidarity and progress did seem intact, a time when the presence of socialism seemed positive and growing, and when the road did indeed seem to stretch out in front of the marchers. So there is talk of 'comrades,' of 'the people,' of 'solidarity' and 'fraternity,' and hackneyed images like the Forward March of Labour are trotted out in comfortable accordance with historical memory.

There need be no apologising for the fact that the labour movement's is a *historical* consciousness, or that its utopianism is counterfactual. But while some of these old values certainly remain vital, they need to be defined in relation to the *present*, rather than just inherited in the often archaic forms of their past expression. The 'solidarity' of Wal Hannington's unemployed heroes can indeed burn bright in the eye of a romanticisation which nevertheless fails to notice that in both the official and the oppositional ceremonies the stage is occupied almost exclusively by men. This sort of unreflected yearning is at best a celebration of defeat: 'solidarity' coming to its purest and most noble expression not just in conditions of unemployment and hunger but also in the imagination of a historical memory which is increasingly incompatible with present political experience.

Alongside this vague hankering there is a related tendency to support and define present activities by aligning them with the more controllable terms of a nostalgically organised 'past' of the labour movement's own. To the extent that it was formed in the imagined mould of Jarrow, the People's March for Jobs (1981 and again—although to a lesser extent—in 1983) can be instanced as an example here. A similarly retrospective appeal to solidarity characterises Tony Benn's more resurrectional invocations of the English 'people' with their own preMarxian drive towards socialism: Peasants' Revolt, Robin Hood and all. The same should also be said for Benn's more recent attempt (1984) to dust off the old Chartist demand for an annual Parliament and beam it into the 1980s. This is an archaic suggestion which can offer little real solution to the problems either of Parliament or of democracy in a world which (according to rumours which should certainly be investigated) has changed somewhat in the last hundred and fifty years.

That this way of gesturing with past resonances works is not in doubt: it works to the extent that it provides some sense of coherence and identity, a vocabulary and *some* sort of public profile for those already embarked on the forward march. But there is surely now overwhelming evidence that the labour movement often only achieves this focus for its faithful by confirming the doubts of a large number of people for whom all this reeks of 'history' in the worst publicly sustained sense of the word—the 'past' as that swamp from which 'we' moderns are struggling to escape. This response can't be treated with contempt or simply written off as middle-class or anti-traditional technicist ideology either, for it is only partly attributable to the dispensation of power biassing the public field of meaning and the media in particular.

If the agencies of public meaning can sustain a 'national past' which functions to disorder, petrify and contain the labour movement, they can only do this because the labour movement itself has a tendency towards the comforting simplicities of an evocative and sentimental nostalgia: in its current uncertainty, it does tend in its radicalism to fall back on the vanished solidarities of a time when a coherent and unified working-class may seem to have been properly resistant, conscious and oppressed (a time—imaginary or not—when the class struggle was pure and simple), or to hanker after a world which corroborates its more exhausted conceptual machinery such as its reduction of all politics to a simple economic opposition between labour and capital, its continuing assumption that the legitimate route to an income leads through fulltime employment, or the theoretical cleaver which still divides mental from manual labour in automatic correlation with class difference, for example. Similarly the trade union movement is in many respects 'backward,' undemocratic and chauvinistic.

So while the public field of meaning is indeed loaded against socialism, it can also be seen as issuing a legitimate reminder that in no sense is socialism somehow 'there' to be dug out of the crypts of history and stood on its feet in the present. This is not to say that the labour movement is doomed by its historical memory to being merely archaic, or

that its cause is in any absolute way outdated. The point is only that if socialism ever does exist this will be because an electorate recognises that it can be made in adequate relation not to the past, but to the complexities (historical indeed) of contemporary social life. In the face of these complexities, and as the Conservative press is only too willing to announce, no mystery cult, however talismanic its vocabulary or moving its stylistic appeals to history, is going to be adequate.

5

Falling Back Together in the 1980s: The Continuing Voyage of the *Mary Rose*

> For if, for example, that ship of Theseus, concerning the difference whereof made by continual repara-tion in taking out of old planks and putting in new, the sophisters of Athens were wont to dispute, were, after all the planks were changed, the same numerical ship it was at the beginning; and if some man kept the old planks as they were taken out, and by putting them afterwards together in the same order, had again made a ship of them, this, without doubt, had also been the same numerical ship with that which was at the beginning; and so there would have been two ships numerically the same, which is absurd.
>
> Thomas Hobbes[1]

Poor old Mary Rose has had quite a bit to contend with these last five centuries.

When she went down, on a sparkling summer's morning in 1545, she was the jewel in the crown of Henry VIII's Navy.

But her 91 guns were no match for the ruthless onslaught of the murderous currents that flow beneath the Solent.

A deep scourpit was eroded on the port side of the hull.

The currents then relentlessly shrouded her in a thick layer of silt.

By the early eighteenth century a hard layer of shelly clay had sealed the once proud warship in her watery grave.

On October 11th 1982, a salvage operation on a scale never before attempted brought the forlorn remains of the Mary Rose to the surface.

Not only the hull, but a host of precious artefacts that tell of life in Tudor England were rescued from the muddy sea-bed. But in the pro-cess of drying them out they could easily be harmed or destroyed.

In order to preserve them, we gave the Mary Rose Trust a chemical solution called polyethylene glycol. Once these items (such as wooden bowls and leather shoes) have been soaked in this solution, they undergo a freeze-drying process that will preserve them for posterity…

You can be sure of Shell.

—Shell advertisement (April 1985)

Ghost Ship 1982: Returning to the Fair Isle

The hulk of the *Mary Rose* was finally lifted from the bed of the Solent estuary at Portsmouth on the morning of 11 October 1982. The recovery marked a triumph for marine archaeology which, with the partial exception of the raising of the early seventeenth century *Wasa* from the bottom of Stockholm harbour in 1959, had achieved nothing like this before. Underwater excavations having already yielded an extraordinarily well-preserved complexity of items which had sunk with the *Mary Rose* in 1545, the successful lifting of the remaining hull now bore witness to substantial developments in the technology of recovery.

The retrieval of the *Mary Rose* also provided clear vindication for Alexander McKee, a writer of popular histories whose search for the *Mary Rose* began with a boyhood fascination and developed through a diving programme which ran more or less continuously from 1965. McKee flew in the face of numerous orthodoxies by insisting that worthwhile archaeological remains could be found in Britain's cold and turbulent waters, and few people are likely to begrudge him the little gibes with which he went on to settle his score with the archaeological establishment. McKee may indeed have seemed like an eccentric maverick to some orthodox archaeologists, but like Schliemann at Troy in the nineteenth century (although without causing the attendant damage) he went on to come up with the goods. There is no proof like that, and in this sense the celebrations were no more than his due.

And celebrations there were. Large crowds attested to a significant degree of public interest, and commemorative pageantry went alongside enthusiasms of a less formal kind. The popular media waxed lyrical, having recourse to the inflated rhetoric which is used to celebrate moments of national significance and recovery. In the words of a special supplement of the *Portsmouth News* (published in October 1982), 'This is the moment when time quite literally stood still'; or again, curiously, in a vocabulary of violation: 'It was a day of champagne and colour, of tears and torment when Mary Rose, a wayward lady to the last, finally gave up the struggle to be dragged into the twentieth century...' Even BBC2's more sober 'Chronicle' team was so moved that in the excitement of the moment its announcer postulated an imaginary collective subject—a transhistorical national identity going by the name of 'we'—as he hailed the moment as 'the first time we have seen this in 437 years.'[2]

People may come and go, but with a little prompting 'we' are evidently elastic enough to make the leap between a disaster which took place 'under the gaze' of Henry VIII in 1545 and the present day. This leap, indeed, is remarkably effortless—perhaps because it really has nothing to do with spanning the ages. What it does instead is to negotiate a far more manageable threshold as it takes 'us' from our particular positions in the prosaic modern world into the more radiant chambers of a well-constructed national imagination. Here, 'we' reconnect with the past, but in a way that has little to do with the historical passage of years. The *Mary Rose* had, after all, been Henry VIII's flagship, and the fact that it sank due to what one commentator admits must have been 'gross mismanagement' before even engaging with the threatening French fleet does not appear to have prevented this from being recognised as the real stuff of history by the thousands who followed and celebrated the recovery.

As Ernle Bradford writes: 'Interest and enthusiasm from all quarters have revealed, in a Britain whose Navy no longer rules the waves, an interest in our maritime past that might prove startling to politicians—but not to those who are in closer contact with the feeling of the people.'[3] However, even in our somewhat immobilised time 'History' doesn't just lie at the bottom of the sea, in museums or under the turf of ancient sites—it isn't just embroidery in the fabric of the present—and Bradford's book was presumably at the press when the Falklands crisis blew up into war. Suddenly there was another task-force churning its way past the carefully exposed site of the *Mary Rose*, and then there were real naval engagements which 'we' actually won. Clear compensation, as it might be thought, for those feelings about no longer ruling the waves or, for that matter, anything much at all.

Of course it was coincidence that the *Mary Rose* was finally recovered in the year of the Falklands crisis, but if coincidence is accidental this certainly doesn't leave it without meaning. For just as it was 'we,' subjects of a publicly sustained national culture, imagination and sense of identity, who were ready to receive the *Mary Rose* in its full contemporary significance, it was also 'we' who were drawn up, with whatever incredulity or passion, into Thatcher's unlikely adventure in the South Atlantic. Their participation in this national culture—and the collective sense of identity which it holds in place—marks the ground held in common by the raising of the *Mary Rose* and the Falklands war. This ground in its turn now stands in need of excavation and survey.

Two basic contours can be sketched in immediately. First of all, it can be said that in the light of this national subjectivity the respective 'recoveries' of the *Mary Rose* and the Falkland Islands appear to have been 'historical' events in the same sense. For in terms of the national imagination what defined these events as bearing 'historical' significance was not just their decisiveness, singularity or uniqueness. It was, above all, their *resonance* of tradition and continuity with the past. For 'us' the contemporary 'historical' event appears increasingly to be the one which marks the *recovery* and reaffirmation of the old ways. In this respect it is intrinsically archaeological. Just as the recovery of the *Mary Rose* was presented as giving 'us' something back—something

which 'we' hadn't seen for 437 years—the Falklands war proved that 'we' are still powerful, still capable of rallying to one flag with confidence and moral righteousness: still, above all, capable of action and therefore no longer the 'waverers and fainthearts' of Thatcher's victorious Cheltenham speech.[4] 'History' in this contemporary sense is evidently not about the *making* of a future, unless we understand that process to be a re-enactment of the imagined past—'our' moment of vindication and perpetuation. In this new guide 'History' is what restores the essential and grander identity of the 'Imaginary Briton' to the modern subject: it is the greatest of contemporary fall-back positions.

The second contour concerns memory. If the event of 'historical' significance now stands more than ever as a binding moment of public revelation rather than the making of change or a decisive event in the struggle for world development, it is not surprising that memory should also achieve a new mode alongside its customary involvement in the ordering of personal life. To an extent this is a shift from private to public, for in its newer mode memory appears as a collective and commemorative form of *anamnesis*.

In Plato's conception *anamnesis* was a process through which true knowledge and understanding were derived by the recollection of 'Ideas' experienced in a transcendental realm before birth. For 'us' too it is another realm which is revealed and remembered in these auguries of the national imagination: a clear although no longer always preindustrial world from which hope, measure, intelligibility and courage have not been banished; a counterposed and authentic world which expresses its incongruity like some strange wild flower forcing its way up through cracks in urban concrete. This is a world in which to be is to belong and where sufficient knowledge and understanding are automatic gifts of entry—a world, in Adorno's phrase, where 'existence itself appears endowed with meaning.'[5] While it may certainly have been betrayed, this is overwhelmingly 'our' world: 'our' birthright and inheritance, a world which 'we,' exiles as we are in the Wasteland of western modernity, can recognise as our own. This world cannot be dated, but then neither could Plato's transcendental realm. It comes simply enough—and the mixture of metaphors is characteristic of the atmosphere—before the Fall.

These modulations of History (of what constitutes historical significance) and memory reflect wider developments in the way British people understand their own relation to the historical process. A desire for continuity develops when the present seems actually to lack the quality, meaning and significance of History—when past and present, in other words, seem disconnected and exterior to one another. History becomes, more urgently, the object of ceremonies of resonance and continuity when it seems actively to be threatened and opposed by an inferior present epoch—when, to put this differently, society is developing (or 'receding') in a way that cuts across the grain of traditional forms of security and self-understanding. More strongly still, we turn to the past when the future seems unattainable or 'utopian' in the wholly negative sense of the word—something that cannot be extrapolated from the present.

Many people have commented in recent years on the failure of confidence in Western societies, and the British experience would certainly seem to corroborate this. We have in the modern period conceived the future through progressivist philosophies of history. In terms of these philosophies (varieties of progressivism have accompanied the development of industrial capitalism, Western imperialism and also Leninism and Stalinism), history is less and less intelligible.[6] The twentieth century has been full of brutal shocks and its projected futures have been falling apart for decades.

In the more particular forms of the British experience since the Second World War, the idea of 'progress,' linked as it has been to the development of liberal market forces or, under Labour, to a statist social democracy, has failed to deliver the promised future. Progressivism still finds resort in technology—another magic carpet ride to the future— but while this vehicle continues to be much vaunted in the eighties, its limits also become clearer. Technological innovation occurs within existing social relations and when it moves these are carried forward with it. It is not, consequently, that the magic carpet won't fly; the difficulty is rather that it will only fly along preprogrammed trajectories, all of which cause justifiable and, as it looks, increasing concern—the concentration of technological power with its threat to civil liberties, the destruction of work, the increasing rationalisation of everyday life....However, nothing debunks 'progress' like the trajectory which, while it may be codenamed 'Defence,' leads in the direction of the most unimaginable future of all—nuclear destruction. In this age of nuclear (and also anti-nuclear) millennialism an antique Tudor war-machine certainly makes a more decorous curio than any Cruise missile.

As for memory and its modulation into a commemorative process resembling *anamnesis*, it is not as if this happens because, in the crisis affecting our orientation towards the future, a shared knowledge of the past is automatically precipitated in public understanding. Wider issues are involved here as well. To start with, a more social and public articulation of memory—one that augments and also changes the co-ordinating role played by memory in relation to the particularities of personal life—follows from the increasing influence which the historical process exerts on personal experience. I am suggesting here that the modern period has seen a sharpening or intensification of the relation between the historical process and the life experience of individual people as they grow up, act and age within the wider society. This sharpening can be attributed to the enormous upheaval and disruption of settled ways of life which followed (and continues to follow) in the wake of the 'developing' capitalist economy.

It seems that History sweeps the board in our time: like Fate, it hangs in the air over an everyday life which can apparently neither control nor influence it. In the turbulence of modernity a great deal that has been stable and traditional for generations is caught up into question and transformation; at the same time an anxious 'sense of historical existence' pervades everyday life.[7] People are likely to be aware of enormous disruption as they think back over their lives: communities have been uprooted and destroyed (often as a result of 'planned' state development); the culture and also the social role of the family have changed; ideas and values have been ripped out of their customary correlation with the empirically given world; norms and ways of life—many of them stemming from an Imperial source—which seemed to stand firm as the ground on which History unfolded have been questioned and dismantled; everyday forms of face-to-face contact (what Goffman/Giddens call forms of 'co-presence') have been devalued; disappointment and disorientation abound in this atmosphere of insecurity—together with confusion, frustrated expectation and apprehension about the future, about what comes next...[8]

Within this jarring present circumstance, memory becomes problematic for people from a variety of social backgrounds, and new coherences within publicly symbolised self-understanding therefore also become possible. Thus for example actual memories of the Second World War can be recuperated to a national mythologisation and redeclaration of that war. Similarly, dislocated experience of family life can be drawn up into (and placated by) the ever escalating celebration of goings-on within the Royal Family. In this way personal memory—with the full and particular intensity of feeling it involves—can be caught up in a wider public process of cultural nationalisation.

So the modern 'sense of historical existence' forms a shared stock onto which ideas and interpretations of the past can be grafted. It is this 'sense of historical existence' which underlies 'our' anxious readiness to receive the past in the mythical and overriding terms of national identity and essence. While this is no place to give a detailed account of the various institutional sites and agencies through which such a rendering of the past is produced, it is important to realise that we are dealing with produced ideas rather than any simple truth about the past. In this respect the national past has been under construction for a long time, but the process seems to have intensified since Britain's social and economic crisis started to escalate in the early 1970s.

It is also worth emphasising that the national past is characterised precisely by the way it blends elements and values drawn from 'the sense of historical existence' with the supposed and often administratively produced facts of the past. Thus, for example, pastoral landscape often blends its reconstruction of 'historical' geography with the invoked ideal of a valued childhood to form images of that earlier world which, while lost or betrayed, still gleams through occasionally. Similarly the traditional ceremonies of state and nation combine their evocation of the past with a desire for solidarity, meaning and continuity which is fundamentally of the present. Then there is the continuing bustle of 'historical' dramas on television. These dramas play out their often trivial stories in reconstructed interiors packed with period objects, all arranged in that slightly obsessive manner which speaks of a present yearning for a time when things at least had the dignity of an indisputable place in an ordered world. Hence, to summarise, the aura of overwhelming Romance—the sense of deep psychological investment and compensatory meaning—that permeates and gives lustre to the national past.

One can indeed get impatient, but the radiance of this essentialised world does, without question, demand respectful treatment. Whatever else it may do, this radiance bears witness to the utopian impulse and hope, the creativity and sense of wonder, the desire for transcendence that such a projection of national identity is able to engage. Such energies may indeed be articulated around ideological fictions (like Thatcher's post-Falklands reconstruction of the 'perennial values of the Victorian era'—thrift, love of country, neighbourliness, hard work and charity) but they should never be treated as if merely ideological or ridiculous in themselves.

This said, however, one must obviously also acknowledge that in its present articulation the national imagination *is* distinctly problematic. For if, as I have suggested, this projected national identity is an Arcadian integration in which all tension between subject and object is reconciled, then all the striving of real consciousness is finished with as well. If we are dealing with an imaginary realm in which 'existence itself' is endowed with meaning—if meaning follows from the mere fact of being rather than from historical activity—then we are also up against a mediocre coalition in which various parties fall back from their different positions to find unity and agreement under a banner reading no more than 'we are what we think we are.'

To put this another way, there is an encompassingly general and complacent sense of identity involved—a sense of identity which, being able to offer a subjectivity existing in harmony with its world, can accommodate and unify a number of different and even opposed experiences. It can offer a home to the well-heeled barbarian—to the self-interested man of 'success' who in these times is also likely to appear as the man of history (of historical and significant action). And yet it also reaches out to shelter the disappointed, the subordinate, the fractured and miserable; for them it offers integration and rest, the settlement of the contented slave.[9] This sense of subjective peace, of being at one with oneself and others finds corroboration in acts of collective aggression, in the exclusion of 'out-groups' (despite the apparent generosity with which Arthur Bryant offers his closed version of the British nation to all legal subjects, the 'Imaginary Briton' is a vibrantly white ghost), in expressions of collective righteousness and as the Falklands crisis revealed, in the excitement of distant war.

North Lighthouse (flashing white)

The recovery of the *Mary Rose* was not an isolated event which had only its ephemeral moment in the passing attention of a detached public eye. The project of recovery came in for repeated discussion and celebration in newspapers and on television from the late 1960s onwards and over this period the national imagination, far from just being well prepared for the eventual appearance of an old wreck in 1982, was actively involved in *producing* the ghost ship which eventually broke into view (disappointingly without its sails up) on that October morning. As things turned out, this present participation in the definition of the *Mary Rose* would extend to the reconsecration and burial of those English (and, if the ceremony is to be believed, also American) bones which were found on the wreck.

The ceremony took place in the presence of 1,000 'mourners' gathered in Portsmouth Cathedral on 19 July 1984. As David Hearst wrote the following morning in the *Guardian*, 'Everything was done to re-enact the forms of the time.' Elements in this ghostly ceremony included the Sarum Mass, incense and sprigs of rosemary, the Sanctus set to an anthem by John Taverner, priests dressed up in fancy costumes beamed in from Alabama (a touristic gesture which made much of the claimed resemblance which these white, patriarchal vestments bore to garments actually worn in sixteenth century England), an oak coffin with nails copied from those found in a seventeenth century coffin in Williamsburg (Virginia), and a bed of New Forest leaves and dried moss for those remaining bones to rest on (the ones which hadn't sensed the prospect of this ghoulish ceremony of authenticity

and taken to rather less publicised resting places in late twentieth century archaeological collections and research laboratories).

Three books on the *Mary Rose* were published in the few weeks preceding the raising of the hulk, and the work of reanimation goes on in them too. Alexander McKee wrote *How We Found the Mary Rose*, while accounts were also produced by Margaret Rule, the archaeologist who co-ordinated the excavation following McKee's discovery, and by Ernle Bradford, a 'historian and writer' who makes a speciality of books about ships (*HMS Hood* for example) and the sea.[10] All three books are of fairly popular orientation, and for all their differences they share an interesting structural characteristic. In all of them two distinct levels of interpretation are evident: one concerned with establishing an empirically orientated historiographical account of the building, sinking and eventual recovery of the *Mary Rose*, and the other with making a more contemporary and subjective sense of this record.

At the first and empirically orientated level the *Mary Rose* is taken as a present occasion for historiographical reconstruction and archaeological description. Accordingly a precise account of the excavation is provided and the historical background is sketched in. In terms that are serious, and indeed often quite sombre, we hear of Henry VIII and the key part played by naval force in the shifting disposition of European power during the sixteenth century—the skills and techniques of production. We are given a touch of social history and detailed accounts of attempts at salvage which were made immediately after the *Mary Rose* sank and again much later in the nineteenth century. At this empirically orientated level there is an evident concern with accuracy and also a fairly close use and display of archival sources, whether these be eyewitness accounts, contemporary descriptions, maps or other images. The excavation of the *Mary Rose* creates in the public a readiness to receive this information, and the three books show no hesitation in delivering to this interest. Indeed some of them make a display of the measure and gravity of serious historiography. They seem to do this partly in order to show that the excavation of the *Mary Rose* contributes to and helps complete the historiographical record (which it indisputably does), partly to flatter a readership which, while it might not exactly be reaching for A.J.P. Taylor's latest tome, does still like its enthusiasm to have an authentic basis in disciplined knowledge, and partly to legitimise the sense of myth and celebration which is brought to bear at the second level of the accounts.

Alongside documentation of this empirically orientated kind the second level of interpretation introduces an openly fictional and imaginative element: it is here that the sober world of factual historiography starts into life. As we enter this second level John Deane is no longer a rather obscure nineteenth-century diver who tried to salvage items from what at the time was the less buried *Mary Rose*; he is suddenly alive and well, an adventurer, one of 'us,' and he goes back to work before our very eyes: 'The weighted rope ladder was already over the side, hanging just clear of the seabed. As, step by step, he entered the water, the pressure pushed in the india-rubber suit, so that Deane could feel the creases and folds; the waves rose above his helmet, and the water rose inside, but not as far as his chin, as long as he kept his head upright.'[11]

As for Henry VIII, he too ceases to be a figure in distant history; he is suddenly a *presence* and actually 'there,' larger than life ('a man of enormous girth'), sitting at Southsea Castle, hearing the 'muffled thudding' of cannon and watching as the *Mary Rose* founders 'beneath his very gaze' and, in Bradford's unforgettable phrase, 'Drowned bodies float upon Solent waters.' Henry is on the scene, and the scene hasn't really changed *that* much. Modern developments haven't totally banished the sacred geography of this national romance, for as Margaret Rule points out quite rightly, there are little tricks of restoration which are available to all of 'us' if we only just half-close our eyes: 'As we go out to the excavation site a mile away in our small twelve man tender we can half close our eyes in order to exclude the modern monuments to Mammon and the municipal blocks of flats and see again the mellow lines of the fortifications and the higgledy-piggledy cluster of ale-houses around Portsmouth Point. Doubtless friends and sweethearts clustered on the beach below the urban ramparts just as they did 400 years later in 1945.'[12] Exit all trace of the post-war mixed economy (including the 'planned' developments of the period). Inner city or country, there aren't many views in Britain which are not amenable to this sort of treatment, and it is not just for Margaret Rule that 1945 is the first essentialised year to appear. For the sake of those who would discriminate between hallucinations, it should also be remarked that 1945 can appear in a similarly exotic light to the left—to people who look through the lens of an insufficiently considered idea of what Gramsci called the 'national–popular', for example.[13]

At this second and mythically orientated level of interpretation vagueness and gestural speculation of a sort which would clearly be inappropriate at the first are both permissible and desirable. This may seem inconsistent and contradictory, but in the dual logic of the books it is no more than what works. At the first level the authors establish a record, submitting openly (even flagrantly) to the discipline of objectivity and truth. At the second the business is to create impressions, imagine we were there and mobilise a plainly mythical form of consciousness. At the first level, therefore, an empirically orientated record is made, while at the second this record is occupied and animated by the subjectivity of our own time. Two different operations are involved, and because they do not take place on the same plane they cannot simply clash or contradict one another.

The raising of the *Mary Rose* provides a striking and in some respects unique opportunity to observe the crystallisation of contemporary meanings around an object which in a certain sense is new, even though it makes its appearance in the familiar garb of the national past. The *Mary Rose* is raised into the present social imagination, and it makes its entrance from the parallel realm of 'nature.' It comes into society as if from nowhere. There is, of course, a readiness to receive it; contemporary understanding is prepared for the *Mary Rose* in a number of ways and anticipates its arrival. Some historiographical information is assumed, public ideologies and philosophies of history are in play, and above all a valuation of the past as priceless and worth recovery is necessary.

Similarly, the 'nature' from which the *Mary Rose* makes its entrance, far from existing in pure separation from the social, has already been interpreted. The hulk, for example, makes its entrance from the 'depths'—a zone with great imaginative appeal and a long cultural history as the domain of the monstrous, the dangerous and the secret, a site of adventure and discovery—the bearer of countless projected meanings. This state of prepared anticipation shows how contemporary concepts are integral to the recovery. Such concepts form the *cultural* machinery with which the *Mary Rose* is drawn up and thematised within the national imagination. In this respect they are every bit as integral to the 'raising' of the *Mary Rose* as marine archaeological technique or the vast lifting technology which was brought in (courtesy of the Howard Doris company) at the last stage. Those concerned with authenticity might well at this point find some entertainment in the famous question which the Athenian Sophists asked of another patriotic relic: is the ship of Theseus still the ship of Theseus after all its planks have been replaced piece by piece—after the entire ship has in this sense been 're-membered' by later times?

What are these concepts, and in what sense are they contemporary? Examples can be found easily enough at the mythical level of the books by Bradford and McKee, examples which refer to the *Mary Rose* itself and sometimes also to the adventure of its discovery. There is the idea of a meaningful and unbroken *natural experience* with its mimetic relation to nature: an unrationalised life-world which has not been colonised by technological science, in which knowledge does not entail a break with the customary measures of being, and in which the traditional 'ways' of the folk remain sufficient. Thus in a passage full of reverie McKee dreams up a time when the *Mary Rose* was lost to all but sea creatures and local fishermen who knew 'the location by marks on land.'[14]

Then there is the idea of a small male *team*: a group of men (the crew of the *Mary Rose* but more specifically McKee's divers) who leave their pining womenfolk on shore to go out and quest against undeniable odds to vindicate a shared vision. This idea of the self-motivating team upholds the possibility of harmony and organised co-operation—of a unity of purpose and endeavour which takes place when particularistic differences are subordinated to a common purpose under the inspiration and benign authority of an accepted leader. Such a conception of the masculine team resonates in a wide variety of contexts—in popular sport, in any number of men-against-nature-or-the-odds activities and films—but for McKee it engages, above all, memories of war.

For McKee the imagined (and perhaps also real) danger of diving into mines still remaining from the war elicits memories of Heinkel minelayers and Stukas over Portsmouth. The discovery of human remains on the wreck leads McKee to reminisce upon 'a farmhouse on the Dutch–German border in March 1945, after the snows melted away from the corpses of the soldiers who had died there many months before.' For McKee the memories seemed direct enough. In his words, 'Such things have been the common coin of my generation.'[15] But whatever their personal integrity, as they become 'common coin' these memories are also articulated into the more mythical and rede-clared presence which the Second World War holds in contemporary British consciousness.

This mythical presence can easily enough engulf the entire *Mary Rose* story, as happens in the following passage from Bradford: 'The whole operation so far had in some ways resembled the pattern for the British during World War Two: the first hard, lonely years with very limited resources and all the odds stacked against a small group of people: to be followed by evidence that their endurance was win-ning; and to be followed again by very great support as it was seen that they had proved their cause.'[16] Once again apparently, much of this 'very great support' came from the United States of America, although this time mostly in the form of donated funds. But this con-ceptualisation of the war is not primarily a fantasy of rescue or of honourably earned assistance. It comes closely connected to the far more powerful idea that *action is still possible*: that it is possible to *be* historical even in the present, immobilised and bureaucratic as these times may be, and that the power of significant action still lies with the British subject.[17] That McKee and his colleagues did act—and that they also succeeded—is undeniably true. One may indeed wonder whether their success is in any way applicable to other citizens' initia-tives (especially those which cannot secure millions of pounds from industry, a favourable media profile and very active Royal patronage), but national mythology doesn't waste time with particulars such as this. Indeed, it actively declares them to be carping details, utterly beside the point.

It is clear then that the mythical concepts which are used to make contemporary sense of the *Mary Rose* are themselves con-stituted in, and remain open to, the historical situation of every-day life in the present. This is the crucial point, for it is here that these apparently fictional concepts find their practical truth, their reality and contemporaneity. They work by articulating not just crude ideological purposes (and, contrary to what muckraking approaches to culture would suggest, not even *primarily* such pur-poses), but also the insecurities, preoccupations, hopes and fears of contemporary everyday consciousness, and they articulate these back onto the more empirically defined meanings of the first level (the archaeological record, the historiographically defined 'truth' of the sixteenth century...). Is the *Mary Rose* still the *Mary Rose*?

While the actual planks remain the same, there can be little doubt that, like the Ship of Theseus, this is a boat which has been thoroughly remade.

History in Reverse

> But this is the famous nature of hindsight: to it everything is inevitable, since everything has already happened.
>
> Philip K. Dick

This mythical intertwining of distinct levels of meaning is nowhere more evident than in the definition which it establishes of history—of the historical process—itself. In amongst the mythical concepts which are used to 'raise' the *Mary Rose* at the second level of the accounts there appears a strikingly fictional, even delirious, conception of history—a conception which is, as I shall suggest, 'mythical' in an anthropological as well as a semiological sense. Distinct from the more sober conception of History produced at the first level, this mythical 'History' is not conceived as a process which moves forward irreversibly through continuity and discontinuity. In sharp contrast, mythical History is incapable of transcending itself or any of its earlier stages; indeed, it appears to flow *backwards* rather than forward in time.

In mythical 'History' we no longer cite nineteenth-century attempts to salvage items from the *Mary Rose* in order to define the developments which eventually made it possible to recover the whole hulk in the late twentieth century. Similarly, we no longer sketch in the sixteenth century background to provide a context in which the sinking of the Mary Rose can be understood. Instead we are suddenly citing the Second World War for the light that it casts on more ancient times. We think of the class structure of Victorian times and this enables us to say (as if there were any historiographic meaning involved at all) of the *Mary Rose*'s sixteenth century crew that 'there was none of that sense of class distinction that prevailed in Victorian times'[18]—another convivial 'team' no doubt. We quote Tennyson on 'immemorial elms' to indicate the nobility of English wood (as found on the wreck), and if the devastation wrought by Dutch Elm Disease in the 1970s comes to mind this just goes to prove the same point—that as time passes we slip further and further away from the national essence.

I say that mythical 'History' flows backwards because it works in a way opposite to those teleological and future-orientated conceptions in which History moves forward through time towards its goal. Contrary to this, the mythical conception of 'History' establishes a national essence which is then postulated as an immutable if not always ancient past. In this chronically and sometimes violently mournful perspective the essential stuff of history remains identical through time—even though it is unfortunately all concentrated at an earlier point in the passage of time. Hence the passage of years becomes entropic, opening up an ever widening gulf between 'us' in the present and what remains 'our' rightful and necessary identity in an increasingly distant past.

The perfect metaphor for this conception of History is the *Mary Rose* itself—an enduring and essential fragment which does not decay so much as it becomes increasingly and irrecoverably 'lost,' sinking each year a bit further down into the total obscurity of Solent silt. Only an act of heroism will reverse this trend, checking the relentless passage of time and restoring to 'us' something that 'we' in our decadence may only just still be able to recognise as 'ours'. McKee located a wreck, but in these mythical terms he also reconnected 'us' to the threatened national identity.

It should certainly be pointed out, if only in passing, that this national identity is sufficiently inclusive to embrace not only all true Britons but also white America as well. This was indicated by the American presence at the 1984 ceremony in which the *Mary Rose*'s crew were 'buried,' but the central point about it can be expressed in the words of England's foremost writer of history-in-reverse. Arthur Bryant, for whom even 'the rocks of Britain have a different past from those of Europe,' was evidently preoccupied by these matters in the forties and fifties. In the first volume of his *The Story of England* Bryant comments that 'England' did indeed exist independently before the union of the crowns that founded 'Britain.' More than this: 'It was in the England of Elizabeth that the earliest colonisers of North America were born. They called their first colony Virginia after her. The great queen—the last English sovereign to reign before the union of the crowns of England and Scotland—belongs as much to American history as British. Without her there would have been neither a United States nor a British Empire.'[19] And even if those expatriates who somehow drifted over the ocean onto 'the hard core of Earth's greatest nation,' also went on to kick 'England' out in a War of

Independence, this only goes to prove their Englishness: how could people of such descent do anything but insist on governing themselves (after 'English ideas of liberty, justice and self-government...')?

Evidently, and as those American vestments and coffin nails at the Portsmouth burial ceremony also showed, history-in-reverse includes among its many capacities the ability to 'derive' contemporary geopolitical alliances from deep in the quasi-genetic mists of time. It is clearly all the more important that these mists be dense and impenetrable if they are really to obscure the appalling third partner who sat down, however awkwardly, with Churchill and Roosevelt at Yalta in 1945.

The fundamental difference between the two conceptions of History at work in the accounts of McKee and, especially, Bradford can be defined in terms of identity and difference. In the empirically orientated 'History' of the first level, historical development moves forward through qualitative change and transformation. Precisely because it takes place in a transformative process a distinction is established between past and present. The 'historical past' is alienated from the present: it becomes other to the extent that it is transcended and therefore no longer identical with the present. This way of conceiving the relation between past and present is founded on a properly historical consciousness (without which it would be impossible to conceive the past as in any way distinct from the present).

In the mythical conception, however, 'History' can be reversed and run backwards because it has identity rather than difference as its theme. What existed then can be retrieved and recognised now because it remains truly 'ours.' In this mode repetition is of the essence, for as Agnes Heller has written: 'whatever happened once will always be repeated, what is ancient serves as a model for repetition; thus the ancient and the present are not distinct. Anyone who repeats the ancient *is* ancient.'[20] There need accordingly be no essential discontinuity between past and present as long as the ceremonies of re-enactment are carried out and respected. As an essence that is embodied in such ceremonies the nation is immutable—either it finds its witness in the present or it is lost and betrayed.

The Nationalist Fable

Like the different levels of interpretation in the books about the *Mary Rose*, these contrary definitions of 'History' are therefore not available as options. They do not exist merely in logical contradiction. Indeed, they are closely interdependent in the accounts and here again one is needed to legitimate or enliven the other. We can certainly take as read Agnes Heller's further point that 'Ever since the emergence of the consciousness of history, the past has become partially alienated.' But what 'consciousness of history' delivers in these times of crisis and insecurity is no longer a promise of progress; rather it is more likely to be a feeling of loss, confusion, disappointment and anxiety. The past may indeed be partially alienated from the present, but in the contemporary context such an alienation of the past is also experienced as deprivation and even emasculation.

At precisely this point the attentions change, shifting from the empirically orientated History of difference to the mythical History of identity. As a result of this shift the partial alienation of the past ceases to mark the properly historical status of the present and is experienced in terms of loss and betrayal. The past becomes a lost inheritance which in its rediscovery (the *Mary Rose*, the sovereignty of the Falkland Islands, the 'Victorian values' of Thatcher's 1983 election campaign) justifies our mythical consciousness, our espousal of a way of thinking which might more normally be thought to stand as an early and transcended stage in the development of historical consciousness, not as a mode of thought which *depends* in this way on historical consciousness (not to say on a relatively accurate historiographical understanding) for its arena. In this mythical framework (and to use Bradford's phrase) the *Mary Rose* becomes a 'time-capsule'—a fragment of idealised history which has borne the national essence and identity down to the present. As such a fragment which can be symbolised in terms of 'our' (threatened) identity, the *Mary Rose* 'endures,' 'embalmed' and 'encapsulated' in a silt where, to quote the *Portsmouth News* again, 'time stands still.' In this sense it is 'we' who ride through time and are still 'there' to be discovered in the sludge of contemporary life, just as it is 'we' who get betrayed or lost, even to ourselves, at the bottom of the sea.

This notion of the time-capsule situates the *Mary Rose* in a narrative structure which comes up again and again in various and diverse fables of nationalism, a structure which consists of a set of necessarily interrelated terms and which speaks very deeply in connection with a dislocated or threatened everyday life. The first of these terms is the postulated purity of an essential identity. This may be constituted specifically as the *Mary Rose*, Mentmore Towers or Calke Abbey, but it may also be 'our' land and way of life as it was both in Thatcher's 1983 election campaign and also in Enoch Powell's racist speeches in the early and mid 1970s. Likewise it could be a cherished national institution such as Parliament or the Monarchy. Whatever its particular content, however, it is always placed in necessary relation to a threat of violation.

This second term of the narrative may be found in public indifference, the stumbling incompetence of bigoted and arrogant professionals (the archaeologists who stood in McKee's way) or the danger of erosion as it was with the *Mary Rose* (perhaps even, as Ernle Bradford speculates, by *teredo navalis*—that southern and 'voracious worm' which may survive around the British coast now that the waters of 'our' polluted realm are unnaturally warmed by industrial 'effluent'). But it may also be presented as the 'Marxist socialism' which Thatcher, riding out from Perth for the 1983 election, promised to banish from the land, as immigrants, extra-parliamentarians, invading 'Argies,' the bureaucracy and regulations of post-war Labour reform, or 'the enemy within' as Thatcher (using the phrase of a Fleet Street rag) called the striking miners (rather than the IRA—who know all about the nationalist fable) in 1984.

The third term of this narrative is struggle and victory for the forces of good—the essence is redeemed (even if legality has to be suspended in the process) and, in this field full of ideological heroism, the threat of violation laid low as the essential order of things is restored. Every bit as much as the Falklands war, Thatcher's 1983 election campaign was fought on this narrative model.

Saint George and the Dragon seem to be fighting it out, not just over again on the contemporary ground of an uncertain everyday life, but increasingly and in a variety of different versions. Thus if the latest phase of the battle has been going on for the length of the century, it is also given to widely divergent forms of presentation and meaning. The classic and perhaps also definitive novelistic manifestation is surely to be found in G.K. Chesterton's *The Flying Inn* (1914) where military and diplomatic upheavals culminate in an agreement that Britain will impose an Islamic ban on alcohol consumption: under this alien legality, the deep nation (the makeshift and wandering 'Inn' of the title) becomes secretive in its particularism, given to the agit-prop life of sudden appearance and disappearance as a mock-heroic publican rolls his fugitive barrel, cheese and sign around the native countryside.

I have already discussed the nationalist fable in the deeply experienced familial and anti-Semitic form which it assumes in Mary Butts's *Death of Felicity Taverner* (1932), and it is certainly also worth mentioning the more innocent variation which appears in the 1940s Ealing comedy *Passport to Pimlico*—a film in which a bomb falls on war-time London only to reveal an old 'Burgundian' national identity hidden under the urban forms of lesser modern society. More recently, the nationalist fable has been put to polemical use by E.P. Thompson in the xenophobic symbolism of 'The Poverty of Theory' (1978)—a dramatically argued essay in which the dragon (or was it actually a cloud of locusts?) of alien 'Theory' lands on green English pastures and (even though in real terms it had already made a good job of setting fire to itself) gets beaten back after a bloody battle in which a lot of native collaborators were slaughtered by their redeeming champion, while others took up wounded and paranoid residence in the hills.

If many pre-war versions of the fable revolved around tea-shacks, litter and speculative plotland development, these seem in recent decades to have given way to ripe stories of immigration, of the socialist 'enemy within', and of treacherous 'moles' in high places (the unmasking of figures like Anthony Blunt has been crucial to the recent redeclaration of the Second World War as a struggle against 'socialism') which are so central to the Thatcherite versions of the nationalist fable. The nation is pure—never mind that its protection demands an increasingly centralised and secretive state machine, extensive official corruption and ministerial dishonesty, brutal and racist immigration controls, the demonisation of 'the enemy within,' extensive state and also 'private' surveillance of people exercising their democratic right to speak at official public enquiries and on occasion, as seems all too likely, the murder of people who get in the way—people like Hilda Murrell, the murdered seventy-eight year old rose-breeder and founding member of the Shropshire Conservation Trust who now seems in some obscure way to have joined the number of those who have 'fallen' for this bright and righteous nation in which 'we' are so proud to live.

Agnes Heller has pointed out that the stories which are such a characteristic feature of everyday life make sense above all in terms of their *endings*. In its connection with everyday life the nationalist fable serves

to prove the point, for whatever variation is in play the crucial questions concern its outcome—who will win, what will be saved, and how will evil be vanquished? The political culture of Thatcher's nation is full not just of publicly fostered anxiety and anticipation, but also of the momentary resolutions and discontinuities which occur when the fable is completed in one form (for instance, the Falklands) and renewed in another (for instance, the 1983 election campaign or the 1984/5 miners' strike). A Conservative journalist has recently commented on one weakness of this style of political leadership. Writing in *The Times*, this columnist has asked what happens to the 'conviction politician' between the moving spasms of her overriding cause (these were not exactly his words). What happens is that a dangerous openness creeps over the scene: political questions start to form as society declares its heterogeneity again, and it becomes advisable for a new version of the fable to be synthesised as soon as possible. As Charles Olson once wrote, 'When the attentions change the jungle leaps in.'[21]

In the contest for the *Mary Rose* Alexander McKee was cast as Saint George to begin with, but as the administration of a growing archaeological operation displaced the adventure of discovery it took Margaret Rule to come in as co-ordinator of the excavation. As it happened, Margaret Rule (since awarded the CBE in the 1983 Honours List) did not get fully drawn into this mythical symbolisation of the recovery. While her arrival on the scene marked the reinstatement of archaeological discipline over maverick adventure, another man waited in the wings—the already fully symbolised Prince Charles— and he took over as President where McKee left off as founder. The predominantly masculine order of adventure was secured over that of professional administration, and the fable was brought through to its triumphant conclusion: the nation rediscovered and reaffirmed.

South Lighthouse (flashing white)

I have said that 'we' provide the essential identity between past and present in mythical 'History,' but what is this essential quality, this supposedly transcendent stuff of history which has conquered time? The answer, obviously enough, is that 'we' is a utopian projection which, while being historically and culturally produced, affects nevertheless to stand above history in a transcendent realm of its own. Reconstructed into a pure form this national identity would be abstract, bearing no necessary or organic relation to people's actual experience. For a few maniacs, and more generally at times of severe crisis, such a fully abstracted and essentialised notion of national identity may become a powerful motivating force in itself.

This century has certainly witnessed more than enough occasions when such a concentrated projection of national identity has recoiled on societies with a vengeance, and recent British experience has included an uncomfortable tightening and concentration of the national essence around the threatened 'sovereignty' of the Falklands. But under normal contemporary circumstances this publicly instituted sense of national identity is far more open and even heterodox. It exists in a state of dispersal—as a fleeting insinuation and challenge, as a million different ways of forgetting all about Northern Ireland or of turning an innocently blind eye to the evidences of contemporary racism, for example—but not as a fully achieved and conscious coherence within the social imagination. Indeed, even in its most extravagant displays this national identity is for many people worth no more than a vague yawn: 'The *Mary Rose*? A piece of over-valued driftwood,' as I've heard it called. Perhaps papers should be written in praise of such little refusals and the boredom they express.

But indifference of this sort—the fact that it is possible to be imaginatively grounded outside or in critical relation to the nation—is in no sense the only factor limiting the political uses to which the nation can be put. There is another very substantial reason why the nation cannot be written off even as an only partially effective ideological construction—or as if it consisted only of bourgeois and imperialist cultural residues which work in easy correlation with Conservative interests in the present. For while it certainly features heavily dominant tendencies, and is capable of truly deadly forms of presentation, the nation remains heterodox in at least two senses.

The first of these applies at the fairly crude level of 'content.' The national past, for example, does indeed include a great weight of originally bourgeois and imperialist cultural material, but over a long period of time these contents have been augmented as a consequence of endeavours which have inserted different and more critical contents into the repertoire. The late nineteenth-century preservation movement forms the obvious example here, especially in its attempt to articulate ideas of beauty, culture and historical significance against the excesses of capitalist development and accumulation. Another example is to be found in the post-war expansion which has widened the repertoire of the National Heritage, establishing the ordinary street alongside the mansion and the early industrial relic alongside the great artistic masterpiece. In this way conflicting cultures may well come to be combined in a bland celebration of mere diversity, but one should never forget that this expansion has often also followed an active *claiming* of national significance in the name of previously excluded cultures and interests.

The same point about the heterodox nature of the nation applies, although differently, with regard to the everyday historical consciousness and also the *values* which are implicit in the way people appropriate and make sense of national culture. These are far from simply or wholly regressive or reactionary. Indeed, they include creativity and aspirations—'hope,' to use Bloch's word—which no reputable socialism should fail to recognise as positive: displaced, maybe, and in all likelihood articulated into a reactionary mode, but positive nonetheless in their active potential—the possible inheritance of very different future development.[22]

What then is the part played by this culturally produced sense of the nation in contemporary British politics? This question brings us up against the familiar characteristics of the continuing British crisis: the collapse of softer (although still imperialistic) organicist ideas of British (or rather generalised English) identity; the widespread anxiety and disorientation (in values, expectations, previously normative ideas...) which has accompanied the disappointment of the post-war settlement; the disintegration and failure of social democratic pragmatism in the Labour Party *and* the continuing inadequacy of what is announced as socialist policy in the same party; the constructed 'consensus' or 'public opinion' of the press and television which makes any full, rational or even active public engagement with political issues almost impossible, and which in turn enables the crudest of the left-wing elements in the Labour Party to persist in the fatuous and damaging illusion that their 'socialism' is 'really' in line with popular feeling (witness Labour's strangely claimed 'victory' in the devastating 1983 election—a claim first made by Tony Benn and later repeated by Ralph Miliband who, after unspecified research into the precise motivations of Labour's remaining 8½ million voters, declared the election result 'testimony to a resilience of popular support of extraordinary strength').[23]

It is in this situation that Thatcher's utopian expression of the nation has been defined and established. It is clear, for example, that the pejorative anti-welfare rhetoric of 'scroungers' and 'handouts' which arose in the late seventies reflected (rather than just contributing to) the corrosion of that coalition of ideas which has formed the basis of consent for the welfare state—a coalition in which moralistic ideas and feelings about personal responsibility came into uneasy settlement with more political and administratively defined ideas of equality and justice.

This development is far from complete (and, of course, its outcome is far from guaranteed). By the time of the 1983 election the New Conservative utopia had gone from 'scroungers' and 'hand outs' to a more syncretic vision of duty and self-reliance. With what should certainly be treated as full (even if not historiographical) conviction and belief, Thatcher has even produced a 'period' so that the public may adopt the stridently contemporary ambitions of the Conservative programme in the comfortable knowledge that they are also falling back into identity with the national past. We have heard, therefore, about the 'perennial values' of the Victorian era, and ideas of 'Charity' have been articulated against notions of social welfare. New post-market authoritarians, such as the much publicised prefect-'philosophers' of Peterhouse, Cambridge, have taken the opportunity of the moment to reinstate ideological pseudo-concepts like the 'weak' or the 'feminine,' and to assert a deformed semi-Kantian argument that execution by hanging provides criminals with a final opportunity to prove their dignity and humanity. Their operation may indeed be crude enough, but the strategies of contemporary Conservatism acknowledge, even thrive on, the extent to which history itself has become utopian in terms of a public culture which has substantial difficulty in conceiving a future at all. This is why the future of the Thatcher project has, in its distinctive way, often also been presented as the past. It is a future in which 'history' is rediscovered and in which traditions find themselves reinstated in the present. This is a revivalist Big Tent Conservatism which has been able, if only temporarily, to fuse its ideology with strong elements in the social imagination of the time.

Anthony Barnett was certainly right in claiming that the Falklands war marked an enormous consolidation of Thatcher's position both within the Conservative Party and in public opinion at large. There are, nevertheless, risks in advancing too far with declaredly provisional notions like 'Churchillism.' While Thatcher did indeed take command of the nation through a gestural repertoire that ceaselessly invoked (and with full Parliamentary support, as Barnett has argued) the glories of wartime unity under Churchill, this does not mean that Thatcher heads a government whose policy amounts only to archaism or, in Barnett's phrase, the 'past's vision of the past.'[24]

Neither does it mean that Thatcher's Conservatism and the everyday 'sense of historical existence' are identical. Before the Falklands the Conservative government was divided between a Tory traditionalism and a modernising anti-traditional monetarism which was seeking to gather forces around a programme aimed to reinstate a technocratic concept of progress. To a considerable extent this modernising tendency, represented by Thatcher, Heseltine, Tebbit and others lacked legitimation. This was so, to a significant degree, because tradition and the 'nation' still lay with the so-called 'wets'—people like Gilmour (Pym was less visible at the time) and St John Stevas who clearly represented a softer one-nation style of Conservatism. This tension within the Conservative Party was exemplified in the fact that while these 'wets' were concerned with preserving the venerable National Heritage (the 1980 National Heritage Act), Heseltine was planning ways of commercialising and repackaging the insufficiently marketed monuments tended for the nation by the Department of the Environment (the 1983 National Heritage Act).

The Falklands adventure made a new combination possible: this small war enabled Thatcher to draw up the legitimising traditions of the 'nation' around a completely unameliorated 'modernising' monetarist programme. This new and charismatic style of legitimation fused a valorisation of national tradition and identity with a policy and programme which is fundamentally destructive of the customary ways and values to which it appeals. An extreme settlement therefore, it has survived very largely on account of what it never ceases to stress as the absence of any credible political alternative. In this respect it is a firmly contemporary project—able to mobilise feelings about past and nationhood which nevertheless remain at least partially distinct and which might, under different circumstances (and here of course the new division of the Parliamentary opposition is crucial), find their way into very different forms of cultural and political expression.

I said earlier that one can get impatient with all this nationalist rhetoric, but the challenge is obviously more difficult than that. The first thing to recognise is that to date there has been no adequate oppositional response to the contemporary rebirth of the 'nation' and the publicly established forms of self-understanding which come with it. The Labour Party has made a few attempts to claim the nation as its own right and inheritance, but these have failed miserably—not least because the 'nation' to which Thatcher appeals so successfully is articulated (both in its own historical formation over the last three decades and in Conservative invocation) against post-war statist reform.

While actually increasing the powers of the centralised state, this Conservatism is also thriving on widespread disillusion with the bureaucratic corporatism of the welfare state and with its extension into everyday life. Successive Labour governments have appealed to the 'national interest' deemed to underlie the development of the welfare state, but this 'national interest' is widely experienced as being as uniformly grey as the local Department of Health and Social Security office, as inhuman as the pettiest of state bureaucrats, and about as dignified in its egalitarian collectivity as the end of the dole queue. Starkly opposed to this, 'the nation' to which Thatcher has learned to

Rule Britannia!

appeal is full of adventure, grandeur, ideas of freedom, ceremony, and conscripted memories (of childhood or war for example). The problem for Labour has certainly seemed dramatic. It is even possible that in the insulated South of England especially, the escalation of unemployment under Thatcher continues to recoil on Labour rather than the Conservatives—at least to the extent that the publicly established images of unemployment (images of dependency and administered welfare) are still strongly associated with the cause, culture and politics of the Labour Party. There are indeed 'two nations' in the symbolism of Thatcher's Britain but these are not the two nations of habitual definition: the division is not so much between rich and poor or North and South, but rather between the grand if not always aura-laden symbolism of Empire and War on one hand and the bureaucratic imagery of the welfare state on the other.

Where efforts to 'claim' the radiant 'nation' for Labour have failed there have been a few attempts to accuse Thatcher's Conservatism of pessimism (citing its claims about the inevitability of unemployment etc)—an argument which fails immediately if only because, since the Falklands especially, the Thatcher project in its strength is precisely *made up* of aspiration and hope (displaced and not *essentially* aligned with Conservatism, but aspiration and hope nevertheless). The third strategy which I shall mention—and I have already alluded to it—is to oppose mythologisations of the past (such as Victorian values) with the real facts of history which such myth usurps. While this strategy has a solid logic on its side, it remains inadequate for two reasons.

First of all, it too fails to acknowledge the complex ways in which such redrafted assertions of the past are received. It is *not* just as 'history' that such ideas are embraced and the historiographic question of their truth or falsity is often peripheral to their practical appropriation in every-day life. In its connection with everyday life even the most manipulative appeal to the 'national past' is likely to be complex. This is surely indicated by the extent to which Thatcher's appeal to 'Victorian values' resonated not just with anti-pornography arguments which are themselves far from essentially Tory, but also with a recent feminist tendency—expressed against the permissive 'freedom' of sixties libertarianism—to revalue the family. The appeal is not just to a crudely falsified image of the past, but to the idea of an ethically integrated subjectivity and to an 'old-fashioned' experience of historicity which does not make a mockery of at least *some* sort of idea of the self-determined personality.

The second reason why such strategies of demythologisation have failed is because the very ways in which the left has recourse to history are negatively over-determined (and to an extent justifiably) in public understanding. There is a wide-spread view, for example, that the Labour Party is inclined to fall back on a redundant past of its own, or to turn so readily to history because it is in fact old-fashioned and incapable of understanding the different political constellation of the present: because the old radical culture has outlived its practical possibilities and, to make a negative use of Zygmunt Bauman's phrase, the labour movement therefore has nothing left but historical 'memories of class.' Thus the painful twist—perfectly, although often too unconsciously, marked by the books of Jeremy Seabrook—whereby an assertion of past oppression, dignity and suffering can be taken to prove current Labour politics a sentimental and anachronistic relic.[25]

Thus also the terrible clarity of the 1984/5 miners' strike. Here was the enormously powerful case of threatened mining communities eclipsed by a leading political culture which was scarcely able to disentangle its present cause (which was about *use*-value and its priority over market considerations) from a rhetoric which was not just excessively economistic in its political understanding, but which on many occasions seemed to go back to assumptions about the inevitability of proletarian victory. As Bauman, among many others, has pointed out, the political situation is different in late capitalism: people understand themselves to be consumers and tax-payers as well as producers (so that 'issues which once catalysed class oppositions embody today the contradictory nature of joint interests'), welfare corporatism has confounded old definitions of public and private interests, and the sharpest forms of exploitation are not simply class-defined.[26]

Other changes could also be mentioned here but while the scene is indeed different, the important point is that it is certainly not empty of political possibility—except, if we are to believe Touraine's somewhat glib phrase, for those who can only think with their memory.[27] The 1984/5 miners' strike indicated a wide range of possibility—not in either the historically pre-ordained class struggle or the curious mixture of syndicalism and unprincipled pro-Sovietism which seems to characterise Arthur Scargill's political understanding, but in the alliances and networks which sustained those communities through month after month of what Thatcher had clearly prepared as starvation, or in the dawning argument that work should be considered as part of the totality of community life and not conceived only through the private contract of employment.

I have argued that the everyday consciousness which is engaged by nationalist articulations of past and identity is to a significant extent *distinct* from the forms through which it is expressed. In the early eighties this everyday consciousness with its hopes and fears has indeed been articulated into the Conservative repertoire, but as analysis of any aspect of the national past—and the sense of identity, propriety and tradition which it promotes—should reveal, the energies engaged by these cultural formations are far from one-sided in allegiance. If this consideration implies that it is not enough to pull out the old standby arguments about ideology and media manipulation, to dismiss as *simply* negative the increasing dominance of the culture of nationalism in public understanding, it also implies that the really important question is much closer to home. For if the energies engaged by the nationalism of contemporary Conservatism are not simply identical with this Conservatism, then why are there so few other publicly instituted forms through which they might find a more democratic kind of articulation?

Relations of domination notwithstanding, this question points directly to the left's failure to develop adequate alternative models for socialist development in a whole range of different fields. Stated more generally, where the Thatcher project has offered actively to *recover* 'History' through its cultivation of falling back, the socialist project cannot seek to thrive on present insecurity in the same way. It faces the very different task of *vindicating* the idea of historical development as a process that can still be moved forward for the better. This will mean reinstating an adequate conception of possible 'progress' (no more *or* less than gain without corresponding loss, as Heller has argued) and proving that a more socialist future is indeed possible—a socialism which is both desirable *and* adequate to the complexities of the present—even after the idea of the necessarily victorious proletariat has passed with its own 'inevitable' progress into the museum of inadequate philosophical constructs.

It will mean establishing that history can be made rather than merely rediscovered, and that it doesn't have to lie behind us as a fetish or as a 'lost' fragment of utopian essence which can only be dug out of the mud. It is certainly possible: a more radically democratic and properly post-imperialist society which is conscious of its place in the historical process but which may also sometimes leave old wrecks to disintegrate in peace on the seabed—as they so often did, one might say for the sake of a flourish, in the 'olden days.' Open-ended indeed, but isn't this the real message which came to the surface with the *Mary Rose*? As for the idea of British 'decline,' does it really take a wreck and a Prince in a wet-suit to show how easily this can function not in connection with any principled concern for the many internal victims of British society, but as background scenery for late melodramas in the ongoing repertoire of Imperialism?

6

Moving House in a Welfare State

An essay prompted by (and incorporating) a consideration of *Miss Savidge*, a film by Danuta and Witold Stok.[1]

> In this town the last house stands as lonely as if it were the last house in the world.
>
> The highway, which the tiny town is not able to stop, slowly goes deeper out into the night.
>
> The tiny town is only a passing-over place, worried and afraid, between two huge spaces—a path running past houses instead of a bridge.
>
> And those who leave the town wander a long way off and many perhaps die on the road.
>
> Rainer Maria Rilke[2]

From Ware to Wells

May Alice Savidge used to live, modestly enough, in Ware, Hertfordshire. For twenty years she inhabited one half of an old building that also housed a bakery. Things have changed and Miss Savidge now lives up on the coast of north Norfolk, a resident of Wells-Next-the-Sea. Miss Savidge, obviously enough, has 'moved house,' but she has done so in a way that finds new meaning in this phrase. While she now resides in a different town, Miss Savidge continues to live in the same house. She has 'moved house' in a literal sense, taking her home with her.

In Miss Savidge's account the story began in the early 1950s when plans for urban redevelopment first loomed, but it was not until the late sixties that the problem became intense. As Miss Savidge puts it in the Stoks' film, it was then that the house somehow 'got onto this roundabout,' and that was the end: a road building scheme was approved and compulsory purchase became inevitable. As can easily be imagined, Miss Savidge took a protective view of her house, one that found expression in ideas of its historical and architectural as well as personal uniqueness. No stately home, certainly, but Miss Savidge discovered that the house had a Tudor chimney and then that the rest of it was even older—a hall-house from a time when smoke was left to find its way out through the rafters of what now turned out actually to be a queen-post roof. Not just home, the full place of her own last twenty or so years, the building was apparently pre-Tudor, 'and there aren't all that number left are there...?'

Miss Savidge tells how at this point she was 'a bit fed up.' As she puts it, 'they keep destroying everything.' The house was listed under the preservation legislation, but only as class three: a since discontinued category which, as a friend told Miss Savidge at the time, the authorities seemed to reserve for precisely those buildings of recognisable architectural and historical interest which they intended to demolish. And yet as it worked out Miss Savidge didn't just grieve and reluctantly settle for *being* moved. With extraordinary resolution she determined not just that she would move herself, but that she would take her house with her. So she bought a piece of land in Wells and then, drawing on the engineering and drafting skills which she had developed in the transformed labour market of the Second World War, she dismantled her house piece by piece.[3] Having numbered all its wooden parts (the house is full of old oak), she saw the whole thing shipped in eleven lorry loads to its new site. And that is where she has been since 1969. Surrounded by her cats, an Alsatian dog and her old, somewhat decrepit things, she lives a life of curious but evidently competent reconstruction. Conditions are harsh. The wind (blowing in, as they say in these parts, from Siberia) makes short work of the plastic sheeting covering unglazed but resolutely Elizabethan windows, and the barn-like interior is so cluttered that there is hardly room to move. But at least no road development is planned. In Wells the authorities only intrude to say that officially Miss Savidge, who is now in her mid-seventies, must continue to live in her adjacent caravan until the plumbing in the house is up to standard. In her own words again, 'You're a bit of a dead loss if you retire and do nothing, aren't you?'

Why Wells? As Miss Savidge said in the discussion which followed a screening of the Stoks' film in the packed Wells centre on Saturday May 5th, this didn't look like a place that was expanding or likely for development. And why so far from Ware? 'Well, it's about a hundred miles and it's a good road.' Distance in the traditional sense evidently posed little problem.

From Warsaw to London

The Stoks, meanwhile, come from Poland. Danuta, more accurately, grew up in Polish West London while her husband Witold comes from Warsaw, where he had been working as a well respected cameraman (not least on films which were prominent in the cultural opposition) and latterly also a director in the Polish film industry. Shortly after settling in London in 1981, the Stoks noticed a passing reference to Miss Savidge in the newspaper (the story forms the classic *Guardian* anecdote) and decided to follow it up. Eastern Arts (a regional wing of the national Arts Council) eventually contributed to the cost of the film's production, and the Stoks scraped up the rest from their own resources. The result of a very specific cultural encounter, therefore, the film comes in from an angle of its own.

One can only wonder about those meetings. Miss Savidge, whose singular magnificence seems to exist at least partly in the dimension of an apparent eccentricity, and the Stoks who themselves carry these Polish perspectives with them, and who are in a sense still finding their unsure way around in this strange land. For one man who saw the film at Ruskin College the connection was overwhelmingly clear. And while Witold Stok resolutely denied any intention of turning Miss Savidge into a story of Polish self-determination, the film leaves little doubt that *something* happened and that some sort of recognition took place on both sides.

Miss Savidge, whose action in a world of noisy and often meretricious publicity is of a strikingly quiet if not guardedly private character, starts to articulate her project. More than this, she even begins (albeit in a fairly restrained way) to *dramatise* herself. She wheels her creaking barrow around, opens the cut on a great oak beam with a tiny handsaw, goes to the baker and buys loaf after loaf (the week's supply—Miss Savidge goes out on Fridays). She occupies herself in this evocative and uncompleted world that she is making on the other side of a garden-gate which is itself not without interest (it has an assortment of signs attached to it ready for display as appropriate— 'Working in the attic' and so on—and is rigged up in Heath Robinson style, so that an old bell starts clanking away up near the house when the gate is opened). We see Miss Savidge talking to her cats, hushing her excitable brute of an Alsatian and playing a piano which, having travelled like its owner in order to stay in the same place (it has its corner in the parlour), is utterly and outrageously out of tune. In a sense then, Miss Savidge co-produces the film. She responds to the sympathetic curiosity of the Stoks, and the result is a delicately humoured and even quizzical film which evokes meaning after meaning without ever seeking to nail its development down to a single interpretation.

The Polish camera seems wide-eyed as it wanders around the densely packed and motionless interior of Ware Hall House (as Miss Savidge now calls her home). It picks some objects out—an old clock as it is being wound, family portraits from a bygone era as Miss Savidge wipes the dust from them—and it lingers over yellowed sheet music ('The Rose of Tralee') near the piano. It gives the impression of a personal world which has needed, somehow, to intensify and fall back on itself, becoming more self-sufficient and also more private and occult in its significance in order to survive not just time (which can indeed appear to be running out on the world rather like Miss Savidge's clock) but also the abrupt and sudden traumas of its recent history. It is a strange still-life that the camera picks out around Miss Savidge: one that speaks of decay, dislocation and also a curiously determined survival.

As for Miss Savidge, she evidently had a view of these interested visitors as well. The day after the screening in Wells she joked about all those Polish names, saying that it was a good thing the credits were clearly written at the end of the film. After all, how else would anyone know who these people really are? And did we by any chance know what had happened to that woman who came up on one occasion as a sound recordist? She was called Aldona, and at the time she was planning to go to Libya with her husband who had just found some sort of job over there. Libya! With all that trouble around the London Embassy! But then perhaps Aldona had a Polish passport and would manage alright after all. Clearly, there is displacement and displacement, and the situation of this film was expressive of both.

The Eccentricity of the Lifeworld

What then does the Stoks' film portray? What does it make of its story? First of all, it stands as testimony to an act of self-determination—one that is remarkable precisely as the act of a woman. The film shows something of Miss Savidge's stand, and in its soundtrack especially it also provides fragmentary insight into her past. Miss

Savidge, responding to questions which are not recorded, mentions her wartime training in technical drawing (and also the fact that her father—who died when she was a young child—was an engineer). She tells of her subsequent work as an illustrator of technical publications with ICI Plastics, remembering a man she had loved and who had died when she was twenty seven (a single woman of twenty seven was apparently 'on the shelf'), and a widowed mother who needed looking after in the years that followed.

While she appears as a woman who has made her way in spite of wider society, Miss Savidge is not presented only as the creative subject of an unproblematically splendid personal drama. The film is not a piece of documentary triumphalism; nor is it a work of feminist-realism of the sort that a few heavily contested members of the Wells audience strongly preferred. For a start the film stresses the singularity of Miss Savidge's project while also edging it with gentle hints of eccentricity. While there is certainly discomfort to be felt here, no jibing or ridicule is involved. For in the same gestures which indicate the eccentricity of Miss Savidge's action the film also establishes an

THE GRASSHOPPER AND THE ANT (after Aesop).

The Grasshopper sang and danced all summer long. The Ant worked hard. Winter came and they met - cold, wet and hungry.

image of its subject as curiously representative precisely *in* her singular eccentricity. In other words the discomfort and uneasiness that viewers are likely to experience is a response to something which the Stoks find in the wider situation rather than the particular character or personality of Miss Savidge.

How can eccentricity be representative? These two ideas may seem irreconcilable, but if we are to understand recent developments in this old country we must start to make connections which would have violated the understanding of earlier times. The Stoks' film is composed in a way that emphasises the difference between Miss Savidge's immediate locale and the wider world in which public significance and national policy are established. As Miss Savidge moves about her house the radio (more accurately, of course, an old 'wireless') is tuned to the BBC. A newscaster announces the death of Brezhnev. There is warning of gales in all areas except Viking and Trafalgar. Prince Charles marries his bride and while the nation follows every little detail of the ceremony, Miss Savidge goes about her life almost regardless. She is not unaware or given to deliberate disregard, and she is certainly not without patriotism; but while brasher flags are displayed everywhere, Miss Savidge's rather more antique union jack nevertheless remains dusty and furled—visibly at rest (if not exactly in decay) among other old things upstairs.

The film poses this difference between Miss Savidge's reality and the world of national significance and official decision as a painful disjunction. It is not treated as if it were only a neutral distinction between different levels of reality or experience—between, say, the particular and the general or the public and the private. Miss Savidge's kingdom—both dislocated and relocated—is precisely *her* world, the world as she inhabits it, shapes it and is conscious of it.

In this intimate realm things exist in meaningful associations which are only appreciable from the point of view of the life which animates and values them. This world is above all resonant: it bears the stamp of a personality with its own history, its own acts of memory and its own orientation towards society. In this respect it is essentially a situated world. It exists in terms of this particular personal disposition but it also takes place in this house, this town, with these people. Thus while it is an intimate world, it is not merely private: it radiates outward into the public culture of neighbourhood and society.

No wonder that, when Miss Savidge starts to speak of her life, Ware and Wells seem to fuse, as if parts of both were just outside the door: double-vision, except that from where Miss Savidge stands it all makes such singular and self-evident sense. No wonder either that Miss Savidge speaks wistfully of apparently discarded values and norms—the traditional meanings of a self-understanding which seems every bit as threatened as her house ('People don't seem to care any more,' as she said more than once in our conversation). As the realm of Miss Savidge's everyday life, therefore, this threatened world is not just local either: it is also intersubjective, constellated according to ethical principles and presuppositions which derive from a time when the meaningful and legitimating worldview was more religious than scientific. Neither entirely private or intimate, nor wholly circumscribed within the boundaries of neighbourhood, Miss Savidge's personal world is also crystallised within a traditionally understood *lifeworld* in which what the phenomenologist Edmund Husserl once called 'the plain certainty of experience' is no longer either so plain or all that certain.[4]

Against this lifeworld the larger, official and political world is a destabilising intrusion. It seems to enter the lifeworld incessantly. And even if reflection suggests that (while it may indeed now seek legitimation for its presence in science rather than religion) it has always been there, the fact remains that its point of determination is always elsewhere. It operates according to a rationalised logic of its own: one which finds no response or echo in the more intimate measure of Miss Savidge's everyday life. In this respect, and as the Stoks' film implies, there is an equation between the public world of the wireless and the road-planning process which one day designated Miss Savidge's home a roundabout. Both break in from outside and both follow a professional and administrative procedure—a rationalised way of going about things—which is taken for granted as they approach Miss Savidge, bringing her news of events which have already happened elsewhere or submitting her to decisions which have already been made. They offer her a curious kind of self-understanding as subject in a wider world which, while it places continuous demands on her, also continues to go on without any specific regard for her.

It is here that the key to Miss Savidge's apparent eccentricity is to be found. This is not just the eccentricity of a woman who thrashes away at a sticking typewriter while the gale warning plays for men at sea, or who is to be seen merely putting on her coat while Lady Diana Spencer sets off on what the commentator announces as 'the longest and happiest walk she will ever take.' The Stoks' film does not present its audience with an image of purely personal idiosyncrasy or peculiarity. What *Miss Savidge* shows is the eccentricity of a traditionally formed everyday life when its meaning and significance are no longer relevant or necessary to the official society which treats it only as the abstract end of the line: not a delicately constellated intersubjective and always personal world, but merely the place where the message finally gets delivered or an anachronistic coherence which can be vapourised by administrative decision. This is the intimate world of a woman who sees, hears and understands, but who herself stands as nothing to what she is given to see, hear and understand.

Eccentric—this is what the lifeworld looks like from the administrative point of view. However, the film does not just languish in the pathos of this situation, for with Miss Savidge there is also a stubborn insistence which sharpens the impression of eccentricity. In Miss Savidge's project of resistance the lifeworld continues to exist, not just as a residue but actively as a coherence which is asserted on its own terms even though the bureaucratic plan has declared it a redundancy which merely gets in the way and public significance is always constituted elsewhere. While the very ground has been pulled from beneath it, this anachronism determinedly lives on. Miss Savidge is perfectly justified in the feeling of triumph which occasionally breaks through—that she, after all, has risen to a peculiarly contemporary challenge.

The Ghost of Citizenship

But how exactly does she rise? If Miss Savidge's story is about the conflict between this personal coherence within a traditionally formed everyday life and the greater public processes which increasingly threaten it, the Stoks' film suggests that this dichotomy also occurs between *self-determination* and the administrative logic of planned social development within a welfare state.

It is noticeable in the film, for example, that Miss Savidge's voice takes on a tone of anger and impatience only once, when she says 'and that's why I'm not keen on the idea of getting pushed into a council flat.' How close such a fate ever came remains unclear.

Miss Savidge's dealings with the local state were complex and evidently well managed from her end. She arranged to clear the other half of the building which had been compulsorily purchased (for a very low £200) from whoever owned the bakery, and to sell the land on which her own half stood, all on the understanding that she would have the entire site cleared within six weeks of an agreed date. This is not the story of a woman who seems ever to have really needed public housing, yet her horror at the very idea should surely be met with a different response than the hissing and muttering of 'reactionary' which came from one woman at the Wells screening. Miss Savidge may have been fighting a ghost of her own conjuring, but like the film her story points in other directions as well. For despite her momentary vehemence on the subject of council flats, Miss Savidge is also revealed to be a woman whose self-understanding is deeply informed by moral values and a traditional ethic of social responsibility. Miss Savidge may hate the idea of 'being moved,' but she also comments (with only the slightest hint of playfulness) that there is a housing shortage and surely 'it's not right to live in a house that someone else could live in. I mean if you've already got one it seems a bit wasteful doesn't it?'

There is a truth as well as a puzzled smile to be found here. The initial question is simple: what is the sense of all this demolition? When I met Miss Savidge the day after the Wells screening her questions weren't addressed crudely against the welfare state. She talked instead of good public housing which she remembered having seen near Amsterdam—blocks of flats with entryphones rather than vandalised and dangerous public hallways, lifts and stairs—and she wondered why the disastrous blocks thrown up in British cities since the war had been allowed or, even more mysterious, considered desirable. It was in this connection that the question of valued architecture came up most strongly. With history running down all the time, old housing is better than its modern equivalents, stagnant towns (where, as Bloch wrote in 1924, everything is immobile and one can only breathe in short gasps) are better than those which are caught in the grip of development and change, and it is an act of civic responsibility to fight for the preservation of what little you may have.[5]

In a situation where development and modernisation are experienced as decline, the good citizen is proudly anachronistic. Miss Savidge even went so far as to mention the Peabody buildings of the late nineteenth century, and her tone of voice as she invoked these terrible old tenements was not entirely critical. 'Model Dwellings' in a new sense perhaps, these buildings which as institutions for housing the urban 'poor' must have echoed with the curse of those constrained if 'deserving' tenants for whom they were designed, reappear a hundred years later as deeply settled and even relatively well-crafted architecture.[6]

This curious architectural perspective reappears over and again with Miss Savidge. In our conversation Miss Savidge recalled her involvement with the East Herts Archaeological Association (of which she is still a member) and also the Society for the Protection of Ancient Buildings. She also remembered lectures given by a man named John Smith at the Ware Workers Educational Association: lectures which told the story of ancient building skills now forgotten, and of techniques which could be traced in still existing buildings as they emerged from their anonymous places of discovery (usually in the London area, but always in the experienced practice of a specific building craft) to extend outwards as craftsmen brought them into use around the country. All this as opposed to the roughcast concrete and glass—to say nothing of curtain walling and modular panelling—of modern prefabrication: discovery in the skilled experience of the world rather than in the passage between an accountant's office and a technological laboratory.

A band of explorers evidently gathered in Ware during the 1950s, and its members were set on nothing less than the discovery of England in their corner of the industrial and bureaucratic modern world. Miss Savidge remembers the involvement of a Mrs Hunt who had authored a History of Ware, and among the great moments she recalls the discovery of an aisled hall in this post-war town. There was John Smith, almost speechless with excitement as he stood in the roof of this building with members of his WEA class able only to repeat, 'well!' But if those evenings took Miss Savidge far from the world of ICI Plastics, the interest in old buildings does not appear to have been merely aesthetic or anti-pragmatic.

Miss Savidge recalls the council worker who agreed that her house was indeed among the oldest in Ware, and cited this as proof that it should come down. With the argument still going on in her mind all these years later Miss Savidge musters different evidence, itemising modern buildings which have failed (like Hatfield swimming pool, where the roof apparently fell in soon after the building's completion) to prove that she is not just grieving nostalgically for traditional skills or for what she nevertheless still names as 'a friendliness in the streets.' These new buildings don't even stand up, to say nothing of four hundred years. Miss Savidge expresses the view—although how much she believes it may well be a different matter—that technology and tradition could always be harmonised. Why, as she put it with an unwittingly postmodernist emphasis, aren't architects, builders and engineers trained in reconstruction? Why, if I may generalise her question, should the restaging of history be merely an impoverished and artificial matter of fictional pageantry or wishful thinking?

As for the welfare state, it is with a sense of threatened history, culture and civic life, rather than any formulated right-wing political antagonism, that Miss Savidge looks at developments in this area as well. Her standpoint is that of a civic life which is nothing if the circumstances under which it can initiate and determine its own actions are destroyed. Just as her interest in old buildings places special value on techniques and skills which testify to their empirical derivation within the lived practice of a traditional craft, so Miss Savidge also favours an idea of citizenship which is active and possessed of its own involvement in public life—and emphatically not that nominal citizenship of passive reception (as 'consumer' or 'client') of administered state services.

So while Miss Savidge won't easily be pushed into a council flat, she is far from simply opposed to public services. On the contrary, in the Stoks' film she recalls a time before state pensions were introduced when there was no question that as an unmarried daughter she should be making the considerable sacrifices involved in caring for her own aged and widowed mother. Miss Savidge speaks of those years in a tone which is significantly double-edged, conveying a sense that the development of the state pension scheme was clearly a good and liberating thing, but also valuing that earlier and remembered climate in which (as she recalls) duty and responsibility, while certainly harder, were also somehow closer to the heart and more enriching to fulfil. While there should be no lapse into cheap sentimentality here, the difficulty of thought still needs to be recognised—together with the ambiguous complexity of feeling which characterises so much contemporary experience of the welfare state.

In the same vein, collecting boxes (of the kind that somebody has to stand behind and shake) for the Royal National Lifeboat Institution and the Church of England Children's Society are hung up inside Miss Savidge's door (in the film she happens to be dusting them off). If asked about these Miss Savidge will joke about the consequences of media exposure, remarking that since her house has been on television people have been wandering in as if it were a National Trust property and open to the public. Why not offer these people a slot or two for their coins? There is, however, a more serious side to all this, for these collecting boxes also stand as testimony to an involvement with voluntary charity work which, as it turned out in our conversation, has also included long service as a volunteer with Saint John Ambulance. It would be too much to say that Miss Savidge positively welcomes the existence of the welfare state; but if she doesn't positively disapprove of it either, she is evidently capable of feeling outraged at what seems to have been forgotten, distorted or merely taken for granted since its installation.

While present times, therefore, are increasingly familiar with opportunistic plans to mobilise voluntary organisations in welfare provision which has until recently been the accepted responsibility of the state, it would still be a mistake to forget the personal forms of action which ideologies of 'self-help' (quite different, as should be remembered, from 'mutual aid') can manipulate and redefine. My purpose here is certainly not to revalue philanthropic notions of charity or to play down the fact that many voluntary agencies, as Alvin Gouldner long ago suggested in an essay about the YMCA in the United States, have an organisational interest in reproducing exactly those social needs which they claim, with suitable vagueness, to be meeting.[7] With Miss Savidge there is simply an objection to register: an objection against the way in which care and social responsibility—traditionally conceived in terms of active commitment ('voluntary' in the sense of being willed by, and therefore meaningful to, the person involved)—have been recalculated in terms of time and money, so that the 'voluntary' reappears in an entirely negative and passive definition as what doesn't cost. It appears now as activity which comes cheap (the only cost being the cost of its organisation and development in 'partnership' with the state) and, in the same calculative logic, it seems to lack rationality—being unreliable, hard to manage and even eccentric precisely because it is not commodified and, finding neither its starting point nor its meaning in money, resists 'development.'

Who is responsible for all this? While Miss Savidge is certainly not given to pointing fingers of accusation, she does seem to be aware that the voluntary organisations themselves have often sought and welcomed this revaluation (or devaluation as it appears from her point of view) of their activities—one that is flattering to the extent that it takes voluntary activity seriously, placing it on some sort of level with state provision. Thus when she talked about Saint John Ambulance Miss Savidge started, perhaps in spite of herself, to speak of 'they' again. Previously journalists and state bureaucrats, 'they' are now the people at the head office of this properly chivalrous organisation—people who, as she recalled, had closed down the Wells branch because it no longer made sense in the national terms of corporate strategy.

On Camping out in the Modern World

> History appears as the derailment, the disruption of the everyday...
>
> Karel Kosik

So far I have not identified the political complexion of the local authority in Ware, not for that matter of the national government when the decision to redevelop Miss Savidge's home was made. This has not been the result of any reluctance to deal with the political implications of Miss Savidge's story. On the contrary, my point is that these implications will not be appreciable unless one also grasps the extent to which politics, at least in the traditional frame of the major electoral parties, have become irrelevant to the issues finding expression in this affair.

In a phrase of Habermas's, the political system is increasingly 'decoupled' from the traditional measures of everyday life, and Miss Savidge cannot be adequately defined as the victim of one party as opposed to another. She fell instead (and, of course, rose again) on the common ground of the post-war settlement, a ground which is made up of rationalised procedures and methods of administration as much as of any shared policies about, say, the efficacy of the mixed economy or the legitimacy of the welfare state. Miss Savidge's house stood in the way of an ethos of development and a practice of social planning and calculation which have formed the procedural basis of the welfare state under both Conservative and Labour administrations. Governments have come and gone (at the behest of an electorate oscillating at a rate which itself reflects the situation), but a professionalised conduct of social administration has persisted throughout.

The professionals of this world are almost bound to see the more traditional forms of self-understanding persisting among the citizenry as merely quaint and eccentric, if not more dismissively as obstructive and inadequate to modern reality. While there is always room for an arrogant contempt to develop here, the most frequent manifestation consists of a resigned and pragmatic realism (the bureaucratic sigh which responds to people's demands by saying that things are always more complicated than that) with which officials draw out and exhaust the discussion and patience of residents' associations around the country. That this system of planning is less than perfect goes without saying, and Miss Savidge is well stocked with complaints on this score. For anyone who stops to ask she will talk about the callousness of the officials who turned up the Saturday before Christmas (1953) to look at the buildings which they had already decided to pull down—even though this was the first the residents had heard of it. She will mention inconsiderate rules applying to council tenants (no cat or dog unless you have a family, and so on). She will also talk about a general bureaucratic incompetence which, in her experience, made it possible to get a council grant towards the cost of installing a bathroom in a house which was already up for demolition, and which was also evident in the many changes of plan regarding the road development itself. Is it to be a new road with a roundabout, or can the old road be widened, and which local authority (town or county) is to be responsible?

Bureaucratic procedure may indeed be conducted as if its rationality were contained entirely within its own calculations, and in this respect it may well seem to stand impervious: free from any responsibility to the world in which its works eventually materialise. But whatever the appearance, this is obviously not a matter of rationality alone. The system of planning into which Miss Savidge was well caught up by 1969 is characteristic of a welfare state that was both corporatist in character (public discussion and political negotiation simulated in thoroughly institutionalised forms), and caught in the contradictions of its commodifying pact with private capital.[8] More than this, the welfare state has developed through a period of extensive cultural upheaval, and Miss Savidge's is therefore a story of the times in its discovery of tradition not just in the lifeworld but also in an apparently hopeless contest with modernity. While the dislocation of traditional self-understanding could indeed prepare the way for better possibilities, Miss Savidge stands there as testimony to another scenario in which the prevailing atmosphere is one of insecurity which develops when extensive cultural dislocation has occurred *without* any better, or even reasonably meaningful, future coming into view.

Miss Savidge's story has its singularity, but it also tells more generally of an everyday life which has been dislocated and devalued rather than simply colonised, of a democratic process which is increasingly simulated, and of official decisions predicated on bureaucratic professionalism and ideas of expertise which are taken for granted from all electorally significant political positions. Given all this, it is not surprising that Miss Savidge doesn't understand her recent experience in conventional party political terms. No mark of ignorance or stupidity on her part, this points instead to the fact that these problems of everyday life lack any organic articulation in current national politics.

But even if the political system is 'decoupled' from everyday life, it certainly doesn't follow from this that there is no political articulation at all. Strange transformations are under way. Thus, for example, ideas of personal responsibility, duty and self-limitation of the sort which historically have functioned to reconcile lower middle-class women to their lot, now appear with Miss Savidge as the driving force of a resistant impulse towards self-determination. Rather than being the result of any change in the meaning of structurally static and persistent ideologies, it is a personal practice of self-regulation (an activity of 'conscience' perhaps) which seems to have shifted. For if a personally willed conformity to ethical norms has traditionally been a part of keeping in one's place, Miss Savidge's story suggests that the business of keeping in one's place may itself now constitute an assertion of autonomy in a world which is out of joint. The ground has shifted and one's place, if I may persist with this usage, has disappeared. It is by now all a matter of *camping-out*, not so much in the 'folds of the downs,' to use a fond southern phrase, but in the windy interstices of a generally hostile society which no longer offers any permanence, corroboration or security to its own traditional forms of everyday life. Like many structures improvised out of tradition, Miss Savidge's reinstated house is really a tent.

This point can also be made in terms of history and the sense which Miss Savidge has of its presence. For Miss Savidge, history is divided and split against itself: it is at once everything which is cherished and at the same time precisely what threatens destruction. On the one hand history is associated with the lifeworld—with that valued realm of personal meaning, traditional integration and predominantly ethical self-understanding—and on the other it is the bulldozer which breaks in from outside. History therefore has two modes of presentation, and in each case a different world-view and even cosmology is implied.

In one mode it seems geocentric—history as meanings which cling to undisturbed ground—while in the other it is more abstract and heliocentric in style: eventful rather than meaningful, this latter is a history which cuts in from above, and if its thunderbolts are not exactly irradiated by the sun they certainly have behind them the full and disenchanting force of state and economic systems. Some people have moved to the country in this confusion, but more of 'us,' following Miss Savidge, are holding out in the small town. Settled into its stasis but all the time fearing the worst, we can meet history only with a tribute or a curse. If we are sustained at all, it is by the miraculous persistence of an underground history which is still somehow foreign to change. Like Bloch's 'Small Town (1924),' this is not a place in which one can breathe easily. But even though it can only be taken in short gasps, there is always the consolation of knowing that the air in such places, while cold, is still indisputably good.

If new political allegiances are being forged around the dislocation of everyday life, these are certainly visible here. For in contemporary political culture it is overwhelmingly the politics of the Labour Party (with its privileging of the state) which stands associated with the technocratic and destructive history which bursts in from outside. Conservative politics—and this especially has been the work of Margaret Thatcher—stands associated with that everyday realm of threatened integration, traditional meaning and self-regulation. Conservatism in this respect has become a politics of self-determination: a politics of camping out in the remaining spaces of a society which, while it is distinctly threatening, seems to be beyond substantial change.

This is certainly a limited and fatalistic style of self-determination, but it also reflects real subjective experience, and is not merely a manipulated ideological trick. Miss Savidge herself is not exactly a representative figure of this Conservatism—at least not in Party terms—and she sometimes seems rather horrified at the elements forming her own story. In our conversation she recalled how some Labour councillors in Ware took the issues of conservation far more seriously than their supposedly 'Conservative' counterparts, but when questioned on her own political alignment Miss Savidge started to float. She looked at the wireless (which was turned off) and said that since long before the 1984 miners' strike she had always found Arthur Scargill reminiscent of Hitler. As for Margaret Thatcher, while she considered there to be one or two good ideas in this particular pro-gramme, Miss Savidge hastened on to add that she herself is no extremist—far more middle of the road. But if Miss Savidge is no resolute Thatcherite, her story nonetheless comes from the heart of Thatcher's Britain: a country made up of old if not always precisely walled towns, tents both opulent and humble, and of tower blocks on grey urban estates for the forlorn and undone—creatures of the modern state.

As Miss Savidge's story becomes a fable of the times, its signifi-cance spreads out along many perspectives. In the Stoks' film these are accumulated, laid one alongside the other. There is the triumph of a woman and her personal activity in a world governed by admin-istrative and rationalised procedure decked out as Fate. With this there comes the related sense of an active kind of citizenship which looks increasingly bizarre in the face of the corporatist state with its simulated democracy. There is the impression of a hobby which has extended itself into all the hours of day and night before finally (for this woman at least) engulfing the entire world. There is also the impres-sion of a task which has absorbed its own goal: the reconstruction has become a way of life for Miss Savidge and while fifteen years have passed, completion remains a distant prospect. Indeed, Miss Savidge is now so devoted to the reconstruction that to have the house finished may even have become unimaginable, the point beyond which there can be no reason for living. So it is appropriate that the day of final accomplishment should always be slipping away, receding impercep-tibly like the rainbow as it is approached.

Somewhere here the perspectives change dramatically, revealing a sadder and forlorn picture in which what had seemed like imaginative triumph starts to resemble instead a condition nearer to cultural psy-chosis. Miss Savidge is still at the centre, but she looks different now as she struggles to reassemble a remembered world against the times. A noticeably old woman with bits of crumbling oak in her hands, she suddenly seems desperate and anachronistic. The new picture is overwhelmingly desolate, and not just because the receding rainbow is replaced by approaching death. Miss Savidge now appears as the figure of a society which is so stuck in its ways, so intent on ghosting itself, that only its ruins appear to have any value. The imagination, at best, has failed, becoming merely symptomatic of the dislocation which in this form it both needs and expresses.

As for that threatened personal world, in this perspective one sees nothing so much as a formless mess of exhausted junk crammed into a house which (unlike Calke Abbey with its higher style of domestic 'junk') also takes a turn for the worse. Pulled from its original place and reconstructed on a piece of land which under no normal circumstances would ever have held such a building, Ware Hall House looks curiously 'jerry-built'—a 'historical' parody of one of those makeshift and much reviled plotland dwellings of the thirties. Pre-Tudor halls don't get built on post-war building plots, or behind what is probably a late nineteenth-century garden gate, and in its new environment this reinstated fragment (among the oldest *and* the newest houses in Wells) seems artificial and grotesque. Certainly, Ware Hall House doesn't fit at all easily into the emphasis of the National Trust or that blue-plaque psychology in which the national past is venerated as a

continuity of place. This building testifies to a more recent and also more desperate sense of preservation. Awkward and of more anxious motivation, this is a preservationist impulse which has not—at least in any disciplined sense—been culturally or aesthetically refined. Far from being another sanctioned site, Ware Hall House is like Arizona's London Bridge, another incongruous edifice in a desert.

What will happen when Miss Savidge is no longer there? With the house still far from officially fit for human habitation, this question comes to mind with some force, even though the answer should probably be that the fate of the building is not of such enormous importance. Whether or not the house is finished, the life which has given it such strange animation will certainly have culminated in something other than empty old age.

But to end here would seem unsatisfactory. I would rather return to Wells and to the debate which met the Stoks' film when it was screened in the Wells Centre. Here the views clashed and contrasted in an active public discussion which was in no way prepared to confine Miss Savidge to an impression of amiable eccentricity such as the one produced through the national media. This local response was both kinder and ruder, more respectful and at the same time more critical.

Some people stood far back from the whole story, one person even muttering that Miss Savidge was something of a canny one who had already manipulated a great deal for nothing and who now, with this film made by gullible outsiders, had won yet another hook on people's sympathy. Others risked proving this point by making strong and well orchestrated pleas that people should give up an afternoon here and there to help Miss Savidge out. An upper middle-class woman resurrected those old pre-war anti-'plotlander' arguments, pointing out that while this story was all very splendid, it would be a disaster if everyone behaved in this way: any more Miss Savidges and the value of property in Wells would surely start to fall. A man, speaking in the tone of the injured rate-payer, complained that the film was not sufficiently informative—he wanted a proper documentary with dates and details, not this wandering impressionistic thing.

Many people made appreciative comments, and hardly anyone got up to leave (which certainly indicates something). A man spoke emotionally of how he had recently driven through Ware only to find that the land on which Miss Savidge's house had stood was still lying unused. There it was as wasteland, he cried as he launched this potent myth of English dereliction and of a state which works only as a destructive agent of nullification: *there was no roundabout.* Rousing stuff indeed, although as Miss Savidge made clear a few weeks later, it had no basis in reality (the road development had gone ahead and the land was used).

Two women speaking in a feminist vocabulary dismissed Miss Savidge—with complete disregard for her presence—as a reactionary figure, and then accused the Stoks of making an exploitative film. When questioned by other women who were considerably irritated by this line of argument, the two outlined the film they *would* have liked—no indication of Miss Savidge's marital status, less concentration on her 'domestic life,' more triumphalist images of Miss Savidge with bricks and trowel in hand, or driving a lorry with her house on it. This argument was being dismantled and rejected by other (far from anti-feminist) women when a man came in to praise the film according to his own bluff lights. As far as he was concerned the two women didn't want a film so much as a City and Guilds course in building skills. He suggested they try the nearest technical college. So much for that conversation.

Throughout all this Miss Savidge sat near the front, dressed for mid-winter on this mild Spring day, occasionally answering questions in a voice which was only audible for a few rows, a distant observer who was visibly rather nervous. She did indeed look somewhat frail, although never exactly bewildered, but for all this it was still curious to see how protective people were: taking her by the arm and treating this woman who had just moved her house as if there was some doubt whether she would be able to move herself up and down a few steps. Civility exposed to a strange light.

Miss Savidge wasn't going to get much sleep that night ('all those people going round in my head,' as she put it the next day), and she was a bit worried by the scene with the piano; or rather she was concerned that people might not have heard the sound-track on which she says that she really must get the thing (which, as she stressed, had been in storage for twelve years) tuned in time for Christmas. As for reciprocity, she had already made her gesture towards the Stoks. There had been some doubt as to whether she would actually come to the screening, and when she eventually turned up she came with a piece of Honesty from her garden. She gave this to Witold Stok in a characteristically understated way—'you wanted to see what this looks like after it has seeded'—but those silvery translucent pods seemed a significant gift all the same, perhaps even something of a challenge. Honesty, as Miss Savidge has found out, is a virtue lacked by many journalists and film-makers from television and elsewhere. She would speak the next day of journalists who had travestied her activities for the sake of a 'good story' (she remarked that if anything sounded particularly unlikely to these journalists they seemed to put it between quotation marks and attribute it to herself).

Did Miss Savidge hope for more 'honesty' from the Stoks? There can be no certainty that any analogical symbolism was intended, but there was the possibility of a gesture here. Honesty as an old virtue—a fragment of natural meaning—to pass across to these people from another ravaged old country? These days a sense of uncertainty is bound to cling to any communication made through the medium of an increasingly occult traditional symbolism like this. As Miss Savidge knows full well, the world doesn't speak that language any more. Perhaps it never really did. It is fitting, in 1984, that the film which also puts this last question should have Polish connections.

7

The Ghosting of the
Inner City

Orwell's Prole Quarter: Humanity as a Good but Utterly Lost Cause

'Who controls the past controls the future: who controls the present controls the past.'[1] Such is the Party's motto in *Nineteen Eighty-Four*, and it should speak to us directly enough in the really existing 1980s. Time has underscored Orwell's suggestion that the past is subject to political manipulation, and not just in its undoubtedly miserable application to the Soviet bloc. In Britain, the 1980s have already seen enough public invocation of a revamped Imperial past to leave no doubt that here too history is capable of serving interests quite other than those of natural curiosity or scholastic research. Orwell, however, did not rest with the general observation that the past can be reworked and conscripted, pressed into the service of present political purposes. *Nineteen Eighty-Four* is more specific, identifying three distinct ways in which a sense of the past is maintained in the present and defining a world as it dramatises some of their possible meanings and connections.

On one side, then, *Nineteen Eighty-Four* presents history in the *archival* sense—the records on which analytical understanding of past and present must depend. These are directly controlled, and Orwell shows Winston Smith working at the heart of the process, rewriting old editions of *The Times* around the ever shifting conveniences of the present and casting previous versions into 'memory holes' which whisk them off (quaintly enough) to be obliterated in vast, all-devouring furnaces. In the imagination of this book the archive is relatively easy to control and the Party has indeed taken it over, dissolving and reconstructing it to produce a mirror of its own intentions in the present. This is airbrushed history in the Soviet style. As Orwell asks in this novel which founds its world on the mutability of the past, 'How could you establish even the most obvious fact when there existed no record out-side your own memory?' With its evidence gone, the thought becomes impossible.

Memory forms a second co-ordinate in Orwell's novel, and here the situation is significantly different. Contrary to the assumption of many commentators, *Nineteen Eighty-Four* does not suggest that memory has been simply expunged by various psychological techniques of thought control. Instead it has been brutally dislocated as its inter-subjective cultural basis is destroyed. There is terror between people (which makes for silence), and if this sort of coercion isn't enough the language itself has been systematically impoverished and the environment refashioned in a style that is free of precedent and therefore supports no meanings or associations not immediately synchronous with the present order of things. As for the media of public com-munication, these have been made inescapable (the omnipresent and watchful telescreen) at the same time as they have been occupied by an incessant presentation of the Party line. In this situation memory is repositioned rather than simply erased: it is detached from an every-day life which is itself totally deformed, and cast into a limbo in which it can only degenerate further. Winston Smith, to quote an obvious example, can scarcely understand what he remembers of his parents (who disappeared in the earliest purges) because tragedy—being dependent on the care of an intimate sphere which no longer exists—is simply not conceivable as experience any longer. So mem-ory doesn't just fade away. It becomes a mutilated anomaly: 'a series of bright-lit tableaux—occurring against no background and mostly unintelligible.'

A third aspect of Orwell's meditation on the past is made up of objects and remaining *presences*. Here are the old buildings and, more emphatically, the cherished bits and pieces from the junk shop in the prole quarter: the creamlaid notebook which Winston Smith uses as a journal and the glass paperweight which is eventually destroyed by the Thought Police. Here also are the Cadburyesque bar of chocolate which sets Smith thinking about a different quality of experience, the picture of Saint Clement Danes, the idyllic rural landscapes in which the most doubtfully 'romantic' parts of the novel are set, and also those traces of popular culture like the nursery rhyme which no-one can entirely remember, or the surviving conviviality of the proles in the pub.

Orwell's novel values these as physical or cultural presences, and distinguishes them from the archival material which the Party controls so thoroughly. Such old presences as these are for the good; they are valued as residues of a more humane order of society. More than this the novel suggests that they have therapeutic and rehumanising power—as if a person coming into contact with such traces can be reintegrated to an extent, with memories beginning to make sense again and externally repressed or uprooted feelings coming back to life. Like Winston Smith's room above the junk shop, these presences stir what Orwell at one point calls 'ancestral memories.'

It is in his definition of the prole quarter that Orwell works through these questions of historicity and the past most closely. The prole quarter is approximately situated 'in the vague, brown coloured slums to the north and east of what had once been Saint Pancras Station.' In this traditionally working-class area life, however hard-pressed and degenerate, goes on. The prole quarter is dingy, full of cobbled streets and 'little two-storey houses with battered doorways giving straight onto the pavement.' These terraced 'ratholes' are boarded up and puddles of filthy water fill their roads. There are street stalls with people queuing, arguing and fighting over scarce goods. There are grimy sawdust-strewn pubs—stinking of beer and urine, but places nevertheless where a version of conviviality is still to be found. Overall there is a sense of density in this atmosphere of decay: not of people as individual subjects but of the thousands of undone and barely distinguishable human objects which compose the 'swarming disregarded masses.'

The prole quarter is a symbolic amalgam in which received ideas, clichés and remembered experience are mixed up together. The old demonology of the depraved, criminal and unhygienic East End 'slum' finds exercise here, and the recent experience of the Second World War also contributes some elements. Thus the arrival of a 'steamer' or rocket bomb which devastates a few hundred metres of housing is evocative of V1 missiles and the blitz, while rationing finds its echoes in the severe shortages affecting this area above all others. Also prominent are the familiar perspectives of class—in this case especially the perspective of those who view the urban working class (fearfully, snobbishly, disdainfully) from above. Hence the view of cultural deprivation—if the proles' lives are full of films, football, beer and gambling, to quote Orwell's list, they are all the emptier of

sanctioned meaning. As for the women, with them such an objectifying perspective is even more prominent. The prole quarter supplies
prostitutes for the whole city. As a voyeuristic Winston Smith wanders
about the area he sees women as the forlorn and numbed figures of
a cycle perceived as more biological than social. There are girls in
'full [if vulgar] bloom, with crudely lipsticked mouths.' Then, with
the generational cycle rolled forward a few years, there are 'swollen
waddling women' who are themselves followed by 'old bent creatures
shuffling along on splayed feet' and tripping over the brats swarming
around them.

If there is some portrayal of endless drudgery here, there is also
more than a little of that iconography which features working-class
women so easily as 'tarts,' 'crones' and 'old bags.' These creatures
of labour and blind generation exist as they are objectified in the
eye of an observer from a different part of town. As the narrative
develops, this objectifying perspective is itself drawn into the account
explicitly enough. Thus there is the female colossus seen by Winston
Smith as he peers out, 'secure in the protection of the muslin curtain,'
from the window of his sanctuary above the junkshop: 'a monstrous
woman, solid as a Norman pillar, with brawny red forearms and a
sacking apron strapped about her middle, was stumping to and fro
between a washtub and a clothes line…Whenever her mouth was
not corked with clothes pegs she was singing in a powerful contralto.'
Orwell eventually redeems this monstrous figure. Just as this appar-
ition sings her song—'dreadful rubbish'—with sufficient animation to
ensure its transfiguration into something meaningful, Winston Smith
eventually performs the same service for her. As he looks down on her
from above he finds a redeeming beauty in this monstrous fusion of
'old bag,' earthmother and Norman pillar. Thus, while Orwell's prole
woman is evidently no classic Madonna to be, the depiction nevertheless still suggests a modernised Annunciation scene, with the ray
of transfiguring light coming down from eyes at an upstairs window
rather than with an attendant angel from the heavens (as it did for so
many old masters).

In a wider sense this is how the whole prole quarter is formed, and
for this reason it oscillates between an emphasised squalor and sudden, sometimes even whimsical, redemptive turns. Orwell forms this
quarter in a negative and often deeply stereotypical register but he
then steps in at the last minute to forgive it, positing the last traces of

a beleaguered humanity as fleeting glimpses within all the emphasised filth and degradation. As this artifice of redemption indicates, there is a creator in the vicinity—looking down on his works from above with muslin curtain in hand. Winston Smith aside, one thinks of Orwell's own flat in Canonbury Square—somewhere 'to the north and east' of Saint Pancras Station, and in the midst of an Islington which in the forties was ungentrified and a more evidently working-class area.

This play between two poles is fundamental to Orwell's evocation of the prole quarter, and the redemptive moments are almost always associated with old survivals from a better past. A pervasive impression of ugliness and degradation is set off against momentary disclosures of remaining beauty. Scarcity and degradation are balanced against enduring possibility; and if there is extensive dislocation and degeneration here, there are also those highly valued signs of continuity and survival. It is *old*, if not always precisely residual, meaning that Orwell values—the only sort, indeed, that can exist in the constrained world of *Nineteen Eighty-Four*. Meaning and value are of the past, and if their traces linger in the prole quarter this is only because they have not been sought out and destroyed.

The basic condition for the continued existence of human and historical meaning, therefore, lies in the fact that the prole quarter is less than fully policed. In this area, where the past is not undergoing constant erasure and rewriting, older and no longer synchronous meanings survive. Shops may change hands, but the old shop-keeper's name ('Weeks') will still be written above the door thirty years after the new proprietor ('Charrington') has moved in. Other survivals are possible in this atmosphere of fortunate neglect. Thus there is also linguistic continuity: 'Oldspeak' (the prole language) brings real meanings through, sustaining a memory which can still talk of pints after metrification has occurred and the litre is the contemporary measure: a memory which can still evoke a time when church bells pealed over London by recollecting snatches of the song 'Oranges and Lemons.' Then there is all the 'beautiful rubbish'—the junkshop which, while it is full of wreckage, is also the blessed realm of the 'beautiful thing.' The antique trade is dwindling, but if brass candlesticks are no longer to be seen, there are still gatefold tables around, along with entrancing glass paperweights and similar objects. The presentation is frankly nostalgic. Winston Smith's bug-infested room above the junkshop is a crystalline and ideal world which, if it can be likened to the inside of a glass paperweight, is also a timecapsule of non-synchronous and therefore still human space: 'the room was a world, a pocket of the past where extinct animals could walk.' There are no stately homes or museums in the prole quarter, but the attention is none the less preservationist for the fact that it focusses on *bric à brac* and fragments of old popular song. If there is hope with the proles, this seems only to be because there is now promise in ordinary remains.

Within Orwell's evocation of the prole quarter there are two distinguishable interpretations of its significance and of the challenge which it may imply for the present. The first, which appears to be considerably more negative than the other as Winston Smith moves between the two, can be described as neo-trotskyist in its theory of revolution and redemptionist in its philosophy of history. In the earlier parts of the novel Winston Smith conceives the 'hope' which lies with the proles as a general and shared *interest*, one which makes it conceivable that the proles might unite to emancipate themselves from the pseudo-revolution consolidated all around them. In this interpretation the past (to the extent that it survives outside the Party's version) is in itself an explosive force. Mere recollection of true history is conceived as a force to be reckoned with: as Smith thinks of an unfalsified photograph which he discovers, the true past 'was enough to blow the Party apart to atoms, if in some way it could be published to the world and its significance made known.' Evidence is evidence, and Smith (rather like the J.H. Plumb who advocates true 'history' as the corrosive answer to the false and ideological 'past') imagines that true recollection would automatically give rise to true historical consciousness.[2] As bearers of such consciousness, the proles would surely cut through the Party regime.

If such hope can be entertained, however, its prospects are drastically limited by the persistent failure of these troublesome proles ever to achieve collective consciousness. Rather than uniting around their general interest, the proles are divided in endless argument. Their common cause remains a vague notion in Smith's head, for the reality is of constant fracturing and the incessant quarrels of petty particularity ('you ain't got the same problems as I've got')—nothing but bickering and despair. As Orwell writes, 'until they become conscious they will never rebel, and until they rebel they will never become conscious.' Going further, as Orwell does when he writes Goldstein's book within the book ('The Theory and Practice of Oligarchical Collectivism'), the 'low' have always been 'too much crushed by drudgery to be more than intermittently conscious of anything outside their daily lives.'

The problem of the proles is carefully, even laboriously, posed in exactly these terms. Thus when Winston Smith engaged an old prole in conversation, what he hears is not historically formulated testimony to pre-Revolutionary truth, but a mess of particularistic recollection and detail. The prole remembers better beer in the old days, and it is the concrete memory of 'top-hats' rather than the more abstract idea of capitalists which sparks off his reverie. He savours words, moments, occasions rather than the generalised meanings of any philosophy of history—thus the mention of 'lackeys' sets him reminiscing on Hyde Park, Speakers Corner and the House of Lords—a flurry of anecdotal recollection rather than any suitably measured memory of class domination. Tied in this way to the recollection of 'old days,' prole memory seems to militate against properly historical consciousness. As Orwell writes, 'the old man's memory was nothing but a rubbish-heap of details.' Nothing which can shatter the Party histories is to be found here, for only a trivially situated (if not entirely false) consciousness of the past remains. The condemnation is complete:

> They remembered a million useless things, a quarrel with a workmate, a hunt for a lost bicycle pump, the expression on a long-dead sister's face, the swirls of dust on a windy morning seventy years ago: but all the relevant facts were outside the range of their vision. They were like the ant, which can see small objects but not large ones. And when memory failed and written records were falsified—when that happened, the claim of the party to have improved the conditions of human life had got to be accepted, because there did not exist, and never again could exist, any standard against which it could be tested.

Why does prole memory 'fail' in this way? While there may be some mockery of its endless details, Orwell's novel eventually suggests that something other than failure is involved and, indeed, that this 'failure' to abstract is in itself a mark of strength.

Prole memory is characterised by the fact that its recollections are filtered through a threatened but still traditionally formed everyday life, and for this reason it resists the generality and abstraction sought by Winston Smith. Prole memory has the floating and even rather apocalyptic quality which is the mark of its experiential basis ('Before the war' says the prole; 'Which war?' asks Smith; 'All war' answers the prole). It is legendary in quality and told as a tale: above all, it is always personally expressed and anthropocentric. The passage of time is experienced in terms of youth and age rather than as more abstract movement between one historical epoch and the next; the old pint measure is preferred on the basis that it is better orientated to the body than the litre (better balanced between thirst and the size of the bladder). Other examples could be quoted, but the main point is that if the experience of particularity leads to endless petty arguments and divisions between the proles, it also includes some common ground—even generality—of its own. Prole memory may well fall short of any consciously adopted and publicly shared values, but it has a recognisable character nevertheless. It works in the experiential terms of everyday life, and this gives it a richness which is superior to anything offered by either the rigged Party histories or the abstracted historical 'truths' sought by Winston Smith.

It is here that a revaluation seems to take place, for Smith starts to see something positive in this prole sense of historical existence and the past. While Smith starts off by associating this largely particularistic memory with cultural degeneration and decay, the picture changes significantly as the book proceeds. The mark of 'daily life' as it is called in Goldstein's tract starts to appear as another redeeming feature, and no longer as a mark of failure. Thus as Winston Smith realises later in the book, the proles (for all their arguing) are still living in a human condition. Just like 'the people of only two generations ago':

> they were governed by private loyalties which they did not question. What mattered were individual relationships, and a completely helpless gesture, an embrace, a tear, a word spoken to a dying man, could have value in itself. The proles, it suddenly occurred to him, had remained in this condition. They were not loyal to a party or a country or an idea, they were loyal to one another. For the first time in his life he did not despise the proles or think of them merely as an inert force which would one day spring to life and regenerate the world. The proles had stayed human. They had not become hardened inside. They had held on to the primitive emotions which he himself had to re-learn by conscious effort.

The fact that the proles are particularistic is now linked with the fact that they live, think, feel and remember in the terms of a traditional everyday life, and in the light of this combination they are now revalued as the last of surviving humanity. After this revaluation the proles are no nearer to being the emancipatory subjects of any generalised philosophy of history. Nor do they become the champions of consciously shared universalistic values, and their lack of public expression remains similarly unchanged. But for all their fundamental and continuing helplessness, they are now seen positively as the bearers of priceless old truths: the human as surviving object. Theirs, finally, is that common sense of the 'eyes and ears' which the Party seeks to destroy. As Smith had earlier mused, 'the obvious, the silly and the true had got to be defended. Truisms are true...the solid world exists, its laws do not change. Stones are hard, water is wet, objects unsupported fall towards the earth's centre.' If such basic but heavily contested truths should go without saying, Winston Smith eventually finds them as mere residues among the proles—those people for whom daily life still has a shred of cultural integrity, and for whom inner experience can still therefore be more than the dull ache of needing to piss.

It is as the bearers of traces like this that the proles are finally forgiven the degraded form in which Orwell had found them to begin with. Incapable as they certainly are of effective social and cultural action (and therefore also incapable of historical influence) the proles are valued as historical objects: like the glass paper-weight, they are objectified as curios or relics which testify passively to old but also defeated human values—preservationism applied this time to people. While historical values may survive in the prole quarter, therefore, every mark of their presence is in the end only further testimony to the impossibility of making new meaning in the present or of actively taking hold of the world in order to change it. In this atmosphere of generalised antiquarianism, neglect is the best that can be hoped for: at least then cultural meaning and value will still be there to flicker among the ruins.

The humanity of the proles is short of any active or practical possibility; like Mary Butts's valued 'being,' it merely resides in them like a threatened ethnicity held passively in common. It may seem a little strange to speak of ethnicity in this context. After all, in Orwell's novel it is not just the prole quarter but the whole of Oceania which is ethnically homogenous: 'foreigners, whether from Eurasia or Eastasia, were a kind of strange animal. One literally never saw them except in the guise of prisoners, and even as prisoners one never got more than

a momentary glimpse of them.' This point, however, needs no immediate elaboration; it will come back soon enough of its own accord.

The Refurbishment of Ancestral Memory

> Anyone seeking refuge in a genuine, but purchased, period-style house,
> embalms himself alive.
>
>   Theodor Adorno (*Minima Moralia*)

Orwell located his imaginary prole quarter somewhere vaguely to the
'north and east' of a no longer existing Saint Pancras Station. While
there is certainly no point in searching out any literal reality which
may be conceived to lie 'behind' the prole quarter, there are certainly
things to be said about the sense of history and tradition as it actually
exists in the inner city areas of the 1980s.

There is a place some miles to the 'north and east' of a still existing Saint Pancras Station called Stoke Newington. In this area (which
has the convenience of being where I live) the terraced houses have a
yard or two of space between their doors and the street. A few years
ago one could probably have distanced Stoke Newington still further
from the prole quarter by saying quite unequivocally that the streets
are of tarmac rather than cobblestones. In Thatcher's years, however,
these incurably Labour voting inner-city areas have been deliberately
deprived of what to start with were less than adequate public funds.
The pavements seem more cracked and broken than in the recent past
and the area's elderly people are falling down more often than they
should be. Similarly, an increasing number of houses—even in the
face of an intense housing shortage—are boarded up empty awaiting repairs which are currently beyond the means of the financially
strapped local authority. As for the roads, they also lack repair; tarmac
is being worn away and in many places the underlying cobbles have
recently risen up into view again. Doubtless we'll be seeing a lot of
them in the rate-capped years to come.

The past reappears in other ways too. Stoke Newington is fairly
typical of many inner-city areas in which a white working-class coexists with a diversity of minority groups and an incoming middle class,
and it is seeing changes which are familiar to other such areas as well.
Thus an increasingly *preservational* emphasis has established itself in

this area over recent years—an emphasis which is more contemporary and ambitious than the one rather tired blue plaque which was put up in 1932 to 'indicate' the spot where Daniel Defoe once lived and wrote *Robinson Crusoe*. This newer emphasis is closely connected with what is often called 'gentrification'—a process which has certainly taken place here between the 1940s (when the area's Victorian terraced houses were scarcely marketable at all) and a present day rich in mortgages (for those who can afford them), MIRAS tax relief (for those who have mortgages) and (until very recently) improvement grants. Even the most caved-in old 'rathole' (to use Orwell's term) is now likely to fetch well over £40,000 as long as it has been emptied of sitting tenants.

The houses which the planners of the 1960s so loudly decried as slums are being refitted in more senses than one. As any observer who walked the streets of this area would be likely to notice, the whirring of industrial sewing machines (on which Asian and Cypriot homeworkers labour for the small sums which must be won in direct competition with third world manufacturers) has recently been augmented

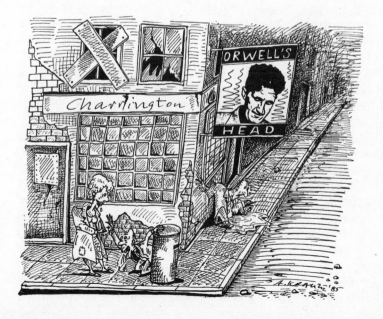

to produce a modified soundscape. There may indeed be reggae and funk in the air, but these days there is also more of the quiet purring associated with consumer durables—along with the resounding bangs and crashes of middle-class self-sufficiency and house renovation. Robinson Crusoe may now be drawing a salary from a job in lecturing, teaching, local government or the probation service, but he's still doing it himself in his own time. His island in the late twentieth century may be no larger than a terraced house, but the same sky stretches out overhead and his garden—with a little extra planting, some additional fencing and the odd trellis—is still idyllic enough. What Raymond Williams has called 'mobile privatisation'—that moveable if not entirely atomised life which brings with it the interior styles of the new *biedermeier*—has certainly found its way into this area of late.[3]

If possessed of a remotely wry inclination, our observer might be impressed by the extent to which such paradoxical forms of coexistence have become the mode in places like this. The clapped out but still powerful old Daimler-Jaguar, even if it is just broken down and rusting at the side of the road (testimony, perhaps, to the long term financial impossibility of a dream-laden purchase), finds itself alongside increasing numbers of expensively renovated Morris Minors. (A 'Morris Traveller Centre' turns a brisk trade restoring these old eco-cars—one imagines green fields wherever they go—on the nearby Lea Bridge Road.) The traditional pushbike rider is liable to be overtaken—especially taking off wheezily from the traffic lights—by more and more correctly clad (sensible shoes included) and non-smoking owners of shining, light-weight Claud Butler or Peugeot racing bicycles. As for the area's many working-class dogs, they are more aggressively regarded by people for whom brown heaps on the pavement or in the park constitute a pressing social problem. The sweated immigrant textile industry has also seen some changes recently, now finding itself in coexistence with a white assertion of ethnicity as style—not just skin-heads but also a somewhat wealthier and more 'cultured' appropriation which finds expression in Palestinian scarves, central American or Indian rugs and fabrics, the hand-knitted sweaters and even the legwarmers of late seventies post-eroticism. So comes the time to diversify—into restaurants perhaps.

The middle classes, in short, have been moving in since the late sixties, and the signs are everywhere to be seen. This new population brings with it a market for wine bars and a new range of culturally defined shops (some of which appeal to tradition directly while others display their more discontinuous modernism against a surrounding background of tradition). It enters the area with an attention of its own—with particular ways of appropriating the place in which it finds and must sustain and understand itself. Alongside the ethnic restaurants (the latest of which is 'Californian' and eking out a living one flight up from Seval and Son's sweat-shop), therefore, this is also where a sense of the past comes in. Suddenly this hardpressed inner city area is a settlement again—a new town in the wood as the name Stoke Newington would suggest to those interested in the historical meanings of place names.

Because this upwardly mobile slum is in an old country, we could easily enough push the reference back to the Domesday Book (which registers this place as 'Newtowne'), but a more informative starting point is provided by Sir Walter Besant who took an interested stroll through the area and reported back to his public in a book called *London North of the Thames* which was published in 1911.[4] Besant concluded that 'almost all there is of history in the Parish' was concentrated around Church Street. Seventy years later, (and if one excludes a cluster of Queen Anne houses on the north end of the High Street) many of the newcomers—owner-occupying residents of what Besant dismissed as the 'little villa houses which the modern builder strings up by the row' along the streets off Church Street—would agree. The new focus is certainly centred on Church Street, even though the commercial and retailing centres are firmly established elsewhere (on the more recession-struck High Street for example), and even though the old Borough of Stoke Newington has been integrated into the bigger administrative quagmire known as Hackney.

Of course Church Street, being westerly, is just that little bit closer to respectable Highbury and further from the rather less gentrified wastes of Clapton and other places east. For this reason among others, perhaps it is not so surprising that a sense of local history should be making its way down to meet the newcomers along this particular road. This, after all, is the road in which the area's great names tend to congregate. Daniel Defoe lived on Church Street and Harriet Beecher Stowe stayed in a house at what used to be its junction with Carysfort Road; Isaac Watts wrote his hymns in a no longer existing mansion off to the north and as a young boy Edgar Allen Poe went to school at the junction with Edwards Lane. There is also the old Victorian Free Library in which this sort of information can be looked up, and eighteenth century 'Tall Houses,' as they were known locally, survive on the south side of the road. For those who want to round the whole atmosphere off, a tradition of dissent can with some limited (in this case that is to say seventeenth century) historical accuracy be imagined to hang over the whole village scene.

I'm not suggesting that these new settlers have exactly researched the history of the area, only that a certain appreciation of the remaining past has facilitated their settlement. This appreciation has much more to do with attitudes towards surviving physical presences than with any formulated historiography. So it happens that old rotting bricks take on an aesthetic aura (there are certainly people here who know what it is to muse on what Mary Butts called the 'brickness of a brick'), testifying now to valued age rather than to bad manufacture, cheap building, dampness or recent urban dereliction and decay. So it happens that there is a market for those very nineteenth-century fittings (cast iron fireplaces, sash windows, cheap pine—which can always be stripped of old paint) which the renovators were ripping out only a couple of years ago when *modernisation* was still the essence of conversion. So it happens that small voluntary associations with an interest in the area's architectural heritage spring up, organising tours of the area and producing booklets like The Hackney Society's *The Victorian Villas of Hackney*. So it happens that the few enamelled signs—'Win her affection with A1 Confections'—remaining above shop fronts or the barely visible traces of wartime camouflage paint on the town-hall are brought to a new kind of focus by some passers-by. So it happens that the classical junkshops of Orwell's prole quarter—shops in which a few ordinary but irreplaceable 'treasures' might be found among the general accumulation of undeniably local detritus—are being augmented by a new kind of 'not-quite-antique' shop in which the selection (which includes nineteenth-century engravings of noteworthy Stoke Newington buildings) has already been made by well-travelled proprietors who value old things rather as Orwell himself did, and who fit well with Orwell's identification of antique dealers as more like collectors than tradesmen. So it happens that one of the several building societies opening branches in the area (often on the back of booming estate agents) fills its windows with eighteenth and nineteenth-century images of the place. So it also happens that this contemporary preservational emphasis comes to be linked with official policy. Stoke Newington Church Street has recently been declared a preservation area, and the newly rediscovered grave of the nineteenth-century Chartist writer Bronterre O'Brien is said to be undergoing some sort of restoration (with the GLC's financial assistance) in the local Abney Park cemetery.

In this new perspective Stoke Newington is not so much a literal place as a cultural oscillation between the prosaic reality of the contemporary inner city and an imaginative reconstruction of the area's past as a dissenting settlement (which it was in Defoe's time) that even the plague, according to some accounts, never really entered. For those who want it, this imagined past will keep looming into view. In the midst of the greyness, the filth and the many evidences of grinding poverty, the incoming imagination can dwell on those redeeming traces which still indicate a momentary 'absence of modernity,' to use Besant's phrase. Thus in Oldfield Road (the northern end, which was formerly known as Cutthroat Alley and which is now bleak in a more municipal sense) there is an old, slightly buttressed brick wall which once marked the end of Daniel Defoe's four-acre garden. The space now holds rows of badly built and subsiding Victorian terraces, cheap post-war council flats (some of which were built after the clearance of bomb damage) and a large depot for the varied machinery of municipal refuse collection. This wall is the last trace of Defoe's abode. Incongruous it may be, but it is there and still capable of supporting little moments of epiphany not just for those in the know—a tiny minority of those who pass by—but for people whose appreciation of pastness is not dependent on precise archival definition. The same old brick that testifies to the eighteenth century at one moment can speak of the early 1940s at the next.

The stroll down Church Street can be full of such moments for those who are inclined to tune into them. What looks like nothing more than a Spar supermarket redeclares itself on the second glance as an eighteenth century hostelry. And underneath the green-grocer's next door there are apparently cellars where the horses used to be stabled. Meanwhile those run-down and densely tenanted houses further to the east are actually four-storey eighteenth-century townhouses—the 'Tall Houses' of Besant's account. Small wonder that one has been bought and properly refurbished by an art-historian—true 'restoration' indeed (and it doesn't take a strict New Georgian to start drawing conclusions from the derelict state of an identical council owned house next door but one).

Traces remain, as one might say, except that this preservationist attention is not automatically granted to residues which have survived neglect, decay and the barbarism of post-war planning. It has a more subjective side as well, involving as it does a contemporary *orientation* towards the past rather than just the survival of old things. As so few guide-books ever recognise, this is not merely a matter of noticing old objects situated in a self-evident reality: the present meaning of historical traces such as these is only to be grasped if one takes account of the doubletake or second glance in which they are recognised. The ordinary and habitual perspectives are jarred as the old declares itself in the midst of all this dross. There is active distantiation and even what some philosophers have called 'astonishment' to be found in their recognition.[5] Like the sculpture in Rilke's poem, 'The Archaic Torso of Apollo,' this past doesn't just endure: it displays itself against the tawdry present which it also actively indicts.

So while there are indeed some fine eighteenth-century town houses, the odd bow window, and other such remains along Church Street, there is also on the subjective side an increased inclination to value the past, to notice and cherish it, to move into it and maintain it as a presence in our lives. To a considerable extent, I suggest, middleclass incomers have brought with them Orwell's fond perspective on the prole quarter—a perspective which is not based on cherishing things and places which have been near and lived with for years, but which finds its basis in a more abstract and artificial aestheticisation of the ordinary and the old. These flashes of redemptive disclosure in which the past is glimpsed as both other and miraculously still present may seem, and in some cases may also be, innocent enough. But before anyone gets too excited about the modernist possibilities of an alienated past which keeps breaking into view in the present it should also be recognised that such moments of sudden disclosure can be deeply problematic in their significance.

Some indication of this is to be found in the example of a largely derelict triangle of ground which lies behind the Red Lion—one of the few pubs on Church Street which hasn't been 'improved' lately, or at least fitted out with the usual selection of 'real ale' to go along-side the ever flowing lager. The familiar inner city wreckage is to be found on this patch of land, but as those who participate in the secret wisdom of the guidebook, the public reference library or even the winebar reverie may well know, this is also where the old village stocks used to stand—along with the cage, the watchhouse and the whip-ping post. There need not be any positive craving for the cagings and whippings of yore for it to become evident that there may be difficult-ies involved in the counter-posing—however momentary—which displays this idealised imagination of an old village against the dingy urbanity of an admittedly less brutal welfare state.

Redemption, critical distantiation and astonishment—these are all aspects of the Orwellian presentation of the past and if they come through directly enough to the inner city of the 1980s they also bring pressing questions with them. For if the 1970s brought the Habitat and Laura Ashley styles of interior decor into this area, they also saw the rise of the National Front. Likewise, if the early eighties have seen the intensified restoration of Victorian Villas in old inner city areas like Stoke Newington, they have also—and still almost unbelievably to many—heard a prime minister advocating what she was pleased to define as a return to Victorian values.

What exactly is it that keeps breaking through? The reappear-ance is not simply of the past as it 'really' was: indeed, sometimes the authentic trace of history is precisely what just has to go. In Thatcher's years old ideas of 'charity' and 'philanthropy' may indeed have been in the air again, but if the 'deserving poor' are still sometimes to be found living in 'model dwellings' of the sort Miss Savidge mused over so ambivalently, the terms of residence are different and a certain remodelling of the original nineteenth-century edifice may also have become necessary. Towards the end of 1984, for example, a small improvement was made to Gibson Gardens, a large model dwelling tenement (dating from 1880) in which flats—among the very cheapest in the area—seem now to be permanently for sale. A chimney had to come down, although not exactly for structural reasons. In these times when the deserving poor are somewhat more likely to become modest owner-occupi-ers (happily relinquishing their status as tenants in council owned post-war tower-blocks?) the problem had far more to do with the old words which were still cut in bold letters on the public face of that chimney: 'The Metropolitan Association for the Improvement of the Dwellings of the Industrious Classes...'

Past Against Past

Although it can be imagined as an English settlement with roots in the Domesday Book, ('There is land for two ploughs and a half... There are four villanes and thirty seven cottagers with ten acres') we should remember that Stoke Newington has recently been administratively integrated into Hackney, a borough which in 1983 was declared the poorest in Britain. This suggests other perceptions of the place. For a start there are clear indications of the ongoing and customary practices of a white working class—indications which may well be resignified and mythologised in the incoming middle-class perspective, but which are not in themselves mere hallucinations.

Within this white working class there is also a sense of the area and its past—one that is significantly different, going to the considerably less aesthetic High Street for its focus far more automatically than to Church Street. There are many older people who remember a more prosperous High Street as it was in the fifties—there was at least one large department store, and the pavements could be so crowded on Saturdays that people had to walk in the road. This remembered past exists in stark contrast with the present, for if the High Street is still the place to shop it has clearly also seen better days. A recently introduced one-way system drove some trade out of what is also an arterial road leading in the direction of Cambridge and other august locations. Though this happens to be the same road that went through Miss Savidge's house in Ware, there is more to the story than road-planning. The big department store was demolished—after years of dereliction—by the beginning of 1984, and many of the more recent shops (like Marks and Spencer) have relocated in the current economic decline. As for the large supermarkets of recent years (Sainsbury's, Safeway and so on), these have started as they mean to go on—elsewhere.

Little has improved recently from this point of view. Some pubs have been extensively smartened rather than gentrified—the old Rochester Castle, for example, used to be a cavernous dive with semi-derelict if not exactly lumpen drinkers at the front and a large, somewhat more purposeful Socialist Workers Party clientele further in. When its doors reopened after renovation this year, they were under a new sign as well as new ownership and management. The Tanners Hall, as it is now called (a name which appeals to the supposed traditions of the area while carefully cancelling out any association with the more grubby and immediate past of the Rochester Castle), has had a hundred or so thousand pounds shoved through it. Where there was Orwellian din-giness there are now stuffed pelicans, copious ferns, a Conservatory like bar, a beer garden and—a pleasantly florid touch—old (although distinctly not antiquarian) books everywhere: these signs of culture and the pre-television age are piled up in heaps as elements of an intensified and slightly manic interiority which must indeed look pretty 'vulgar' from many a Church Street perspective (people who persist in thinking that books should be *read*). And it remains a mixed crowd which drinks at the Tanners Hall, not least because the more derelict and SWP constituencies don't seem completely to have got the idea and moved on.

While some of the cultural relations of the white working class have survived the upheavals of the post-war period they have done so most strongly off either of the main streets, in amongst those rows of 'little village houses' which Besant found so meaningless. Here the pub may still be the 'local,' but it is also clear that cultural survival has often occurred alongside a growing sense of anxiety. It only took one per-son (an incomer) to walk into The Prince of Wales (a backstreet pub) not so long ago with a jug, and the intention of taking beer home, for conversation to pause before a torrent of memories started to flow: 'When I was a girl I used to fetch for my Grandad' and 'Of course that's a four pint jug—what do you think it was made for?' Such dis-cussion forms an act of commemoration in a full sense of that word—a sharing of memories, certainly, but also tribute and testimony to a valued time which is increasingly alienated from the present and only to be recalled occasionally. The streets were cleaner and the chil-dren less disorderly: faces were whiter in those days, and doubtless the grass was greener too. There were indeed some people in that pub for whom this sort of replay was uneasy—the younger people, by and large, who distinctly didn't join in this ceremony of remembrance and who may have gone further, saying that they wanted nothing to do with all that. A few weeks later during the 1983 election campaign, these same sceptics would sit at the bar scoffing at Michael Foot as the television showed him evading questions about defence and going on about the Forties and the traditions of the Labour Party. 'There he goes, Old Worzel...' And these weren't even the people who remembered that before 1945 Stoke Newington was a Tory Borough.

A similar sense of upheaval was evident during the encounters at-the-standpipe which were laid on for us during the water strike at the beginning of 1983. 'Just like the old days,' as one woman remarked in the cold but almost convivial misery of a momentarily reactivated street corner, an only partly ironic remark which also resounded with ambiguity, contradiction of feeling and (once uttered) embarrassment—perhaps at the way deep feeling and cliché can run so cruelly together. As for the embitterment and reaction which grows in such a context, it will take me a few years to forget the somewhat dishevelled elderly man who happened to make his way down the pavement as we were moving in. 'People moving in,' he said with affected surprise and a certain amount of contempt in his voice: 'people (by which he meant white people) still moving in.' He went on to comment that, had he been able, he would have moved *out* years ago, along with the many he had known leave for the suburbs and new towns in the sixties and seventies. Too many 'rusty spoons' around here as it's sometimes put in rhyming slang. Encounters such as these indicate the extent to which this traditional white working class has been affected by a dislocation of culture and memory like that which Orwell describes in *Nineteen Eighty-Four*. In this situation the recourse to racism can provide easy compensation.

And of course things have changed, although not simply in the ways suggested by compensatory understanding. Early in 1983 there were police helicopters hovering overhead, and shoppers emerged onto the High Street to find it filled with men and women in blue engaged in community policing. There have been demonstrations and arrests, and graffiti has been appearing on the walls: 'Police scum killed Colin Roach—We are getting angry' and 'Police pigs murdered Colin Roach.' Graffiti has also been disappearing, the large and loud letters sprayed along the length of Church Street quickly silenced by someone who followed the same route with brush and yellow paint—not a 'memory hole' exactly but another act, no doubt, of community policing.[6]

When we come to the minority communities that form a significant part of the Hackney population we ought to leave Orwell behind completely, and not just out of recognition for settlements which have occurred since Orwell was writing in the forties. There is a long established Jewish population in the area with its Hasidic community concentrated slightly to the north of Stoke Newington in Stamford Hill. There are Irish, African, Italian, Asian, Cypriot (both Greek and Turkish) and West Indian people in the area—people who have their own routes through the place, although not necessarily ones that move in any easy accordance with the imaginative reconstructions and memories which hold the measure of the place for many white inhabitants.

Given the prevailing white criteria, which measure belonging and cultural authenticity in terms of continuity of place and an imaginary valuation of the remaining trace, it is entirely consistent that the belonging for these people should seem (and I speak here from a dominant point of view) more makeshift and improvised. For people excluded from conventional identification with the area's historical geography, the traditional structure of the place is still there to be dealt with. Sometimes, courtesy not least of imperial history, old centres can be adopted—like the sixteenth-century church on the edge of Clissold Park which, while it looks exactly like the fragment of old Elizabethan village that in one limited respect it is, seems now to be used most actively by a Nigerian congregation—but at other times the connections appear more strained. Thus on the High Street there is a Turkish mosque and community centre. This is housed in a building which until recently was being used as a cinema and which was originally built as an entertainment palace with exotic domes thrown in for orientalist effect. While transcultural forms of identification should certainly not be judged inauthentic, there is no conventionally sanctioned dream of ancestral continuity or home-coming about that connection.

The different populations in the Stoke Newington area have different senses of the place and these are certainly not always congruent with one another. Thus, for example, I recall walking through Stoke Newington with Annette, a twenty-one-year-old white woman who has lived her entire life in Hoxton (a more thoroughly working-class area which lies a few miles south of Stoke Newington). Annette comes from what years of ethnographic sociology have treated as the classic East End background and she finds it hard to believe that anyone would ever *choose* to live in this borough: she herself has eyes set on Kent or, failing that, Essex.

As we walk through streets of Besant's 'little villa houses,' she comments approvingly on a house which from any culturally sanctioned perspective is a complete eyesore. Its bricks have recently been covered with a fake stone cladding, the sash windows have been replaced with cheap louvres, and the whole place is painted up in gloss so that it shines like a birthday cake. These 'improvements' certainly stand out, and it seems very likely that the quieter neighbours (subtler greys and whites, carefully restored wooden shutters...) might be among those who see them as acts of vandalism. They might even be interested to read in a recent issue of *Heritage Outlook* (magazine of the Civic Trust) that Leicester City Council has recently been *removing* such 'insensitive improvements' as imitation stone cladding and taking their Victorian terraces back to their now valued original condition.[7]

Annette, meanwhile, sees it differently. Somebody *owns* this place and their renovation of it speaks of pride, self-determination and freedom to this woman who has lived her whole life in council flats. For her it is exactly the point that this house stands out from the rest. The uniformity of the street is merely the grey background against which this improved house glows—a well packaged interior and 'home.' As for all that stripped pine to be seen in other houses around here, what about painting it? And what are all these enormous plants doing in some front windows—the ones without net curtains (now *there's* a sign of a likely haul—insured videos, stereos etc. Talk about inviting trouble...)?

These tensions between different appropriations of the place are articulated around many different phenomena or issues. Thus, for example, middle-class incomers value Abney Park cemetery precisely because it is overgrown and four-fifths wild—a good place for a Gothic stroll. A very different view is taken by some working-class people (far more likely to have relatives buried in the place), who find the unknown and neglected appearance of this nineteenth-century cemetery a mark of decay, and argue that it should definitely be tidied up.[8] The same contest of views occurs over the bay windows in the area's terraced houses. Many house owners—working class, black, Cypriot (although very rarely if ever incoming middle class) rip these out, throw the whole front of the house forward with an extension which opens up considerably increased space inside. None of this looks good from the point of view of the Hackney Society. In his preservationist pamphlet on *The Victorian Villas of Hackney* Michael

Hunter (himself a relatively early settler in the area) celebrates every feature of these little villa houses—from plaster cornices, ceiling roses, moulded skirting boards and door frames through to the floral capitals above the bay windows and those touches of Italianate influence which come to these slum houses 'from the Renaissance palaces of Venice, Florence and Rome' no less. The plea is straightforward and direct:[9]

> Above all, if you live in a Victorian house and are considering altering it in any way, please respect the aesthetic merits of this type of building which have been outlined here. Each Victorian house is, in its way, a period piece and worth respecting as such; many form part of terraces which have an aesthetic unity that is easily destroyed by piecemeal, unsympathetic alterations to individual houses.

The row is no longer the line along which speculative jerry-builders strung their cheap 'little villa houses.' Since 1911, when Besant found nothing of historical or aesthetic interest in streets of this sort, the row has become a precious aesthetic unity which present-day inhabitants are all too likely to misunderstand and abuse—especially those whose history goes back into a very different experience of the nineteenth century.

In this view all is well with the original buildings, and with an impoverished local state planning less demolition these days the problem now
seems increasingly to lie with the heedless people who live in them.
Perhaps this is why so many of the photographs in books like this evict
the contemporary inhabitants and their various furnishings altogether,
concentrating instead on bare rooms and empty streets. They are like
stills of a clear and surviving old world—the aesthetic attention can evidently work like a neutron bomb. What would the Hackney Society say to
the Irish carpet layer who looked up at the cornices in our front room and
said that he would love to own one of these houses—he would start by
putting strip lighting *inside* the cornices? Is it all just a matter of bad taste?
Certainly not. Here was another person who as a financially hard-pressed
council tenant imagined a freedom of action that he currently lacked.

   The point should be clear enough. People live in different worlds
even though they share the same locality: *there is no single community or
quarter*. What is pleasantly 'old' for one person is decayed and broken
for another. Just as a person with money has a different experience of
shopping in the area than someone with almost none, a white homeowner is likely to have a different experience of the police (the con-
siderate homebeat officer who comes round to commiserate after yet
another stereo or colour television has been stolen) than a black person—homeowner or not. Likewise, if I read the *Guardian* or *The Times*
and can substantially determine my own relation to the borough, then
maybe I don't actually need to read the *Hackney Gazette*. Those stories
of daily misery and violent horror can stay local to someone else's
paper, together with the job advertisements (although, of course, I'll
keep a close eye on the rising house prices).

   The Colin Roach case indicated such differences very clearly. For
many residents Colin Roach's death in the foyer of Stoke Newington
police station on 12 January 1983 was scarcely more 'local' than any
other event in the media—something one read about in the national
press or heard about on the news. But if there is no single community
here, events such as this make it obvious that we are not dealing with
any free plurality either. The distances between different people or
groups is not just a matter of neutral space—of relations which are
merely absent or yet to be made—for one can't consider them without also raising the larger question of domination and subordination:
without, in other words, recognising that relations *do* exist even though
they are not always directly or deliberately experienced.

For the worlds inhabited by some groups work against the needs and interests of others, defining them according to an imported logic, romanticising and mythologising them, confining them to the margins of public life and defining them as 'makeshift.' The sense of history plays its part in all this. It seems unlikely, for example, (and I can't speak with any legitimate certainty here), that the people who took up Colin Roach as cause and symbol are much concerned about old enamelled signs, the architectural merits of Victorian villas, old Chartists or the fact that Church Street has been officially designated a preservation area. For in the midst of all this romantic attachment to old brick and earth, the large and mixed ethnic minority and black populations in the Hackney area are still struggling against formidable odds for the basic constitutional and cultural rights of a citizenship which is itself far from secure.

History from this point of view remains to be made, as do the cultural means of developing and expressing a different past or, in wider terms, a different experience of the same imperialist history. From this perspective (a perspective which, far from being a 'minority' matter, is central to the democratic development of the borough) the other appropriations of the area's past may well constitute part of the problem, valuing as they do a time before much recent immigration took place. In the case of preservationism this danger is almost self-evident. What should also be said is that the problem may also be expressed in the historiosophical dreams of the area's new Robinson Crusoes—figures who, left-leaning or not, can certainly be caught in an imaginary and less than emancipatory relation to Friday.

After all, progressive credentials can be drawn from living in mixed areas without anything actually being done to contribute to the social welfare or development of the minority groups which lend such exuberant colour to incoming life. I recently heard a woman say that she wanted her child to go to a school with children of all races. Why not indeed, but isn't the wish itself curiously specific to an incoming white imagination, and isn't it insultingly abstract? While this sort of cultural consumerism may not be deliberately practised, it doesn't exist any the less for the fact that it is passive. Similar questions are brought to mind by Fox's Winebar—a relatively new establishment on Church Street which is already fabled as a convenient day-time rendezvous for those young women from the North who are now finding employment as resident (if not precisely Victorian) nannies with the area's new middle class.[10] Fox's has the somewhat curious distinction of being remarkably white in its clientele whilst at the same time being packed to the ceiling with members of the anti-racist and professional left.

Such difficulties were raised into the sharpest relief in the reception which greeted publication of Paul Harrison's book *Inside the Inner City* in 1983.[11] Here were over four hundred pages of closely described social disaster. Harrison describes the miseries and deprivations of Hackney with an eye to shattering national myths about the adequacy of the welfare state, the absence of real poverty in Britain. This is not a book that seeks to be local in its solidarity with the poor. In the view of this modern-day Charles Booth, Hackney is (as a policeman put it to Harrison) a 'bloody awful place, a stinking cesspit' and a strong contender for the title of most awful place in Britain.

Brittle romanticisations of the area don't last a minute here, and certain local myths also come under attack. As Harrison writes, 'there are many people who live in Hackney who will deny this: middle-class owner occupiers who will tell you aggressively that it is not at all such a bad place to live.' Harrison hints that it is not just houses that can be gentrified: the number of councillors who are graduates has risen dramatically in recent years, and the local Labour Party has a new kind of membership as well. As for that 'rich diversity of colourful cultures' which the 'chic radical' may see in this area, this is just so much voyeurism. Harrison reports on (yet more) grinding poverty and concludes in an Orwellian mode that the oppressed are hopelessly divided against themselves. Turkish against Greek Cypriots, people from large West Indian islands against those from small islands, Indians against Pakistanis, Muslims against Hindus. The spiral plunges downward, in his view, with nothing to check it.

If there were some cavills from the local left when Harrison's book came out (some complained, truthfully enough, that Harrison overlooked the things that Hackney people were doing to overcome their plight, while others dismissed it all as more middle-class parasitism and issued another of those timeless calls for imminent revolution), the right also felt provoked to reply and for a while the national press was full of discussion. Paul Johnson dutifully hacked out a repudiation of 'the poverty myth that can make us all paupers.'[12] Disregarding all the evidences of the book, Johnson blithely reasserted his own pet dogmas: people are poor because they are paid too much, or because they are robbed and crime is unchecked (in turn because the police are distrusted); housing is inadequate and insecure because private tenants still have some security of tenure. As for the profusion of one parent families, all this goes to show that the priests are behaving like 'social workers' rather than doing their jobs. Hackney needs the Ten Commandments rather than public money or the social services department, says this deeply caring and Christian man—a soothing message, no doubt, for an autocratic government which has cheated this borough of funding even according to the already corrupt norms of a system of allocation devised to redistribute wealth from the inner city areas to the rich Tory shires.

If this was the *Daily Mail*'s predictable response, *The Times* came up with more interesting goods. David Walker replied to the book, arguing that the poor are 'inadequate' and that, contrary to the suggestions of the 'poverty lobby' and the ethos of the 1960s (that evil decade), the poor need 'to be taught the virtues of thrift.' As Walker continued, 'affecting vignettes of life among the Hackney poor do not of themselves make a case for increased social security payments. They might, instead, suggest that the women of poor families need help and guidance on household management.'[13]

This, of course, is not to exclude 'affecting vignettes' of life among the Hackney gentrifiers, which is precisely what Philippa Toomey hastened to contribute in an article entitled 'Hooray for Hackney' and published in next day's *Times*. For Toomey the fuss was frankly unbelievable— she actually *lives* in Hackney and, like a good pioneer (a middle-class plotlander in this urban jungle), she intends to stay there for the rest of her days. Her article (which reeks of De Beauvoir, that part of East Islington which somehow slipped over the borough line into Hackney one night) denies it all: 'As I walked home along the canal in the blazing sunshine...' Her folksong continues in the Percy Grainger mode: there are ducks and ducklings on the canal rather than condoms and cadavers; little boys fish and lovers 'dawdle' on the towpath. Can this be a 'no-go area for almost all except those compelled to remain here?' Toomey thinks of her 'gracious home' (perhaps even older than a Victorian Villa), of the public libraries, of her Church with its mixed congregation, of the improvements which she and her friends have brought to the area. She thinks of walking home safely, of her good neighbours (who once helped the police apprehend her burglars), and of the ethnic radiance of Ridley Road with its 'lively' street market. Here is yet another way of camping out in the modern world. What can the problem be?[14]

It took another *Times* journalist to answer that question, for if there is a touristic appropriation of poverty as local colour in East Islington, Richard North seems to live further into the abyss called Hackney. In an article published on September 7th, North told readers of *The Times* how to go about 'making life tolerable in the urban jungle.' North admits that his own good influence on the area will only be a temporary one. Like some of the immigrants, as he puts it, his residence here is merely a stage in his family's upward mobility. North acknowledges the existence of a 'seriously deprived minority' in the area and thinks that government should do something for these people rather than just subsidising the mortgages of the well off. But North says all this in order to rise above politics into the realm of absolution he calls 'busybody activism.' What the deprived really need is to be reformed by good fellows like himself. Their children should be chided, corrected and 'talked to' by middle-class people in the area. Somebody needs to take an old-fashioned upper middle-class *stand* around here: stickers should be stuck on misparked cars by middle-class vigilantes and the 'burly little goys' who insult Hasidic families in Clissold Park should be 'cuffed' by the same good people. The middle classes are said to be 'good at poverty': like the hippies among their offspring, they know how to do it. It is these virtues that are needed in Hackney—'the WRVS and the WI: good, stout sure women who know what's what and don't mind saying so to those unfortunate enough not to have heard yet.' The working class should be 'taught how to do it': they should be encouraged to make their own wine, form free creches, adopt appropriate technology (the bicycle and the black and white television) and return to the good and cheap nourishment of lentil soup. The people are there, forlorn and dying to be 'talked to,' and they will soon learn to love those like North who start teaching them superior but simple adequacies and truths like these.

In this perspective what is valuable in the area's past belongs to the stern and self-sacrificing philanthropists of yore, and North seems to claim this largely invented tradition for himself. His very presence in the area is an act of generosity, and the people need only attune their ears to his words for the improvements to begin. Toomey and North may both take a narcissistic approach to the area, but between them the relationship to Hackney is still significantly different. Where

Toomey loves her own aestheticised view (her gentrification) of the inner city with its colour and liveliness, North goes beyond such trivial denial and actually acknowledges the abyss.

What he appears to love, however, is the light that he himself becomes in the darkness of this place. More precisely, if I get the logic of this argument right, he *needs* the darkness that is all around him, for the darker it is the brighter this human beacon will shine. He expects to be loved by the people of the abyss, who will surely recognise the voice of their superior redeemer every time he opens his gifted mouth and 'talks to' them. These are the narcissistic perspectives of a false Christ, and whether or not North understands the implications of his stance, it certainly also seems consistent that when he finally consented to listen rather than 'talk to' young people in the area (which he did a year later for a series in *The Times* entitled 'The Docile Generation') all he heard was acquiescence and calm. Here is a man who should perhaps try to read the papers before he writes for them. A careful reading of the press during the 1984/5 miners' strike might even have revealed that when hard-pressed working-class people do resort to cheap nourishment and home-made wine and beer,

this is not because they have been 'taught how to do it' by middle-class
hippies or philanthropists.

The True Past Which Finally Crawls Out From Under A Stone in Lambeth

Henri Lefebvre once wrote that 'in the name of memory history
has been abolished,' and an abolition of this sort is implicit in the
memory which still clings to Orwell's prole quarter as well.[15] While
he stages the past as the only hope, Orwell also presents it as a cause
that has been lost, irreparably broken. To the extent that it remains
at all, memory marks the defeat and disconnection of history. The
styles and potentials of the past are finished with: their persistence as
residue only testifies to the fact that they lack any leverage or active
historicity in the present. Thus there is the antinomy in which (old)
beauty is only possible against an over-whelming background of (contemporary) squalor and degradation. Thus the past is imagined as the
hopelessly redemptive trace of values which are all but totally buried
by a destructive and inferior present. Thus human value comes to
be associated with an everyday life which has been shredded and is
no longer capable of supporting anything except particularistic argument and quarrel.

I have suggested that more recent appropriations of the inner city
work within the same symbolic repertoire as Orwell's prole quarter,
imagining the past in ways which stand in problematic if not always
exactly helpless relation to the present. From a political perspective it
should also be made clear that these difficulties find expression on the
left as well as the right. Thus, for example, there is a focus associated
with labour or people's history which, while it may feel very much at
home in Hackney, can easily get lost in an entirely archival definition
of the 'people' and which on occasion seems only to enter the present
in support of a ludicrous snobbery about how Bethnal Green, say, is
more authentically 'working class' and part of the 'East End' than
those parts of Hackney lying elsewhere.

It should certainly be acknowledged that the sort of historiographical activism which confines itself to casting light on what was hidden
from history in earlier times can itself contribute to the maintenance
of the often very different forms of domination which exist in the
present. Such historiography can produce a valued past which is not

just Orwellian in its helplessness, but fortunately so—at least from the perspectives of a great deal that has happened since. My point is that a simplifying nostalgia can replace any principled democratic consideration here, one that is happier in its romantic identification with the nineteenth-century working class, or with the remaining traces of earlier Huguenot immigrants, than with the challenging and complex situation of the area's population now. The fact, moreover, that the endless details of an obsessive historiography can be used to support a past of this kind doesn't necessarily make the initial identification any more adequate: just as the radical historian can degenerate into the connoisseur of past suffering, the archive itself can function as an Orwellian 'memory-hole.' 'In the name of memory history has been abolished...'

But if difficulties of this sort exist on the left (and if they raise questions which should be put to all the decent nostalgists of the white left) it is on the right that an Orwellian stylisation of the past has been deliberately adopted and taken through to the explicit political conclusions which it holds for the 1980s. Thus in 1982 the Salisbury Group, which is on the authoritarian rather than libertarian right-wing of the Conservative Party, met the publication of Lord Scarman's report on the Brixton Disorders by commissioning a friendly 'professional journalist' to go out and talk to the *really* oppressed people of the area. These are defined as the 'elderly, white people of Lambeth'—people 'whose voice has not been heard in the national debate.' The 'professional journalist' who invited these people 'to speak for themselves' turned out to be Charles Moore, a 25-year-old graduate of Trinity College Cambridge who was at the time employed by the *Daily Telegraph*. Moore's professionalism would soon land him the editorship of the *Spectator*, but his standards are already evident in this early work on 'The Old People of Lambeth.'[16] Moore starts from the set of assumptions which he was predisposed and doubtless also given to prove. The riots were black (not, as Bauman has pointed out, a good example of inter-racial co-operation);[17] post-war immigration was an unmitigated disaster responsible for all ills anyone might care to mention; soft social-workerism has made the word 'community' a euphemism for young blacks...As for his evidence, Moore interviewed a number of people and then expunged his own questions and goadings to produce three seamless narratives as representative life stories—three unbroken tales from three horses' mouths.

There is Mrs E.R.J., a seventy-four-year-old widow who lives on the Duchy of Cornwall Estate in Kennington. Her story begins with the Second World War, that overriding moment of national dignity and worth: 'We saw our first aeroplanes in that war, fighting in the sky over us. We thought they were lovely, like silver birds.' Then there is the fall when the blacks arrive: 'We did make a terrible mistake letting them in. To think our men died to let that lot in.' Mr P.B. is about sixty years old and lives in a council-owned terraced house in Brixton. His narrative begins with his training as a skilled cabinet maker and then plunges soon enough into the same abyss. He has 'brought up 12 kids. I like kids. Some of them are bright boys, but with so many blacks in the schools they get retarded.' As for Mr T.J.S. who has just moved from Stockwell to a home in Woking, he's still thanking his lucky stars (or was it the Labour controlled Lambeth Council, or even the Greater London Council?) for the move. His tale opens with memories of his war-wounded father and closes with predictable views from Woking. Since the blacks came (of course), London is no longer London. 'It's a dustbin.'

These carefully presented stories have more shared features than this basic narrative structure (the nationalist fable once again) which moves them from a state of grace to The Fall which is said to occur when the blacks and the Welfare State arrive. In the beginning there was order, friendliness, dignity, sharing and mutual respect: 'Everyone mucked in and was properly neighbourly.' Along with this communal solidarity, these good old people have never wanted anything from the state except law and order. One of their kin even refused a War Pension because it could only be gained after the indignity of stripping naked in front of an Inspection Board. They have worked for starvation wages and never complained (four pence a day as it was for a man who cut wood for the Salvation Army), and most decidedly they have been betrayed. There were the towerblocks certainly, but mostly there were the blacks who spit, break queues and mug (as Mrs E.R.J. testifies ripely, 'they mugged an old lady here with a cataract who was helping a blind friend of hers back from church'). These old white people love the police (whose strength has been sapped by hypocritical liberal and left-wing criticism): 'The more police the better' as one of them expresses the equation of political desire. Finally, of course, there is Royalty and the Crown overall. Mrs E.R.J. lives on the Duchy of Cornwall Estate and, as she says, 'the rent's high but I

won't ask for it off because I want Prince Charles to have that money.'
Moore ends his pamphlet (the 'professional' upturn to round it all off
no doubt) with further testimony to abject loyalty: 'As one old man
said simply, It's our country and our Queen. Why should we be afraid
to go out?'

There is no reason to deny the existence of uprooted and rancorous
old white people like those that Moore and the Salisbury Group here
exploit. Almost every week the letters column of the *Hackney Gazette*
features similar voices (the white man in a wheelchair who has been
told that he can't have a social worker any longer and blames it on the
cost of council services to the ethnic minorities, or the woman whose
bitter letter advertises for 'another white person' to share memories of
a golden age gone down ...). There are indeed frightened and resent-
ful people who have been thrust back into a sullenly defended particularity, and for whom racism provides an easy and compensatory
self-understanding.

The real criticism, however, should certainly be reserved for Moore
himself, with his 'professional' approach to his subject. Nowhere does
Moore indicate how he questioned people or for that matter who he
selected for interview—matters of this sort are 'professionally' left out
of the picture. Similarly, nowhere does Moore engage with the terms
of these stories, or with the actual historical situation of the post-war
inner city in this country. All he does in the end is to exploit his old
people, shaping their voices from behind and then interpreting what
they have said to produce the mythical and ideological effects that he
wants. The old people are absolved of any charge of racism ('They
feel sorry for the black people, lost in a strange land,' and generally
take a 'Christian' view of things). As for the National Front and all the
multiple evidences of discrimination, Moore merely brackets them
out: 'The National Front found no support. The violence of their
attitude was repudiated, and they were criticised for wanting "lynch
law".'

Moore presents these old people as merely loyal subjects: as good
patriots who have been betrayed, their freedoms eroded by liberal
hypocrisy and black terror. Nowhere does he look for any potential in
their experience which might lead towards a more actively democratic
form of citizenship, but then of course it is far from Moore's aim that
such people should ever rise to anything except grateful obedience to
the next round of hard, white, authoritarian government. As Moore

claims, Lambeth is traditionally a Labour borough, but these loyalties are eroding. The old and more organic political forms of these people are breaking down and where there was, at least to some extent, democratic political expression, there are now merely forlorn loyal subjects regretting any previous indiscretion (like voting Churchill out in 1945) and craving righteous government from above. Moore complains about mugging, but as a 'professional' journalist he has merely mugged these old white people himself, knocking them down with a microphone and taking from them what he needs to make the story of his own ends: the Second World War remembered and redeclared once again.

Moore's old white people are certainly comparable with Orwell's proles. They are the battered repositories of old decencies which are fading and which can no longer hope to influence or change the world. They live on with memories that are increasingly dislocated and crave reintegration. Where Orwell has the all destroying Party, Moore has both the unnatural and demeaning welfare state and that horde of black primitives in the same structural position. In one respect Moore's 'old people of Lambeth' are worse than Orwell's proles. They are like *good* proles in the sense that they crave their own submission. They no longer make any demands except that authority should be established all around them, and they would probably apologise for ever having dreamed of the Labour Party. They now crave the status of pawns in a game where the rules are at least to be reinforced. It was by appealing to 'primitive patriotism' that Orwell's Party controlled the proles, and Moore clearly saw similar possibilities in Lambeth. His pamphlet gives a clear picture of the sort of loyal subject some Tories crave.

In one passage Moore gives his own game away. Where his ideological forebears would joke endlessly at the vulgarity and ignorance of the uncultured urban working class, it now suits Moore to find these old whites decidedly civilised: 'Without having an arrogant or dogmatic theory of racial superiority, the old people of Lambeth can see with their own eyes that they are surrounded by people more primitive than they, who lack their respect for law and privacy.' Racist theory is collapsed into the self-evident reality which Orwell associated with 'the eyes and ears'—part of a right-wing appropriation of the 'lifeworld.' In Orwell the proles are precisely the helpless bearers of threatened but largely unspoken truths which are defined as the essential core of humanity—truths which reside in them like an ethnicity at the quasi-natural level of 'being' rather than of social practice. The dangers of such a strategy may not have been so clear in Orwell's time but they certainly burst into view forty years later with Moore, who champions a similar set of self-evident truths at the threatened and helpless heart of old white Lambeth.

And whose truths are these anyway? The racist assumptions which are most important in Moore's text—the one's which *really* go without saying—are not actually those of the old white people of Lambeth at all. They are attributes instead of the readership to which Moore and the Salisbury Group make their appeal, a readership made up of people who are unlikely, by and large, to come from Lambeth (except, of course, when passing through on the way to somewhere else). These projected readers are people whose unspoken racism is of a more distant kind—more abstract, more like the earlier anti-Semitism which finds expression in Mary Butts's writing. It is the physiognomy of *this* onlooking racism which Moore sketches out in the old white people of Lambeth. Moore nails these people to an idea of their existence which can only be desperate and fearful, and he does so in order to present an authoritarian Tory readership with an image of the white working class with which it can readily sympathise and get along: an obedient white plebiscite which recognises its previous political mistakes and longs to be rescued by those who in their minds are still capable of setting sail from the shires. Helpless kelpers and old proles, the rescue fantasy goes on. Agnes Heller has written that it is *right*-wing radicalism which treats people as objects, and this is what we are looking at now: the proles as battered ornaments still waiting to be dug out of the ever-collapsing junk-shop of modern history in which Orwell hesitated before leaving them all those recent years ago.[18]

Afterword:
Everyday Life and the
Aura of the
Modern Past

In a brief but very interesting discussion of official policy regarding 'Patrimony' in Giscard d'Estaing's France, Philippe Hoyau has argued that the contemporary emphasis on the national past 'derives less from a will to preserve and value a "monumental" and academic past than from the promotion of new values articulated on a largely transformed conception of inheritance and tradition.'[1]

Hoyau does not conceive the expansion of the national heritage as a simple addition of new contents which may be considered merely to augment a traditional repertoire; on the contrary, he suggests that the whole frame of reference has shifted in a new and vernacular direction. 'The past' may still be an imaginary object, but it is now organised around three major models: the family, conviviality and the countryside. Purged of its leading political tensions, the past can then be offered to one and all in newly inclusive ceremonies of collective identification: 'History annuls itself in ethnology...it dissolves itself in the circumscribed depth of the countryside and congeals in the time of repetition.' Hoyau suggests that a new and hybrid discipline is being forged around these recent measures of conservation—a discipline which he names 'Ethno-history' and sees as being focussed above all on the previously spurned details of everyday life. As a celebration of the immobile fabric of cultural difference, Ethno-history manages a redeployment of French ethnology—its advocates holding that the latter 'has for too long been held distant from its true inspiration (obligations of a colonial past) which is the metropolitan domain, a particularly rich mixture of the archaic and the modern.' The main merit of Ethno-history, however, is to be found in its ability to 'adjust ethnological and historical research to the ideological demands of the time...and above all to rationalise nostalgias, offering them "real" contents.' In addition, as Hoyau adds, 'by revaluing "poor" forms of knowledge and despised objects, Ethno-history affirms its spirit of openness, and at the same time makes its appeal to as widespread an audience as possible.'

Hoyau's account of the hegemonic past, and of its recent reorientation, has considerable application to the British scene as the essays in this book have described it. Hoyau writes of industrial archaeology with its 'restaging of dead labour' (a 'revenge of the infrastructure' which can indeed look peculiar from a perspective which has habitually assimilated the factory to a forced labour camp), and if this sounds familiar we can surely also recognise something of the 'soft socialism' which Hoyau identifies as a new form of 'relief from below': here as in France there are scarcely examined if always ambivalent pacts between oppositional history, say, and the expanding national past of a modern society which is indiscriminately hungry for the traditional meanings which alone appear able to legitimise its development.

Hoyau may well seem to underestimate the extent to which the transformation of the national past has been won by people championing the previously despised histories of the oppressed, but his challenge should still be acknowledged. The point is not just that oppositional or 'committed' historiography can get lost in an obsessive accumulation of comfortably archival detail—first the wood disappears behind the trees, and then each tree becomes unrecognisable for all the twigs. The more serious difficulty is that the assertion of, say, working class or colonial history can now be appropriated in such a way as to suggest that political domination is just 'history' these days. What is more, this is not just something that happens *to* history; it is not just the consequence of a recontextualisation which occurs when the ostensibly innocent results of historiographical research are taken up in the wider public sphere. For there are times when committed historians seem unwittingly to collude with the oppression of those whose cause they follow—declaring them to be authentic only as they appear in the traditional cast of their subordination, and refusing any political discussion which would question the adequacy of a historical memory which limits itself to the moving resurrection of dead misery, time-expired utopias and failed (but all the more heroic) resistance.

However, if Hoyau is right to argue that the national heritage has undergone transformation rather than mere augmentation over recent years, the question of everyday life must also be raised in a more positive way than Hoyau's predominantly negative critique allows. More specifically, if the past now includes the ordinary traces of old everyday life among its valued contents, there are different things to be said about the sense of *uniqueness* which hangs over the celebrated objects within its changing repertoire. This sense of uniqueness may indeed still characterise precious works of art, but in recent times it has drifted far from its old academic moorings and it can now be held in common by, say, a phrase of rhyming slang, an old piece of industrial machinery (preferably *in situ*), a hand-painted plate from the turn of the century and a cherished landscape or place. It is not merely official cultural policy which determines the meaning or the extent of the modern past. The uniqueness of heritage objects may indeed be pointed out in official guidebooks, but it is far more power-fully expressed in the vernacular measures of everyday life. For the perspectives of everyday life, the unique heritage object has *aura*, and in this respect the national heritage seems to have a persistent connec-tion with earlier traditions of bourgeois culture—a connection which may even be *especially* strong as the modern past reaches out to include not masterpieces but the modest objects of bygone everyday life in its repertoire. More than this, and contrary to the assumptions guiding much work on 'popular culture,' I refer to this connection with the bourgeois tradition in order to indicate a critical rather than merely 'ideological' potential within the national past.[2]

As my use of the word 'aura' may already have implied, my argu-ment here is close to the work of the Frankfurt School, for whom art was above all an area of high negation. Habermas has put it as follows:[3]

> Only bourgeois art, which has become autonomous in the face of demands for employment extrinsic to art, has taken up positions on behalf of the victims of bourgeois rationalisation. Bourgeois art has become the refuge for a satisfaction, even if only virtual, of those needs that have become, as it were, illegal in the material life-process of bourgeois society. I refer here to the desire for a mimetic relation with nature; the need for living together in solidarity outside the group egoism of the immediate family; the longing for the happiness of a communicative experience exempt from imperatives of rationality and giving scope to imagination as well as spontaneity...Thus, along with moral universalism, art and aesthetics (from Schiller to Marcuse) are explosive ingredients built into bourgeois ideology.

Where Habermas follows the Frankfurt School in focussing on art as an exclusive and autonomous sphere, the aura of the national past is both more secular and also more problematic in the way it is expressed at the level of everyday life. On the positive side, the aura of the modern past can indeed speak against rationalised experience; it can celebrate a contemplative rather than instrumental or pragmatic relation to nature, just as it can pose the question of an unalienated rationality and of a social experience in which to be human is to be a personality as a whole rather than the subordinate or merely special-ised subject of so much modern activity. The modern past may cer-tainly invoke a different relationship between freedom and necessity or between imagination and technical knowledge, just as it may also project a broader circumference of personal action than is available in the manipulating and procuring of so much everyday activity under the modern division of labour.

However, if the aura of the modern past can testify to the exist-ence of radical needs in this way, it also has other implications—no less critical or negative in their relation to the present—which can't in any way be approved. Just as the green world of Mary Butts came to be tinged with anti-Semitism, the national past is capable of find-ing splendour in old styles of political domination and of making an alluring romance out of atrocious colonial exploitation. Similarly, it can affirm the complex and differentiated culture of colonialist expec-tation which, no longer finding its customary outlets in the periphery of a mastered world, recoils bitterly on its disappointing home terri-tory. As for the idea of the lifeworld—the central ambivalence of Miss Savidge's story (a story which could indeed, and the Stoks' film seems aware of the temptation, be reconfigured as a Conservative fable of national decline)—this has its unquestionably reactionary appropri-ation as the severely 'natural' if also somewhat psychotic phenom-enology of an agitated establishment.[4]

So the aura of the national past does indeed involve negation, but in no sense does this negation amount only to humane nostalgia. Bloch saw something like it in the 1920s when he watched the non-synchro-nous culture of the German countryside migrate into the hideous but nonetheless 'hopeful' symbolism of National Socialism, and while the situation is different the perspective now should be just as watchful and critical as was Bloch's own.[5] For all its difficulty, however, the aura of the national past testifies to the fact that even the most authoritar-ian expression of the nation is responding to crucial questions which are experienced in everyday life and *which remain open*—questions of historicity, political and cultural authenticity or freedom, questions of rationality and personality which are not obliterated even by the most destructively jingoistic and racist answers with which the culture of the nation can so copiously provide them. The essential point, then is to comprehend the nation (and the modern past in which the nation finds such expression) in terms of these questions. Rather than seeking to 'claim' the nation and its symbolism for an oppositional cause, and rather than merely dismissing it with negative hermeneutics, the aim should surely be to derive practical answers to these questions: answers which are democratic rather than authoritarian, appropriate to a post-Imperialist and markedly heterogeneous society rather than ghosted by aggressively mournful fantasies of the old Imperial nation.

Let there indeed be a greater expression of cultural particularity in this society, but let it be articulated according to democratic principles and let it therefore also reflect a truly heterogeneous *society* rather than the unitary image of a privileged national identity which has been raised to the level of exclusive and normative essence. And if everything possible should be done to enable a more diversified public expression of social imagination, isn't this also to say that there should be a movement (both economic and cultural) towards a *democratic* (rather than merely spell-binding) re-enchantment of everyday life? Against the unitary nation, special attention might well be paid to local moments of self-determination—moments of republican space in which an increase in both rationality and personality is possible. More than ever in the shadow of a vividly imagined nuclear millennium, it is important to remember that the radicalisation of democracy doesn't easily proceed in quantum leaps, and that the small step (as distinct from the compromise) matters a lot.

And what about history? While I have spoken against the revivalist utopianism which seeks to dust off, say, Chartist aspiration and beam it into the present as adequate political analysis, I do not conclude that history now stands utterly debunked. To the contrary, I accept Heller's claim that, against the already completed 'past' of nationalist encouragement (or of left-wing nostalgia), History should be the name of a future-orientated *project*: history-which-is-to-be-made rather than stately history-which-is-already-made and demands only veneration in what it also dismisses as an abjectly inferior and declining present.

While the earlier marxist philosophy of history with its assumptions about the inevitable progress of the universal working class should certainly be discarded, there is continuing need for a theory of *possible* history which can be fought for in accordance with the political principles of socialism. For Heller this theory is based on the historical logic of democracy and also on the supreme (and, indeed, universal) guiding value which she defines as humankind. This is indeed to identify history as a utopia, but it is a disciplined, rational and informed utopia—one which, while it is counterfactual, is also formed on the basis of empirical knowledge about the present rather than in spite of it.[6] Within these limits there need be no embarassment about imagining ways of life different from those that currently exist—just as long (and this again is a reminder that Heller herself adds) as there is no contradiction between the aspiration and the measures which are taken in the attempt to realise it. As for all those recent 'farewells' to the working class, while contemporary forms of exploitation certainly demand that socialist politics no longer be defined only in the traditional economic terms of industrial production, this should be seen as an urgent question for working-class organisations and not as a mark of their final disqualification from the field of political relevance. In this old imperial country, it would be altogether preferable to say farewell to the elegant but also grievous culture of national 'decline.'

Appendix to the Oxford Edition

Sneering at the Theme Parks: An Encounter with the Heritage Industry

Patrick Wright in conversation
with Tim Putnam

(This exchange was first published in the journal *Block*, No. 15, Spring 1989, pp. 48–55. Since a computer error resulted in an only half corrected version being printed, the text below has been reformed in places to bring into conformity with original intentions)

TP: After the recent Council of Europe Conference on Heritage and Urban Regeneration at Halifax, Robert Hewison led off a public debate with the observation that the enemy of heritage was the heritage industry. This was not an easy line of argument to sustain in the face of such formidable figures as Peter Addyman from the Yorkshire Archaeological Trust, creators of Jorvik. Addyman was easily able to show that Jorvik provided an effective way of extending their programme of archaeological research. Hewison was forced to retreat into conjuring up an image of a decadent country dotted with Jorvik clones, which didn't go down very well in an old industrial area where conjuring with heritage has brought new jobs and increased investment, reversing decades of decline and outmigration. It all made one wonder what was really at stake in the debate which has circled round the notion of 'heritage industry.'

PW: There is more than one issue in play here. To begin with, we are seeing an apparent rise of interest in questions of tradition—in old buildings, in the way things were. So we've got all that going on, and it is obviously mixed up with the memory of colonial forms and imperial dramas. Yet this interest in the past is also a response to modern disruptions about which one can't simply be disdainful. It can't just be dismissed as backward hankering.

We've then got the different question of the nationalisation of those feelings and meanings, a present movement towards the manipulation of those concerns. In other words the sense of history can be produced, and deflected and used. There's surely no doubt about that. We've seen it at work in the curious kind of nationalism that came up during the second phase of Thatcher government.

But finally we've also got the whole curatorial agenda—a legitimate area of activity for museums—and that seems to me to have been vaporised and ignored in the recent critique, just as much as what it is that actually drives and defines people's interest in the past, whether it be strictly true or accurate or not.

With such a tangle of issues, what should we expect criticism to do?

We need critical argument here for two reasons. First, it is vital to be able to differentiate within any cultural practice, and there is no shortage of developments in the heritage area which should be robustly opposed. Take the case in Avebury where the new, and decidedly nouveau, owner of the manor house is presently proposing to open an Elizabethan theme park right next to those massive stones.

This is just one example of a kind of private development which, for all its invocation of 'heritage' and 'public access,' would actually over-exploit and destroy a place and atmosphere that is already under public protection. Other examples come immediately to mind. Not so long ago, a 'wild west' theme park was proposed for the Rhondda valley and justified, most insultingly, as the answer to the employment problems of the area. Meanwhile, over in Bow you've got the old Bryant and May factory being themed up and marketed as the 'Bow Quarter.' The brochure, which compared this estate agent's invention with the Latin Quarter of Paris, stresses the stylistic attractions of the designer flats which are now available where Annie Besant helped organise the famous matchgirls' strike a hundred years ago. If enough historians protest, Annie Besant might even get a statue as the development continues, but the main attraction will remain what the brochure, in an unlikely gesture towards lower Manhattan, calls those 'lofty' apartments. We have to be able to make critical comments in this field, if only in order to define and promote better practice. In the end, though, it's not good enough just to crack easy jokes and sneer. If that's Addyman's point, I accept it.

In this respect, the publication of Hewison's The Heritage Industry *has muddied the water in the way that it criticises important developments such as Wigan or Ironbridge. While there are quite a lot of things which could be said in criticism of either, it needs to be recognised that such institutions were pioneers and are still leaders in their field. They are exemplary, not typical. To discuss them as though they are symptoms of some general malaise mocks any attempt to raise*

standards of interpretation, and makes intervention within it impossible. No won-
der it makes people like Peter Addyman mad.

At the same time, contemporary characterisations of heritage often do seem to be
symptomatic of processes beyond curatorial practice.

Yes. Critical discussion is also vital here because the whole heritage
agenda has become mixed up in a much wider symbolic and, indeed,
polemical drama. It is significant, for example, that such a major
national debate about Britain and its post-war history should have
been conducted in terms of architecture. The 'heritage' has become
a national theme, partly because it is the bearer of wider, and often
less explicit, arguments about what the nation is and what the legitimacy of the state may be. Archaeologists, conservationists, planners
and museum curators sometimes express irritation at the difficulties
this additional metaphorical dimension brings to their work. I'm not
surprised they get impatient with commentators who have scarcely
even bothered to find out what their day to day practice involves. But
even so, this wider dimension is there, and its part of what has caused
the increased popularity of the cultural heritage. It also demands a
broader kind of discussion than many of the curatorial professions
are accustomed to.

There is more to this larger dimension than the 'wallowing in nostalgia' which
some papers tell you is 'stopping us going forward from modernism.' Accounts like
Fiona McCarthy's in the Guardian *assume everyone knows what nostalgia is, but*
they actually confuse various kinds of historical reference.

A lot of this talk of 'nostalgia' is hopelessly general. It conflates
any number of different impulses, and it also seems to assume that
the desirable state for a society is to be untroubled by any sort of
historical awareness at all. As for the idea that heritage-obsession is a
symptom—or rather a cause—of economic decline, this is in Hewison,
but only because he took it from Martin Wiener's *English Culture and
the Decline of the Industrial Spirit.* I don't think this idea is sustainable.
In the last few years it has become quite obvious that 'heritage' and
'conservation' are fundamentally involved in various programmes of
urban regeneration and economic restructuring.

Of course, everything depends on what you mean by 'decline' and
what you think of as renewal. For most of the post-war period British
culture has featured a persistent opposition between the imagery of the
traditional nation and the modernising imagery of reform—Brideshead
and the tower blocks, as I've put it. In this opposition, 'heritage' has been

asserted against modernisation. Its rise as a national theme may certainly have contributed to 'decline'—of the welfare state, not the 'industrial spirit' Wiener writes about. His book put Raymond Williams—or a gloss of Williams' idea of culture—onto the curriculum of the business schools. It was also taken to justify Thatcher's assault on the public institutions of culture, from universities through to the public museums. There is a partial convergence between this argument and some attacks on the 'heritage industry'—not just Hewison's either…

But it's not making enterprise with heritage that would have upset Wiener (or his Thatcherite followers) but the appeal to 'heritage values' to shield us from change and risk. Hewison's attack on the former is actually an example of the decline that Wiener laments. The scope of this mythic opposition between 'culture' and 'enterprise' has become so vast that it can contain its own negation. As with most polemics, the self-evidence of Wiener's argument has been rapidly eroded, and it makes better evidence of late twentieth century decadence-obsession than it provides of late nineteenth-century decline. The slippery Weberian concepts and casual assumptions about what evidence texts provide about culture don't provide much of a foundation for work in this area, either.

In your view, what kind of theoretical framework is needed to support the lines of critical argument we have been talking about?

I remember finding current theories of culture distinctly unhelpful when I started to write about these issues. There was endless over-elaborate talk about how culture wasn't natural, how meanings were 'constructed,' how subjectivity was the effect of texts, but there seemed to be very little engagement with the world beyond the theorist's cinema where people still insist on getting up out of their seats and putting what they think into action. I was trying to produce an analysis which was able to address the politics of nationalised tradition but was also able to base that critique in a sensitivity towards people's involvement in those ideas of nation-hood and tradition. This can't be done merely within an ideology-spotting mode, and it also demands some respect for the policy issues involved in the conservation and administration of tradition. Meanings may well be constructed, but we only gain from saying this if we use the observation as a starting point rather than a con-clusion. Some recent writing about the 'heritage industry' seems to assume that if a meaning or tradition is 'constructed' then there is nothing more to say about it except that it is also false. End of story, start of sneer.

It's not as if we haven't been here before, either. This, or something very like it, was J.H. Plumb's position in the sixties. In *The Death of the Past* he described 'the past' as 'a created ideology with a purpose,' an area of complete illusion and mystification. He claimed that the task of the historian was to come up with superior knowledge (those were confident days), and then, by some sort of process of argument that he never fully explained, dispel the clouds of popular misapprehension...

rather than making them thicker...

which is indeed what often seems to have happened. Now this idea of history and the past certainly has convenience and simplicity on its side. Everything that isn't approved and date-stamped by the proper authorities, in this case the historian, is simply written off as rubbish. And who really needs to discriminate between one pile of rubbish and the next? The same kind of generalisation is assumed in Hewison's book. In his perspective it doesn't really matter whether we're dealing with a Labour council in the North trying to do something about a run-down industrial area, or some sleazy hotel group in the South who have realised in a cynical way that if you put a bit more historical patina on your building you can make that much more money out of it. The difference between, say, Beamish and the 'Bow Quarter,' is of no interest from this viewpoint. Indeed, the only difference that seems to matter in the end is the one that comes between the 'heritage culture,' which Hewison generalises as backward, manipulated and sentimental, and the 'critical culture' which he invokes as superior but leaves almost entirely unspecified.

And this involves the heritage critic in a dubious and quixotic pursuit of 'authenticity,' which turns out to be rather self-referring. Criticism risks becoming just a privileged taste, and is thus easily outflanked by the populist Government line on heritage, exemplified by the Conservative minister Virginia Bottomley's speech at Halifax: 'heritage is not just for toffs,' that is, no longer safe to be left to publically funded cultural cognoscenti.

Yes, it looks suspiciously like another 'them and us' job to me. We are back at sneering at the theme park, and at the dupes who are seduced by it. We're back in the worst traditions of educated snobbery. There should be a moratorium on this sort of writing, which is now becoming commonplace in papers like the *Guardian*. In its place there should be some decent visitor research to find out how people actually use these places and what they actually think about them.

This would provide a much sounder foundation for a critical response to the 'heritage industry.'

For example, there has been a very precise and, I'm bound to say, classically organic critique of the heritage industry which has escaped notice, and that has gone on in the world of the metal detector enthusiasts. It's quite an intriguing story this, as far as I've been able to trace it out. There were mine detectors in use in this country after the war, but they were great cumbersome things and not very effective, but then in the Sixties quite refined portable metal detectors were on the market in the USA and imported into this country through US Air Force bases: USAF personnel are coming out at the weekends or at night and wandering around Essex or wherever digging things up. By the late seventies, there is a very large network of people using portable metal detectors. The practitioners will deny this absolutely, but it looks to me as though it's a pretty exclusively male working-class activity. The practitioners will admit its male—they're trying to do things about that, to get more women involved, but they're deeply, deeply resistant to the idea that it's working class, partly I think because once that is said about them they've basically been written off as ignorant freebooters.

This concept of the metal detectorist would probably have been invented by the archaeologists in any case.

That's true. But in fact, the metal detector fraternity, and that's precisely what it is, supports 162 federated clubs throughout the country and two national magazines which come out on a monthly basis, which are fairly glossy; one has to say that's a pretty good comparison to *History Workshop*. We're dealing here with something that is quite major, and if you look at those magazines you'll see intriguing signs of development: in the original ones most of the articles are made up of bits of plagiarised academic writing. They aren't very knowledgeable, to put it crudely; they are the works of people sort of expressing their initial enthusiasm. But, five years in, there's a qualitative change and the kind of material that's coming out is very impressive.

If you go to the metal detectorists' clubs, you'll find a discussion that reflects a disciplined and often very knowledgeable appreciation of history through the found object. Of course the archaeologists' response to this was completely panic-ridden. In the early eighties there was an anti-detectorist campaign co-ordinated by the Council of British Archaeology with the museum professionals. One of the most interesting county archaeologists who had worked in this area, Tony Gregory, was even censured by his professional body because he had co-operated with detectorists. These people were seen as vandals. They were seen as land pirates. There were enough people looting historical sites with these machines to justify professional concern, but the archaeologists' attempt to close down the hobby, by trying to get legislative change, backfired. The detectorists defended themselves very interestingly. They claimed to be the inheritors of old rights of common. They argued very strongly that, while private land is private, municipal parks should be absolutely open to detectorists to do exactly what they wanted—after all, that is common land. I suspect their culture also links them quite explicitly to poaching.

The detectorists have done very well in this argument. They were being accused of being big business. Because three people got together and started manufacturing detectors in this country, capitalism was moving in, this was literally how the archaeologists were phrasing it, and the counter accusation, which was launched in the pages of *Farmers' Weekly* was about how the CBA is run by Dr Henry Cleere, who was alleged to be an East European-style Marxist. The way they got to him was by associating him with the New Archaeology. They went through all the archaeological journals of the seventies—you know, Althusser and the trowel, that kind of thing—and they found articles about the New Archaeology and its roots in Marxism. They got Dr Henry Cleere to repeat this argument, which is of course about methodology, it's about how archaeologists don't dig for objects but in order to verify hypotheses. They're more interested in stains left by rotted sill beams than in treasure or gold coins.

The detectorists didn't believe a word of this and started making coarse remarks about the site archaeologist's preference for broad-brimmed wellies (good coin catchers). They considered the archaeological profession an embodiment of the usurping state, the overweening state that is crushing native Brits' rights of common, and they actually seem to have done quite well, in the early eighties, in preventing any reform of the treasure trove laws. So what one sees there is a powerful 'organic' critique which is confused, which is messy, and about which no one could take a simple stand, because while there is a legitimate issue raised by the archaeologists—and there is a question of regulation of archaeological sites in the face of this new portable technology

—at the same time the demonology launched against the detectorists was so excessive that it just made the necessary co-operation between these two parties more difficult.

If you stand back from that polarisation you could say that the difference between the professional archaeologists and the detectorists is really less important than the difference between those who are reading books and watching television, on the one hand, and those who actually go to find something out, on the other. From that point of view, the stance of the archaeologists was wasteful in spurning new sources of enthusiasm and interest.

I think that's right. What is extremely interesting about the metal detectorists is that historically, they came at the very point where the heritage professions—the museum people, the curators, the archaeologist—were being strapped, squeezed from above financially and were being encouraged to turn against the idea of their collections. (The left intellectuals were in this too, saying nothing is worse than the object in itself, nothing is worse than to go to a museum full of boring glass cases with bits and pieces inside.) The museums were running from that: they were into contextualisation, they were using audio-visual techniques and all sorts of special effects to get away from their object-oriented collections. At the same time the detectorists were actually reinventing the high cultural styles of appreciation, in other words they were entering into the object itself. Their collections were a reproduction of the old cabinet of curiosities. In many ways, their sense of historical knowledge is like that of the eighteenth-century museum. So much for popularisation!

In a sense what we are seeing is the reinvention of field archaeology. You can see the problem this poses for professional archaeologists, and it has to be a legitimate problem: how do you get these people in line? They spent a hundred years disciplining their own amateurs who were county-based and middle or upper class...

No easy task, especially when they're on their own land!

Yes, they've just got them incorporated into the procedures of the discipline when these wild characters come along. So the response is that the metal detector is evil, we mustn't use it, it's a piece of technology with no apparent use to archaeologists—a completely crazy situation to be in. The only conceivable way of regulating that activity and of knowing what is coming out of the ground is for museums and archaeologists to be in touch with those people, and to be assisting them by giving them knowledge and defining what they are finding and helping build connections so at least they can register what's coming up where.

The polemic which The Heritage Industry *launched is not going to help us to overcome that sort of problem.*

Quite. There are two reasons why that book is worrying—well, there are several, but two which concern me: one is, that we've heard a lot about the collapse of history and this present situation in which the left's theories of history are in disarray. Now, I'm quite sure that the teleologies are genuinely in disarray but it's not the fault of curators and heritage entrepreneurs.

If you look at the background of the conservation organisations you find yourself repeatedly facing a kind of social reform tendency. We are not talking about communist organisations, obviously, but we are often talking about Victorian liberal reform campaigns, which have very clear roots in attempting to democratise, in attempting to establish the public interest in areas where private property has ruled before. We've also got the fact that the most significant cultural theories on the left or even of the centre have been deeply concerned with a sense of history, with a sense of the useable past. To be a critical thinker is in its own way to be a curator of history.

All that disappears, the minute you allow the argument of *The Heritage Industry*; you're basically vaporising that field under a crude definition of ideology, and you're probably also blaming a collection of rather surprised museum professionals for the collapse of your own theory of history. That seems to me to be the hidden implication.

Museum professionals say things like: here we've been, working away in a field of limited interest, involving local government because of the potential of doing something with totally undervalued assets, and we've put this together into something fundable, which has revalued neglected assets, which is attracting people to somewhere where no one ever thought people would want to go, and everyone is having a good time and then along comes this jerk who says it's degrading and a fake. What do you want us to do?

The first Director of Wigan Pier, set up as a theatre of inauthenticity in Hewison's book, has sensed that there is a weakness in the attack, and asked what so-called 'cultural historians' think they're doing with history. But, as he's addressed his remarks chiefly to fellow museum professionals, he's not really expecting a reply.

So that's one difficulty. The other is that if you actually look at the way in which the forms and methods of the 'heritage industry' got assembled, it really isn't good enough to say that these techniques of display and of simulation are manipulative con tricks. If you look at the pioneers of the open-air museum, for example, you are looking at people whose intention is extremely worthy. It's a democratic intention, connected with adult education, it's about reaching new constituencies, it's about giving people a way of thinking about things that had previously been the domain of exclusive professions. And the same applies, it seems to me, to the National Trust. Within the Trust, there's a house which marks very precisely the paradigm shift, a house called Erdigg, on the Welsh border, which is a house which you now enter through the kitchen, through the service rooms . . .

And you encounter not only the 'workings' of a big house, but an extraordinary document of its paternalistic social relations in the portraits and verse which generations of the family commissioned and composed about their servants.

When that house came into the Trust, there was a significant argument internally about how you administer the visitors going through them. Advocates of the art historical paradigm claimed that these mansions are places with grand rooms and you go in through the front door, properly, and look at the grand rooms and the paintings and furniture. Others said, no they're not, they're social institutions. You can see, in a way, it's Mark Girouard's argument, it's the arrival of social history, which moves here into the practice of display. Many of the developments that are being written off as spurious and 'heritagey' are, if you look where they come from, produced by people arguing from such positions—from social history through to History Workshop. So there is a real problem about this, if you're actually dismissing the whole thing, you're really not doing anything better than those old sods sneering at *Coronation Street*.

Yet the discussion of heritage at the most recent History Workshop was preoccupied with the commercial and political 'misuse' of history rather than examining the nature of public involvement in heritage questions. It was as if Hewison had provoked a knee-jerk reaction against the industry which would turn your heritage into trifles.

A bit of history might help here too. You go to Exeter Exchange in London in 1790 and look at what's going on there. You look at the panoramas. It's not as though gaudy display is something that's been invented in the last few years.

Certainly not, and one is entitled to ask questions about where such moral aesthetics come from with their proprietorial stance towards 'the past.' What people in the History Workshop context seemed to be missing was the extent to which the phenomena and paraphernalia, such as they are, designated by the term 'heritage industry' have been drawing out very important quasi-political amateur popular movements over some time, and the last twenty-five or thirty years in particular. Metal detectorists form one strand of this, and another is drawn from the serried ranks of the railway enthusiasts, the architectural preservationists, the industrial archaeologists, the oral historians, and the original project of History Workshop. The confluence of these quite distinct currents in the 1970s created a new kind of amenity politics in which conservation was the focus, and in the 1980s, in a changed field of public responsibility and governmental initiative, they have actually become things to conjure with. They have made it possible to contemplate investment on a speculative basis, and in that sense, they justify the phrase, literally, of 'heritage industry.' Whatever issues must be faced now about the effects of commercial forms and practices in this area, we need to remember who has created, and what sustains, the basis of interest and involvement.

The first time I came across the phrase 'heritage industry' was with Colin Ward, who uses the phrase very much from inside those movements you're talking about. He was closely involved in the arguments in the sixties and early seventies to do with interpretation and interpretative technique, where again what you're seeing is a whole set of people figuring out how to enable people of a diverse background, people who are not of an academic orientation or of any given set of skills or qualification, to appropriate in their own terms or in terms that they can at least make sense of, a particular given landscape or industrial site or whatever. So when Colin Ward talks critically about 'the heritage industry,' he is concerned about the way in which public statutory policy has since come along and lumped all this stuff together.

And, equally, the transformation of aspects of heritage into a kind of business also needs to be closely studied because both have implications for the choices being made now. Museums which are being pressed to follow a commercial paradigm have somehow to make imaginative design decisions which don't put their fundamental cultural assets and messages at risk, and they're not getting much of the right kind of help. Equally, the sort of market or audience research that is appropriate to their very sophisticated offerings isn't provided off the peg, at a price they can afford. Pertinent assistance could help avert the drift towards a uniform, plastic fronted, heritage industry which is the surest solvent of public enthusiasm and involvement in their own history.

But the external critique which finds 'heritage' a problem itself arises from a set of transformations, a kind of banalisation of cultural studies.

Yes, some of the critical arguments that are made about developments in the heritage field are produced almost entirely at the level of ideology. They're following fairly tired methodologies which are to do with deconstructing meaning. The thesis about the 'invention of tradition,' for example, has been cheapened to the point where the minute you can prove that any tradition is constructed—an expression which is over-used—you've falsified it. Well this is just completely ridiculous. First of all there is no tradition which isn't constantly under reproduction, which isn't being re-synthesised if you like. And secondly, the important questions begin after that initial and rather banal observation and you go on to ask: by whom, and for whom, and what are its potentials as a synthesised tradition?

To take another example: it's been quite clear for the last five years in this country that heritage, rather like avant-garde artists and gay communities, can play a crucial role in urban regeneration. The shrewd estate agents follow the gays into areas and the market moves after them because basically they're the beachhead marines—they go to areas where no one else would choose to live. They start reclaiming old buildings; they start developing forms of life that eventually become tradeable. Now it's quite clear that preservationists have done that sort of thing in various places. The most obvious example in East London is in Spitalfields where you have those early Georgian houses which ten years ago you couldn't have raised a bean on and were empty and rotting. Now they are coming onto the market at £400,000 a piece and the bankers have started to move in. All of this seems to justify an argument which says that the whole preservationist thing is just a sop for redevelopment. Having said that, however, and agreed with the strengths of its assertion—this is the process that Sharon Zukin spotted in New York with Manhattan loft development—you still have this genuine set of questions, which is concerned with what you might do with endangered early Georgian buildings.

Having gone through various levels of analysis you have to return to the question of the range of choice available in the context, given this or that horizon of possibility and level of contingency.

Absolutely. And where it may be going.

That would place heritage within a grounded perspective of cultural policy and the management of cultural resources in a practical sense. For example, take any area which has seen a form of property cycle. The alternative to some sort of revaluation of the existing premises because of change in the estimation of their cultural potential and possible use is going to be piecemeal or comprehensive redevelopment, whatever the regime of property or planning control.

So what one regrets is first that the revaluation may be purely monetary and secondly that it only applies to certain limited numbers of buildings. I remember feeling this very strongly, when I went to Brick Lane for the ten-year celebratory meeting of the Spitalfields Trust and I noticed that not a single person of any of the cultural minority populations or post-immigrant populations of the area was present. Now I don't say that lightly, because clearly it is difficult to establish links between communities that may indeed have very different interests. You're coming along trying to preserve historical buildings while others are trying to preserve footholds in the area: these are different interests and there are difficulties there. What one regretted was not that the conservationists' agenda—to the extent that one existed—was caught up with property valuations, but that it was exclusively framed in architectural language, that there didn't seem to be a policy for the area beyond its selected buildings.

There have been similar problems where those agenda haven't been framed exclusively in architectural terms. In the case of Ironbridge for example, there has been an editing process which is more than architectural but still privileges a particular notion and particular periods of history, to make a story which could be retailed outside the Gorge more than within it. Historians have pointed out that in some respects the story as presented doesn't make sense, but arguably the more important problem is the very considerable amount of the history of the Gorge which isn't validated—there are virtually no connections, for example, with living memory, and this dispossesses both new and old residents.

The whole area was going through a massive process of redevelopment as a New Town. The making of the Ironbridge Gorge Museum was part of the making of the myth of the new community.

Indeed, and it was part of the initial studies for the New Town that there should be a recreational and historic zone in the Gorge. This made a more complex context for heritage management than that at Williamsburg, for example, where hundreds of post-1800 buildings were simply removed in the restoration of the colonial settlement. In Ironbridge there was an interesting relationship between redevelopment and conservation. Tower blocks were at one point proposed right in the Gorge; what did take place was a destruction of large numbers of dwellings in the historic area as well as huge tracts of existing settlement in those parts which were not considered historic and the simultaneous building of new housing estates, though not high-rise estates. So the heritage dimension was part of comprehensive redevelop-ment from the start and not a reaction to it, as one is generally led to think.

This leads to something you have written about: how it was made to appear as though there had been previously a kind of polarisation where aspects of herit-age which had been rediscovered through housing history for example had been set against the terrible social democratic mistakes that we made.

That re-establishment of the preserved English country house is certainly where some of the simplification took place. This polarity exists within a single memorial span, from the Second World War to the present. One only has to look at the present iconography of the war, with its endless references to traditional values that were proved then, and have since been upset or lost or are being recovered. The revivalist speeches of Prince Charles have recently put a gloss on that for us. The whole repertoire of heritage as we know it now has been shaped in this broad opposition which has been proliferating in the national culture since the forties.

It has always seemed interesting to me that Evelyn Waugh has a Georgian Group in *Brideshead Revisited* (1945) and what they're com-plaining about is old buildings being demolished to make way for modern luxury flats. The 'modernist' threat isn't yet expressed in terms of council housing; we're talking about events near Mayfair, perhaps, I don't know.

It's interesting to talk to someone like James Lees-Milne. In his imagination, as expressed in his autobiography *Another Self*, the English country house was lined up against the thought of Communism. A polarising imagery is in play, and in the post-war years it seems to me to quite overwhelm the actual problems of the country house. The real threats get understated and even ignored as the polemical metaphors take over. Of course you turn over the coin and you're looking at the tower block, and while it is clear that Labour authorities were far from innocent of these developments, as Jules Lubbock has suggested, it is still the case, I think, that the metaphors have taken over. Stephen Haseler writes of 'Fabian' tower blocks of the East End, Witold Rybczinski has spoken of post-war Labour councils 'grasping the high rise,' which of course is a gross oversimplification of what happened...

They ignore the role, for example, of Keith Joseph.

I believe he inherited the Bovis fortune... So that opposition [between Brideshead and the tower blocks] which became a commonplace, we can't rest with its definition of cultural themes. The main thing I'm concerned with now is to see the whole conservationist terrain, with its increasing linkage through to ecological questions, pulled away from the polemical formations which have shaped up around it since the war. What I fear is that a lot of the discussion has only been interested in the polemic.

This problem hasn't really been taken up by much of what's been written about the 'heritage industry.' Case studies such as Bob West's about Ironbridge in The Museum Time Machine *are more concerned with placing the phenomena in an ideological firmament than with the sort of repositioning you're talking about. There's a sense of distance rather than involvement, and in Bob's case that certainly doesn't arise from lack of knowledge.*

I have some recollection of that moment where you walk into a museum or, these days, a hotel, and you think 'this is all a fix, it's all terribly fake.' Now this is an initial perception and we're all familiar with it. Bob West's article seemed to me to be rooted in that perception. But having made that observation you have to move very fast, because if you rest with it you build arguments which are turned in on themselves and you vaporise the field in which important issues have to be decided.

It is a problem to decide what the object of West's critique of Ironbridge is: is it a particular practice of museology, historical representation at all, or 'late' capitalism? The contextualisation is out of control, and there is a loss of actuality as a result. This may be a problem of method, but it's also one of address.

The big gap in most of such work is that if you're sitting in a library, you're producing arguments from that basis. What is badly needed to take these arguments forward for those who are particularly concerned with the museum question, is some kind of analysis of what people are doing when they go and visit these places.

Now I simply don't believe that they are gulled, that the people who visit the National Trust are all involved in the ceremony of lamentation and mournfulness which is part of the interpretative script of so many of those buildings. Somebody should put some research together—somebody with a budget. After fifty years of the country house scheme, the National Trust should go out there and investigate what use people actually make of those places. It's the same with Ironbridge; you can make the point, and Bob West does this well, about MSC (Manpower Services Commission—a quango responsible for running youth employment schemes) slaves and staging the revival of forms of misery we should be pleased to abolish, but I don't believe visitors to Ironbridge are all dying to revive work practices from the early industrial revolution. So little of what is happening when people visit that place is actually about the consumption of representations of history. It's that wretched film theory scenario again: people constructed out of representations.

We certainly oughtn't to assume that any of the phenomena associated with heritage necessarily arises out of or leads back to some central relationship with history. I recently heard a group of adult education tutors analysing what their people got out of visiting the Blists Hill open-air museum at Ironbridge, and history of any sort hardly came into it. I'd agree with what you're saying about the National Trust. Whatever criticisms one might make of the country house programme, it has continued to move and change and the use which people make of it will continue to move and change.

It's very interesting, that. The history of the country houses scheme is very alive now and one has to be careful that the critique of the Brideshead cult doesn't feed exactly the wrong end of the debate. There has been a definite change of agenda from the beginning when these big buildings were in trouble. A number of the founding figures, including James Lees-Milne, were closely connected with Mosley and the New Party in the thirties. There's a curious circle of people which includes Harold Nicholson and Lord Lothian, of course, who gave Blickling to the Trust during the war. Basically these characters were saying that these houses are going to go down, they are already going down; there are problems with taxation, there are problems with labour supply—all the rest of it. There are problems of owners not wanting to maintain them: the modern luxury dwelling was beginning to look pretty attractive to a lot of people in the thirties.

You then have the whole movement which defends the buildings, which takes the Trust away from its previous concerns with landscape and small buildings. The journalism about the Trust in the forties doesn't see that as a dichotomy, but it becomes one, and you get this art historical discourse developing around the country house which is quite interesting—along with the attempt, by Vita Sackville West among others, to establish what makes a house distinct from a public museum. What you're effectively seeing with the country houses scheme is the state, not the state literally, but the Trust as a statutory body, doing everything it can to preserve things while at the same time effacing its own presence. We act to preserve your house, Lord and

Lady whoever, as a public body, but what we most like about it is that it's not a public institution, and we're going to make sure that it retains that distinction. We're going to make sure that it's not clinical, that it's not museum-like, we're going to keep you in residence, even if it's not in the style to which you are accustomed.

...a kind of simulacrum...

Now what seems to me to have happened is that the thing comes forward into the seventies and you get a very strong politicisation. It is evident that the Attlee government of 1945 was the first one fully committed to the Trust, and perhaps there is some truth in the idea that they took the Trust seriously, because they intended that the old world should only remain in scattered fragments preserved by these rather crusty and eccentric characters. Anyway that gave the Trust far more than they had from any other government. Yet by the time you get into the late sixties the conservationist lobby as it is formed up around the country house is entirely horrified at the post-war scene. The mythologies of the tower block have come in, we're no longer protesting against property development and mindless speculative profiteering, we're ideologising against the state, against egalitarianism. Those arguments that people like David Watkin eventually use: you criticise the modernist Zeitgeist and then you put the classical revivalist one in its place; it's a completely disgraceful development that.

Having had that polarisation and the country house having become the emblem of everything that the post-war settlement was meant to have destroyed, we now have a situation where those of us who have criticised the way the preserved country house has been interpreted have been placed in a new quandary. We've been sitting there saying that the National Trust has been taking on the values of the private aristocratic ancestralised home all too sincerely and all too fully but our criticisms have also been joined by others who would like the Trust to get out of the country house for very different reasons indeed.

But we can't rest with that curious kind of reversal, because the latest phase is altogether more worrying. The Trust has started to be attacked in its dealings with country houses, from all sorts of unexpected quarters. Recent issues of *Country Life* have claimed that the officers of the Trust behave like barons, that they're insolent, and make decisions about the management of properties that are aesthetically ignorant. We've had the *Daily Mail* sniffing repeatedly around the mortgage arrangements of the Trust's finance director. Every sign suggests that the post-war consensus about the worth of the National Trust is breaking up. We've got Roger Scruton writing, in 1984, that the Trust has extinguished, one by one, the little fires of our national inheritance by plunging them into the ice-cold waters of the bureau-cratic state and we've got the *Spectator* publishing articles praising very fulsomely the work of James Lees-Milne and celebrating the fiftieth anniversary of the country houses scheme but leaving no doubt that the Trust is no longer needed and that these houses are capable of looking after themselves again: that is, a return to private ownership.

So what is going on at the moment is a process of de-legitimisation and an attack on the values that supported the trust and sustained it and enabled people to feel that it was a generally acceptable good thing. Interestingly, it is James Lees-Milne who is now the most vehement advocate of the Trust's continuing involvement in country houses. He is arguing with a lot of people on the right in the *Sunday Telegraph*, defending the public interest in these houses which others, like Scruton, would apparently reprivatise.

Because in that respect, what the Trust has done, for whatever reasons, with whatever terms of reference, is to have taken these things and made them accessible to the general public.

Yes, though some have tried to establish these buildings as weapons of imperial nostalgia. Others did not, of course, and in any case the public has been able to find its own uses for them.

Yes, we come back to the question of what do people make of these things. I think it's clear from observing people visiting the National Trust properties that you would need a fairly complicated checklist to describe their range of enjoyments.

Indeed. How many people are going there in reverence to the cult set up by some of the Trust's historical advisors? The answer is, I think, very few. The Trust's reluctance to establish guided tours may initially have been based on the assumption that its visiting public could rely on its cultural instincts to see it down the hallways, but it also means that these houses are remarkably open to diverse use and interpretation.

In any event, what a museum can do is affected more by changes in its audience than by its own interpretive programme.

It has to be a key priority to take on that question of audience and use. The problem is that the analysis that has been produced so far has simply been read out of the display and its representations. If one doesn't go further it is difficult to ground a critical discussion in anything other than disdain. What we need now is to differentiate and move beyond the refusal which says it's all fake, it's all constructed, and get into a situation where the arguments are based on the ability to support and develop the kinds of practice which are valuable while also consistently de-polemicising where necessary. One can't do that by sneering at every theme park that comes up as one drives down the motorway, tempted as one may certainly be.

Notes

Preface

1. J.H. Plumb, *The Death of the Past*, (1969) London 2004, pp. 12 and 17.
2. Ibid., p. 14.
3. As an early 'teledon,' Plumb himself wrote for the popular market: indeed, he would go on to produce two different books entitled *Royal Heritage* and published in association with television programmes by the BBC. See J.H. Plumb, *Royal Heritage: The Story of Britain's Royal Builders and Collectors*, London 1977 and J.H. Plumb, *Royal Heritage: The Reign of Elizabeth II*, London 1982.
4. E.D. Morel, 'The Fruits of Victory,' *The U.D.C.*, Vol.4, No.8, June 1919.
5. Rex Warner, *Why Was I Killed?*, London 1943, p. 22.
6. André Malraux, 'Our Cultural Heritage,' *Left Review*, Vol.2 No.1, July 1936, p. 491.
7. Hannah Arendt, *The Burden of Our Time* [later known as *The Origins of Totalitarianism*], London 1951, p. ix.
8. David Brett, *The Construction of Heritage*, Cork 1996, p. 8.
9. Raymond Williams, *The Volunteers*, London 1978, p. 28.
10. Ibid., pp. 27, 28.
11. Ibid., p. 27.
12. Peter Mandler, *The English National Character: The History of an Idea from Edmund Burke to Tony Blair*, New Haven and London 2006, p. 234.
13. Richard Weight, *Patriots: National Identity in Britain 1940–2000*, London 2002, p. 583.
14. Neal Ascherson, 'A Society that Falls Back on Miming the Creation of its Wealth…,' *The Independent*, 19 February 1995.
15. Raphael Samuel, *Theatres of Memory. Volume 1: Past and Present in Contemporary Culture*, London 1994, pp. 259–73.
16. P. Wright, 'Heritage clubs slug it out,' *Guardian*, 4 February 1995.
17. Mark Leonard, *Britain™: Renewing our Identity*, London 1997.
18. Weight, *Patriots*, p. 585.
19. François Hartog, 'Time and Heritage,' *International Museum*, 227, September 2007, pp. 7–10.
20. François Hartog, *Régimes d'Historicité*, Paris 2003, p. 218.
21. Ibid., p. 218.
22. François Hartog, 'Temps et histoire. Comment écrire l'histoire de France?' *Annales. Histoires, Sciences Socials*, Nov.–Dec. 1995, pp. 1219–36.
23. Hartog, *Régimes d'Historicité*, p. 200.
24. Ibid., p. 201.
25. Ibid., pp. 203–4.
26. Hartog, 'Time and Heritage,' p. 10.
27. Brett, *The Construction of Heritage*, p. 22.

28 Quoted from Peter Mandler, *History and National Life*, London 2002, p. 72.

29 Dated Christmas 1918, Vernon Lee's 'The Muse of History' is published in Lee's *Satan the Waster: A Philosophic War Trilogy with Notes & Introduction*, London 1920, pp. 219–28. For a fuller discussion of Lee's thought, see my *Iron Curtain: From Stage to Cold War*, Oxford 2007, pp. 76–95 and 109–27.

30 Lee, *Satan the Waster*, p. 224.

31 Stephen Fry, 'The future's in the past,' *Observer*, 9 July 2006.

32 Vernon Lee, 'The Narthex of Vézelay,' *The Golden Keys*, London 1925, p. 169.

33 For a fuller account of Goldring's project see my 'Little England,' *London Review of Books*, Vol.28, No.17, 7 September 2006, pp. 19–22.

34 In the blurb on the back cover of his subsequent tract *Future Tense: A New Art for the Nineties* (London 1990) Hewison is said to have given 'a new phrase to the language' with *The Heritage Industry*.

35 Weight, *Patriots*, p. 581

36 Colin Ward, 'Blue plaques and dead elms', *Times Education Supplement*, 11 October 1985. I am confident that this is the source of the phrase, not least because this review was among the photocopies I sent to Hewison at his request when he approached me with the idea that we should jointly write the book eventually published as *The Heritage Industry*.

37 Colin Ward and Andrew Fyson, *Streetwork: The Exploding School*, London 1973, p. 1.

38 Colin Ward and Malcolm MacEwen, 'Architecture in school,' *RIBA Journal*, May 1973, pp. 251–61.

39 Ward and Fyson, *Streetwork*, pp. 3–4.

40 Colin Ward, 'Can We Teach the Art of Seeing?', *The Architectural Review*, May, 1978, pp. 297–300.

41 Raphael Samuel, 'Utopian Sociology,' *New Society*, 2 October 1987.

1 Introduction

1 Tom Nairn, 'The English Literary Intelligentsia,' in Emma Tennant (ed.), *Bananas*, London 1977, pp. 57–83.

2 Ferenc Fehér and Agnes Heller make an important distinction between Liberalism with its '*contractual* arrangement of the state of social affairs' and the kind of nationalism which postulates an *organic* arrangement of social affairs and which is 'by its very nature intolerant towards the idea of choice, elective affinities, contract, and especially towards the cancelling of contract.' See Ferenc Fehér and Agnes Heller, *Hungary 1956 Revisited: The Message of a Revolution—A Quarter of a Century After*, London 1983, pp. 79–80.

3 Tony Wilden, *The Imaginary Canadian*, Vancouver 1980.

4 Guy Konopnicki, *La Place de la Nation*, Paris 1983, p. 9.

5   While there is still ample reason to repeat it, this point was well made in
    the 1960s. See Cornelius Castoriadis, *L'institution Imaginaire de la Société*,
    Paris 1975, p. 208.
6   Karel Kosik, *Dialectics of the Concrete: A Study on Problems of Man and World*,
    Dordrecht 1976, pp. 42–3.
7   Ibid., p. 43.
8   Agnes Heller, *Everyday Life*, London 1984. For a fine critique of Lukács's
    formulation of 'species-Being' see Gáspár Tamás, 'Lukács's *Ontology*:
    a Metacritical Letter' in A. Heller (ed.), *Lukács Revalued*, Oxford 1983,
    pp. 154–76. See also, more generally, Mihaly Vajda, *The State and
    Socialism*, London 1981.
9   The essay 'Everyday Life, Rationality of Reason, Rationality of Intellect'
    appears in Agnes Heller, *The Power of Shame: A Rational Perspective*, London
    1985. I have drawn extensively from this essay, but because I have worked
    from a typescript I am not able to give page references.
        It is worth contrasting Heller's strong opening claim that the prob-
    lematisation of everyday life is historical and occurs in the social world
    with Raymond Williams's recent suggestion that the motivation for the
    Lukácsian 'return to everyday life' is rather to be found in the abstract
    arrogance of high philosophers (see Williams's review essay 'A man
    without frustration,' *London Review of Books*, 17 May–6 June 1984).
    A comparable point is made even more critically by Gáspár Tamás
    in *Lukács Revalued*, the book which Williams reviews (Williams must
    have been very short of space, for his review also passes straight over
    Heller's magnificent essay on 'George Lukács and Irma Seidler'). This
    high and austere Lukácsian humanism certainly bears the mark of its
    context: it was formed as part of an oppositional—and perhaps exces-
    sively philosophical—'Renaissance of Marxism' which was forged
    against a surrounding Stalinism. While this may indeed merit some
    respect, Williams's question should be answered at the level of the
    theory itself. What is the connection between this philosophy of every-
    day life and the actual historical everyday lives of people in modern
    societies? The early conceptualisation of 'species-Being' is thoroughly
    problematic, yet Heller's recent work is concerned with precisely the
    same question.
        Arnason has recently suggested that, because it is still conceived in
    terms of objectivation, Heller's anthropology also still postulates an
    'expressive relationship between man and history' (Johan P. Arnason,
    'Progress and Pluralism: Reflections on Agnes Heller's *Theory of History*,'
    Praxis International, Vol.3, No.4, January 1984, pp. 423–38). In my view
    Heller's recent work on everyday life is far less tied to a unificatory
    philosophy of history than Arnason suggests. The various spheres of
    objectivation are not defined evaluatively and neither are they proposed
    as identities which persist unchanged through history: indeed, it is of
    their anthropological essence to be historically elaborated, developed
    and changed (and this change is not defined as an inevitably teleological

unfolding either). Heller does insist on certain empirical universals, but these come increasingly at the end of the day. Like the definition of rationality, they are universals which seem to me far more openly defined than I take Arnason to imply. While these questions remain, and while they certainly merit more theoretical discussion, my own approach here has been much more pragmatic. I have used Heller's theorisation in an endeavour to elucidate actual cultural phenomena. Crudely put, I consider the problematisation of everyday life to be a historical fact—one that is closely connected with the deepest difficulties of class theory—and I find Heller's work very useful in the analysis of this fact.

10   *Everyday Life*, p. 6.
11   Ibid., p. 12.
12   Agnes Heller, *A Theory of Feelings*, Assen 1979, p. 155.
13   *Everyday Life*, pp. 22–3. See also *A Theory of Feelings*, pp. 156–7.
14   It is on the basis of this possibility—that of a principled and also pleasurable life being made in a countervailing world—that Heller advocates a consideration of Stoic–Epicurean ethics.
15   *Everyday Life*, p. 239.
16   *A Theory of Feelings*, p. 184.
17   Ibid., p. 197.
18   Ibid., p. 213.
19   I quote from 'Maximus Letter #Whatever' in Charles Olson, *Maximus Poems IV, V, VI*, London 1968.
20   Agnes Heller, *A Radical Philosophy*, Oxford 1984, p. 134.
21   *Everyday Life*, p. 15.
22   Raymond Williams, 'Problems of the Coming Period,' *New Left Review* 140 (July–August 1983), p. 16.
23   *A Theory of Feelings*, p. 183.
24   Ibid., p. 184.
25   Heller's analysis of conscience is to be found in the title essay of *The Power of Shame*.
26   Agnes Heller, *A Theory of History*, London 1983, p. 51.
27   Alain Touraine, *The Self-Production of Society*, Chicago 1977, p. 15.
28   *A Theory of History*, p. 55.
29   Ibid., p. 61.
30   Ibid., p. 57.
31   Ibid., p. 65.
32   Bauman, *Memories of Class*, pp. 2 and 27. Bauman's concept of 'historical memory' has certain advantages over the notion, originally sketched by Foucault, of 'popular memory.' To quote Bauman more fully: 'the problem with "remembered history" of virtually all groups except the educated elite is not merely that it has not been recorded in writing but that it rarely, if ever, surfaces to the level of verbal communication, written or oral. The historical memory of a group which has been ploughed into its collective actions, which finds its expression in the group's proclivities to some rather than other behavioural responses, is not necessarily

recognised by the group as a particular concept of the past' (p. 2). For a discussion of 'popular memory' see Popular Memory Group, 'Popular Memory: theory, politics, method,' in R. Johnson et al. (eds.), *Making Histories: Studies in History-Writing and Politics*, London 1982, pp. 203–52.

33 Ibid., p. 64.
34 Ibid., p. 69.
35 Marshall Berman, *All That is Solid Melts in the Air: The Experience of Modernity*. Perry Anderson's critical discussion of this book, 'Modernity and Revolution,' is printed along with Berman's 'The Signs in the Street: a response to Perry Anderson' in *New Left Review* 144 (March–April 1984)—an argument which is surely about everyday life and its expression of human nature *in* modern experience, rather than (as Anderson seems to suggest) about a modernity which could ever be demolished in the name of a distinct human nature.

Anderson is certainly right to ask for some clarification of the term 'modernity'—a term for which Berman is not concerned to give a theoretical account. The theory of modernity which informs the essays in this book comes from Ferenc Fehér and Agnes Heller, who have defined modernity as 'the period (and the region) in which capitalism, industrialisation and democracy appear *simultaneously*, reacting to, reinforcing, complementing and checking each other' (Ferenc Fehér and Agnes Heller, 'Class, Democracy, Modernity,' *Theory and Society* 12 (1983), p. 211). 'The West' appears as one formation within modernity (differentiated, but for all its variation a formation within which the three dynamics are all present), whereas the Soviet system represents another (in which the dynamic of industrialisation, with its associated systems of control, has been raised to an exclusive and hitherto unimaginable eminence). As for the 'region' of modernity, this—courtesy of imperialism and multinational capitalism—has been extended to the farthest reaches of the globe.

This theory of modernity is still being defined, but some of its more important features are already clear enough. It is a theory which does not see history as a series of discrete modes of production, and neither does it confine all politics to the economy with its opposed classes. While not dismissive of class as a social category, Heller and Fehér insist on the existence of democratic norms and values which have not all evolved out of socio-economic functions (see also Heller's review of Jean Cohen's *Class and Civil Society* in *New German Critique* 32, Spring–Summer 1984, p. 183). Heller and Fehér forcefully reject the idea of modernity as only a dichotomy between capitalism (the west) and 'socialism' (understood as the Soviet bloc). In this regard the theory is certainly irreconcilable with the muddled kind of theoretical diplomacy on the Soviet system that seems to characterise the thought of anti-'revisionists' like Ralph Miliband—a perspective which seems all too ready (if only by innuendo and reference to France) to associate leftist criticism of the Soviet system with Reaganite anti-communism. The existence of Reaganism cannot from any principled socialist point of view be taken as reason to moderate criticism of the Soviet system (limiting it, as Miliband seems to suggest, to particular 'policies' or 'actions'). On the contrary, rather than raising the whole either/or dichotomy of Cold War thinking into theoretical discussion, it is the fundamental and essential link between socialism and democracy which should be stressed again and again. In the century of Stalin and Pol Pot it is not enough just to say that socialism has, in the words of *New Left Review*, 'a great and abiding need for democracy,' or that 'only socialism can secure democracy's full flowering.' It should be accepted that socialism is inconceivable as distinct from (or as existing in any way prior to) the radicalisation of democracy. (For the last two passages quoted see 'Introduction to Nikolic,' *New Left Review* 150, March/April 1985, p. 133. Miliband's studiously noncommittal words are to be found in his 'The New Revisionism in Britain' in the same issue of NLR, pp. 24–5.)

36   While this point is stressed in the account of everyday life, it is also made in *A Theory of History*, p. 289.

37   In this respect History becomes like fate to the particularistic person. *Everyday Life*, p. 24.

38   *A Theory of History*, p. 30. In general this account of the transformation of everyday life rests on Heller's 'Everyday Life, Rationality of Reason, Rationality of Intellect.'

39   See Raymond Williams, *The Country and the City*, St Albans 1975, pp. 149–57.

40   See, for example, Jürgen Habermas, 'New Social Movements,' *Telos* No.49 (Fall 1981), p. 37.

41   *Everyday Life*, p. 251. The same point is made by Raymond Williams who finds this nostalgia 'universal and persistent' in *The Country and the City*, p. 21.

42   Stephen Graham, *The Gentle Art of Tramping*, London 1927. The passages quoted here are from pp. 73, 24 and 11 respectively.

43   *Everyday Life*, p. 39.

44   *A Theory of Feelings*, p. 184. In the same book Heller writes that 'from the 1930s on the bourgeois world of feeling gradually loses its representative character, and even in artistic creations it is represented only as history, as the past' (p. 192).

45   These remarks of Terry's were quoted in an article by Maureen Cleeve, 'God's Architect' in the *Observer* (colour magazine), 23 September 1984. See also Quinlan Terry, 'Seven Misunderstandings About Classical Architecture' in Frank Russell (ed.), *Quinlan Terry*, London 1981, pp. XII–XIV (sic). The critique of Pevsner—in its theoretically presented version (it circulates more generally as scurrilous accusation)—is to be found in David Watkin, *Morality and Architecture*, London 1977. By mentioning Terry's work I may well put some people in mind of Mussolini's Rome, but I also bring my argument to the ground on which Peter Fuller (a man of the left) seems recently to have found himself close to agreement with Roger Scruton (a man of the far right) in the defence of architectural tradition.

While I do not oppose Fuller's search for cultural value (or, for that matter, his impatience with the vain posturings of much late 1970s poststructuralism), I think he is fundamentally mistaken to join Scruton in grounding value—human, moral or philosophical—in art rather than in the intersubjectivity of everyday life. There is a choice here and, whatever else may be said about them the familiar and well-beaten gestures of particularistic retreat into the national landscape (the kind of retreat that Fuller seems recently to have made) cannot be dignified by just claims of necessity—cultural or otherwise. Fuller accepts Scruton's aesthetics but argues that they point in a different political direction than the extreme authoritarianism espoused by Scruton himself. In my view Scruton is entirely consistent in deriving a Conservative elitism from his theory of cultural value. As for tradition, I accept the stress that Fuller places on its often critical presence in contemporary society and also on related questions of its erosion and preservation. But here again, as I see it, this emphasis should be placed on tradition as it exists (and, indeed, as it really *lives*) in present everyday life, rather than on tradition conceived only as or through art. Readers of Roger Scruton's *The Aesthetics of Architecture* (London, 1979) may object that this book argues its case in relation to everyday life rather than any autonomous sphere of 'art.' But while Scruton does indeed connect aesthetic understanding as it applies to architecture with the 'practical reason' of everyday life, the connection is carefully made and more than a little colonialist in character. While Scruton certainly approaches everyday life, he does so in such a way as to freeze it over. What emerges is an aestheticised, and indeed severely 'classical,' definition of *appropriate* everyday life. For Agnes Heller's discussion of some previous, and far more consequential, attempts to derive philosophy from art see her 'Lukacs and the Holy Family,' *Telos* No.62, Winter 1984–5, pp. 145–54. For Peter Fuller's article on 'Roger Scruton and Right Thinking' see his *Images of God: The Consolations of Lost Illusions*, London 1985, pp. 36–40.

To touch on Terry is also to raise the question of Postmodernism. Considering the country-houses that Terry has already built, it seems possible that his testimony to Lutyens could easily extend to the building of castles (Lutyens's Castle Drogo in Devon may not be 'the last castle in England' for very much longer—cheers from Peterhouse, Cambridge, where castles are second in popularity only to war memorials and little English churches); but if, as Fredric Jameson has recently argued, Postmodernism is the cultural logic of late capitalism, it would be wrong to judge Terry's classical revivalism as only another variation within historical *pastiche*. My point here is not the same as that of David Watkin, who has argued with 'classically' English smugness that 'Terry's architecture…is as different from the so-called neo-classicism of Post-modernism, which is simply meretricious American window dressing, as chalk and cheese' (see Watkin's 'The House of Joy' in the collection edited by Russell and mentioned above). Nevertheless, Terry's assertion of a reimagined traditional lifeworld seems more powerful in its formality, more to do with an elitist and austere *return* to style and a cult of the unique than with its final passing. (See Fredric Jameson, 'Postmodernism, or The Cultural Logic of Late Capitalism,' *New Left Review* 146, July–August 1984, pp. 53–92.)

While Terry's star is still rising (and also being pushed up by a number of Tory authoritarians), there is already little room left for doubting that his style of classical revivalism finds strong resonances beyond itself in British everyday life—and not just in its obvious references to the imperialist past. Compared with any postwar towerblock, Terry's classy and expensive classical buildings may indeed, in a limited but nonetheless strong sense, form a 'popular' style of architecture.

46 Stephen Graham, *Russia and the World*, London 1915, p. 96. Heller's comments on modern nostalgia for war are to be found in *The Power of Shame*, pp. 19–20.

47 Heller talks of the re-enchantment of the lifeworld in *The Power of Shame*, although not in connection with the nation.

48 See Benedict Anderson, *Imagined Communities* (London 1983) for an important argument on racism and the development of its ideologies and stereotypes in the class-based culture of Imperialism (pp. 129–40). There should, however, be no doubt that the continuing use and appeal of racist stereotypes is integrally connected to the sense of nationhood. In this respect I see no contradiction between Anderson's arguments and those which he criticises in Tom Nairn's *The Break-Up of Britain* (London 1977).

49 Arthur Bryant, *The Spirit of England*, London 1982. Bryant's discovery that 'the rocks of Britain have a different past from those of Europe' was made in the light of the Second World War and announced in his *The Story of Britain: Makers of the Realm*, London 1953. The 'Spirit of England' (which, to judge by the title of a book published in 1929, Bryant used to know as 'The Spirit of Conservatism') was similarly 'quickened' by the recent Falklands War. As Bryant writes of Margaret Thatcher, 'By her courage and resolution she reminded a people, who for a generation had forgotten, that the finest moments in their past had been those when they had staked their own safety to defend the liberties of the weak against the strong' (*The Spirit of England*, p. 9). Despite the fully justified incredulity which is likely to be provoked by these remarks from a best-selling 'historian' who was himself made into a knight of the realm, it should be noticed that there is a brutal generosity in the way Bryant wields his nation. While the definition of the mythologised nation is definitely not open to question—indeed, all the present can do is to honour it as an already achieved identity which demands only that it be put into practice in the present— Bryant does nevertheless make a point of offering this nation to all legal subjects. Regardless of race, class or creed, this is your inheritance and you must learn to love and even fear it. Of course the national symbolism is massively loaded, and of course all sorts of present interests and attitudes are sanctioned by it, but Bryant differs—at least in which he is prepared to say—from Conservative figures who would use the nation in an openly

racist way to differentiate authentic from inauthentic subjects in terms of ancestral continuity.

50   Geoffrey Grigson's mapping of *anathoths* (places with an echo) was mentioned in Simon Rae's review of Grigson's *Country Writings* (London 1984), *New Statesman*, 11 January 1985, p. 33.

51   On Ernst Bloch and his *The Principle of Hope* see Wayne Hudson, *The Marxist Philosophy of Ernst Bloch*, London 1982. Fredric Jameson has also written on Bloch in his *Marxism and Form* (Princeton 1974) and *The Political Unconscious* (London 1981). Jameson's extension of the Althusserian definition of ideology is certainly comparable with what I, through Heller, have been calling 'making sense'—both, for example, stress the importance of narrative. Another likely connection concerns the utopian resonance of ideology. Jameson draws on Bloch to suggest that 'all class consciousness—or in other words, all ideology in the strongest sense, including the most exclusive forms of ruling-class consciousness just as much as that of oppositional or oppressed classes—is in its very nature Utopian' (*The Political Unconscious*, p. 289). This is clearly an important proposition, although in my attempts to define the utopian elements—the 'hope'—which are articulated in the symbolism of the British nation I have chosen not to become too involved in defining utopianism as an allegorical characteristic of *all* ideology. The issue is not merely generic to ideology and it seems to me that Jameson risks losing the strength of Bloch's concrete analysis of utopian 'hope' in the formal limbo of Althusser's conceptualisation of ideology as opposed to 'science.' As Pauline Johnson has argued, the Althusserian concept of 'ideology' leaves no space for true knowledge except as it comes in from outside in the form of 'science.' The possibility of everyday life having any emancipatory potential is inconceivable from this perspective—as indeed is the very existence of everyday life. If utopianism is merely a formal principle in the operation of *all* ideology conceived through Althusser's definition, then we can legitimately ask what positive difference it could ever make. See Pauline Johnson, *Marxist Aesthetics: The Foundations within Everyday Life for an Enlightened Consciousness*, London 1984.

2 Trafficking in History

1   SAVE Britain's Heritage published their leaflet 'Save Mentmore for the Nation' in February 1977. These passages are quoted from Marcus Binney's 'Introduction.' The Mentmore story is here reconstructed from its coverage in *The Times*.

2   I quote Céline from Wayne Burn's essay '*Journey to the End of the Night*; a Primer to the Novel.' See James Flynn (ed.), *Understanding Céline*, Seattle 1984, p. 36.

3   On Calke Abbey see Marcus Binney, *Our Vanishing Heritage*, London 1984, pp. 74–83. Here again, my account is also informed by contemporary newspaper coverage. See especially the colour supplement of the *Observer*, 25 March 1984.

4   *Hansard* (Commons), Vol.975, No.79, Col.55.

5   Ibid., Col.69.

6   On Hazells Hall see SAVE Britain's Heritage, *Silent Mansions: More Country Houses at Risk*, London 1981, p. 11.

7   Quoted in *The Times*, 5 July 1980.

8   Quoted in N. Hodgkinson, 'Alice-in-Wonderland World of the National Land Fund,' *The Times*, 22 April 1977.

9   *Hansard* (Lords), Vol.405, No.89, Col.1525.

10   On the passing of hortatory commemoration in the United States see John Brinckerhoff Jackson, *The Necessity of Ruins*, Amherst 1980 (and especially the title essay), pp. 89–102.

11   *Hansard* (Commons), Vol.95, No.79, Col.60.

12   *Hansard* (Lords), Vol.405, No.89, Col.1572.

13   National Heritage Memorial Fund, *Annual Report 1980/81*, London 1981, p. 2.

14   *Guardian*, 23 August 1979.

15   Michael Hunter, 'The Preconditions of Preservation: A Historical Perspective,' in D. Lowenthal and M. Binney (eds.), *Our Past Before Us: Why Do We Save It?*, London 1981, pp. 22–32. For the more pastoral argument see Jan Marsh, *Back to the Land: The Pastoral Impulse in Victorian England from 1880 to 1914*, London 1982 and also Martin J. Wiener, *English Culture and the Decline of the Industrial Spirit 1850–1980*, Cambridge 1981.

16   See Patrick Cormack, *Heritage in Danger*, London 1978. The general information used in this account of preservationism is largely drawn from Cormack's book, David Elliston Allen's *The Naturalist in Britain: A Social History* (Harmondsworth 1978), Robin Fedden's 'official' history of the National Trust, *The Continuing Purpose* (London 1968) and John Lowerson's 'Battles for the Countryside' in F. Gloversmith (ed.), *Class Culture and Social Change: A New View of the 1930's*, Brighton 1980, pp. 258–80.

17   Quoted in Cormack, *Heritage in Danger*, p. 17.

18   Fedden, *The Continuing Purpose*, p. 6.

19   Cormack, *Heritage in Danger*, p. 20.

20   Arthur Bryant, *The Spirit of Conservatism*, London 1929, pp. 74–5.

21   Marsh, *Back to the Land*, pp. 52–3.

22   On the popular land-usage of the interwar years and the conflict between preservationism and the makeshift plotland buildings (shacks, railway carriages etc) which were erected on marginal land, see Dennis Hardy and Colin Ward, *Arcadia for All: The Legacy of a Makeshift Landscape*, London 1984.

23   For a 'socialist' argument that the people are not yet properly 'ready' for their inheritance see C.E.M. Joad, 'The People's Claim' in Clough Williams-Ellis (ed.), *Britain and the Beast*, London 1938, pp. 64–85.

24   I quote this passage from Karl Kraus, 'The world of Posters' in H. Zohn (ed.), *In These Great Times: A Karl Kraus Reader*, Manchester 1984, p. 45.

25   The Shell material discussed in this section cannot be itemised piece by piece. Except where otherwise mentioned all images and writing described were examined (in 1980) in the British Petroleum archive at BP's Britannic House, London.

26   Walter Benjamin, 'The Work of Art in the Age of Mechanical
     Reproduction,' *Illuminations*, London 1973, p. 235.

27   On the political landscape (and the part played in it by boundaries) see John
     Brinckerhoff Jackson, *Discovering the Vernacular Landscape*, London 1984.

28   It should certainly be mentioned that while the interrelation between
     'nature' and 'technology' forms one theme in Shell's advertising reper-
     toire, there is also a contemporary series of advertisements which appeal
     to the technological imagination alone.

29   While Ogilvy and Mather, the advertising agency currently holding the
     Shell contract in Britain, was awarded the Creative Circle Silver award
     for these advertisements in 1985, there were contemporary conservation-
     ists who had a different view of the Mosmorran plant. Scottish Friends of
     the Earth insisted that 'You can't say a project is environmentally acceptable
     just by taking a picture of the nearest convenient hill' and pointed out that
     the gas liquids plant at Mosmorran exists as a massive eyesore—visible from
     Edinburgh and shooting flames two hundred feet high from its chimneys.
     The Advertising Standards Authority were apparently unimpressed by
     the complaint (reported in *New Statesman*, 22 March 1985). As Ogilvy and
     Mather know so well, it's all a matter of perspective.

30   Some important remarks on the homogenisation of space and 'The
     Organisation of Territory' are to be found in Guy Debord, *Society of the
     Spectacle*, Detroit 1970.

31   The figures for 1974 are quoted by Marcus Binney in *Save Mentmore for the
     Nation*; those for 1983 come from the English Tourist Board's *Sightseeing
     in 1983*, London 1984.

32   The significance of the car was disputed in the interwar years. For
     G.K. Chesterton the car was an emblem of 'the mechanical forces which
     are laying waste to this country.' The fact that the modern car 'com-
     pletely shuts in the motorist' is proof that these enclosed vehicles are
     really the tanks of an invading army:

     > So the new and narrow type of trader or traveller spreads ruin and
     > destruction along his essentially solitary journey, precisely because it is
     > essentially solitary; and the more introspectively he looks inward at his
     > speedometer or his road book, the more certainly and sweepingly does
     > he in practice wither the woods on the remote horizon or shake the very
     > shrines in the heart of every human town.
     >
     >   The roads designed by this spirit are not roads to places; but through
     > places. It does not entertain the old idea of reaching the gates of a town,
     > but rather of shooting a town full of holes by which it can reach out
     > beyond.

     (from Chesterton's 'Introduction' to Council for the Preservation of Rural
     England, *The Penn Country of Buckinghamshire*, London 1933, pp. 7–8.)
         J.B. Priestley took up the preservationist cause with comparable ardour
     in the thirties, but he tried desperately hard to see the positive side of this
     new experience of 'speed':

I shall be told that the newer generations care nothing for the beauty of the countryside, that all they want is to go rushing about on motor-cycles or in fast cars. Speed is not one of my gods; rather one of my devils; but we must give this devil his due. I believe that swift motion across a countryside does not necessarily take away all appreciation of its charm. It depends on the nature of the country. With some types of landscape there is a definite gain simply because we are moving so swiftly across the face of the country. There is a certain kind of pleasant but dullish, rolling country, not very attractive to the walker or slow traveller, that becomes alive if you go quickly across it, for it is turned into a kind of sculptured landscape. As your car rushes along the rolling road, it is as if you were passing a hand over a relief map. Here, obviously there has been a gain, not a loss, and this is worth remembering. The newer generations, with their passion for speed, are probably far more sensitive than they are thought to be. Probably they are all enjoying aesthetic experiences that so far they have been unable to communicate to the rest of us.

(quoted from Priestley's 'Introduction' to Batsford's *The Beauty of Britain: A Pictorial Survey*, London 1935, pp. 2–3).

33 Harry Batsford, *How to See the Country*, London 1940 and Edmund Vale, *How to Look at Old Buildings*, London 1940.

34 Batsford, *How to See the Country*, p. 3.

35 J. Wentworth Day, 'The Most English Corner of all England,' in Richard Harman (ed.), *Countryside Mood*, London 1943, pp. 173–4. A similar contempt for 'those who like beauty-spots but are completely bored by beauty' (ie the urban working and lower-middle classes) informed the advocacy of a policy to establish National Parks (another of Hugh Dalton's achievements) in the years following the Second World War. As Ivor Brown wrote 'A National Park must never be just a national car-park.' Brown may have argued for a balance between the needs of the soft, unimaginative 'beauty spot drone' and those of the person who can really take to the hills, but there is never any doubt which side he is really on. See Ivor Brown, 'National Trust and National Parks,' in James Lees-Milne (ed.), *The National Trust: A Record of Fifty Years Achievement*, London 1945, pp. 1–8.

There is a remarkable persistence to this sort of snobbery, with its often desperate attempts to distinguish what it values as the authentic cultural relation to traditional town and landscape from the gawping curiosity of the messy democratic masses. Peter Fuller, for example, has recently found occasion to praise John Piper, a long-established Shell artist. Fuller writes that 'Piper was not interested in the blinkered glances of the busy, snap-happy tourist.' This is a curious claim, since Piper—and not only in his employment with Shell—might reasonably be thought to have played a part in *creating* the clichés (if this is what they are) of modern touristic understanding and of helping to put the 'blinkers' onto the very 'glance' at which Fuller sneers so disdainfully. As for fond John Betjeman, he may not have been so 'snap-happy' himself, but as time went on this was only because there was a bevy of technicians to hold the television cameras as he trailed from little English church to little English church. It is hard to figure out what Fuller considers to be the superiority of Piper and Betjeman's self-styled 'church-crawling'—non-touristic, as Fuller insists, but still capable of taking in ten village churches in a day. Is it really only that Piper (far from just having gone to the same school as Fuller) had read Ruskin and therefore knew how to take what Fuller knows to be a truly *English* perspective on 'the particular essence of a given place...'? Is this really only another claim for the superiority of the cultured nation over the unsanctioned enthusiasm of mere society? Here again, I think, we see the consequences of grounding a theory of cultural value in art as distinct from present, although certainly also historical, everyday life. See 'Pleasing Decay: John Piper' in Peter Fuller, *Images of God: The Consolations of Lost Illusions*, London 1985, pp. 92–7.

36 Wyndham Lewis, *Rotting Hill*, London 1951.
37 The phrase recurs as a motif in Flann O'Brien, *The Poor Mouth*, London 1975.
38 See Department of the Environment, *What is Our Heritage? United Kingdom Achievements for European Architectural Heritage Year 1975*, London 1975.
39 I take the phrase 'age of dead statues' from Ariel Dorfmann and Armand Mattelart, *How to Read Donald Duck: Imperialist Ideology in the Disney Comic*, New York 1975.
40 Quoted on the front page of Cormack, *Heritage in Danger*.
41 On Technostyle see Jackson, *Discovering the Vernacular Landscape*, pp. 113–24.
42 Roy Strong, 'Home is where the art is,' *The Times*, 10 Nov 1984.
43 Cormack, *Heritage in Danger*, pp. 51–2.
44 Agatha Christie, *At Bertram's Hotel*, London 1984, p. 11.
45 Reported in the *Guardian*, 13 March 1980.
46 Esmond Knight, 'The Archer's Tale,' BBC2, 30 October 1980.
47 Jean-Paul Sartre, *Anti-Semite and Jew*, New York 1948. Sartre writes as follows:

> In a bourgeois society it is the constant movement of people, the collective currents, the styles, the customs, all these things, that in effect create values. The value of poems, of furniture, of houses, of landscapes derives in large part from the spontaneous condensations that fall on these objects like a light dew; they are strictly national and result from the normal functioning of a traditionalist and historical society. To be a Frenchman is not merely to have been born in France, to vote and pay taxes; it is above all to have the use and sense of these values. And when a man shares in their creation, he is in some degree reassured about himself; he has a justification for existence through a sort of adhesion to the whole of society. To know how to appreciate a piece of Louis Seize furniture, the delicacy of a saying by Chamfort, a landscape of the Ile de France, a painting by Claude Lorraine, is to affirm and to feel that one belongs to French society; it is to renew a tacit social contract with all members of

that society. At one stroke the vague contingency of our existence vanishes and gives way to the necessity of an existence by right. Every Frenchman who is moved by reading Villon or by looking at the Palace of Versailles becomes a public functionary and the subject of imprescriptible rights.

Now a Jew is a man who is refused access to these values on principle…He can indeed acquire all the goods he wants, lands and castles if he has the wherewithal; but at the very moment when he becomes a legal proprietor the property undergoes a subtle change in meaning and value.

Only a Frenchman, the son of a Frenchman, son or grandson of a peasant, is capable of possessing it really. To own a hut in a village, it is not enough to have bought it with hard cash. One must know all the neighbours, their parents and grandparents, the surrounding farms, the beeches and oaks of the forest; one must know how to work, fish, hunt; one must have made notches in the trees in childhood and have found them enlarged in ripe old age. You may be sure that the Jew does not fulfil these conditions. For that matter, perhaps the Frenchman doesn't either, but he is granted a certain indulgence. There is a French way and a Jewish way of confusing oats and wheat. (pp. 80–3)

48 *The Birmingham Evening Mail*, 6 May 1980.
49 Edited by Roy Faiers, *This England* is published from Cheltenham, Gloucester, for 'all who love our green and pleasant land.' *Heritage: The British Review* is edited for a comparable readership by Peter Shephard and published from London. Both publications testify amply to the cultural psychosis of modern English/British nationalism.
50 Franco Moretti, *Signs Taken for Wonders*, London 1983, p. 190.
51 Raymond Williams points to the peculiarity of this sense of the 'timeless' which is ensconced where a sense of history should be, in *The English Novel from Dickens to Lawrence*, Harmondsworth 1974, p. 89.
52 Donald Horne, *The Great Museum: The Re-presentation of History*, London 1984, p. 249.
53 See the passage on 'Old Saint Pauls' which is excerpted from Twain's English Notebook in B. DeVoto's edition of Mark Twain, *Letters from the Earth*, Greenwich (Connecticut) 1962, pp. 140–3.
54 Quoted from Heller's essay 'George Lukács and Irma Seidler' in Agnes Heller (ed.), *Lukács Revalued*, Oxford 1983, p. 44.
55 On Zimbabwe see E.R. Chamberlain, *Preserving the Past*, London 1979, pp. 27–35.
56 See John Stevenson, *Popular Disturbances in England 1700–1870*, London 1979, p. 47.
57 Cormack, *Heritage in Danger*, p. 14.
58 Stanley Baldwin, *On England*, London 1926, p. 7. See also Bill Schwarz, 'The Language of Constitutionalism; Baldwinite Conservatism,' in *Formations of Nation and People*, London 1984.
59 H.A.L. Fisher, 'The Beauty of England' in CPRE, *The Penn Country of Buckinghamshire*, p. 15.
60 Hermann Glaser, *The Cultural Roots of National Socialism*, London 1978, p. 61.
61 Peter Scott as quoted in the Foreword to Harman, *Countryside Mood*, p. 5.

62   Rex Weldon Finn, *The English Heritage*, London 1948, p. 22.

63   Harman, *Countryside Mood*, p. 5.

64   Two important essays on the elaboration of tradition within imperialism are Bernard S. Cohen, 'Representing Authority in Victorian India' and Terence Ranger, 'The Invention of Tradition in Colonial Africa,' both in Eric Hobsbawm and Terence Ranger (eds.), *The Invention of Tradition*, Cambridge 1983, pp. 165–264.

65   Rainer Maria Rilke, *The Notebook of Malte Laurids Brigge*, Oxford 1984, p. 20. Parts of this chapter first appeared in a paper by Michael Bommes and myself called ' "Charms of Residence"; the public and the past' in R. Johnson et al. (eds.), *Making Histories*, London 1982.

3 Coming Back to the Shores of Albion

1   Mary Butts, *The Crystal Cabinet*, London 1937, p. 20.

2   Ibid., p. 21.

3   Ibid., p. 16.

4   I take the idea of non-synchronism from Ernst Bloch. See his 'Non-synchronism and the obligation to its dialectics' in *New German Critique*, No.11, 1977, pp. 22–38.

5   Mary Butts, *Armed With Madness*, New York 1928, p. 134.

6   Mary Butts, *Warning to Hikers*, London 1932, p. 6.

7   *The Crystal Cabinet*, p. 62.

8   In the closing pages of her *Scenes from the Life of Cleopatra* (New York 1974 [reprint of 1935 edition]) Butts considers the historical reputation of a woman who has been represented entirely by men. The same process is repeated on a different scale in the case of Butts herself. The text of *The Crystal Cabinet* was softened at the suggestion of Angus Davidson and Father Bernard Walke (an Anglo-Catholic priest at Marazion who became important to Mary Butts in her last years), and what little reputation Butts has had since her death seems mostly to have fallen into two related categories. In the first Butts appears as the alluring and fascinating object of a male romanticisation which can be both gossipy and possessive (see Douglas Goldring, to an extent Virgil Thompson, and perhaps more recently R.H. Byington and Glen Morgan). In the second, Butts appears as the target of rabidly misogynistic attack from men who take evident pleasure in remembering her as a 'maggot' (Aleister Crowley—see R. Blaser's Afterword in *Imaginary Letters*) or as an 'old bag' (William Plomer, the author of *Museum Pieces* [1952] with its portrait of Lydia Delap). As Butts says of Cleopatra, 'there is a tradition of memoirs,' but it is such that it is 'hardly the testimony to take seriously.' Hopefully more adequate accounts are yet to come, for there are certainly many parts of this story which remain untold.

9   *The Crystal Cabinet*, p. 20.

10   Mary Butts, *Ashe of Rings*, London 1933 (Revised version of 1925 edition), p. 267.

11 *The Crystal Cabinet*, pp. 266–7.

12 *Ashe of Rings*, pp. 114 and 80.

13 For this biographical information see Douglas Goldring's *South Lodge*, London 1943; *Odd Man Out*, London 1935; and *The Nineteen Twenties*, London 1945. Also R.H. Byington and Glen E. Morgan, 'Selections from the Journal of Mary Butts,' in *Art and Literature* (Lausanne) Vol.7, Winter 1965, pp. 163–79. Cecil Maitland, Mary Butts's apparently very dissolute and war-damaged companion of the early twenties, can be traced to a fishing village in Brittany where he and a few other deracinated British drifters (*les mauvais anglais* as the locals knew them) were found in impoverished but thoroughly instituted, and in Maitland's case apparently terminal, intoxication—by the busy Goldring once again, who described what he saw in *Northern Lights and Southern Shade*, Boston and New York 1926, pp. 169–90.

14 See Robin Blaser's 'Afterword' to Mary Butts, *Imaginary Letters*, Vancouver 1979 (reprint of 1928 edition).

15 One such translation of Meleager was by Richard Aldington (see his *Medallions in Clay*, New York 1921) whereas Cavalcanti was translated by Ezra Pound. One of the bombs fell on a house in Mecklenburg Square next to that in which H.D. had a flat. Aldington was H.D.'s husband at the time and he is a good candidate for the man who returned to the damaged flat and 'gave a decisive football kick with his army boot' to a volume of Browning that lay on the floor, demanding dramatically 'What is the use of this now?' See H.D., 'A Note on Poetry' in W.R. Benet and N.H. Pearson (eds.) *Oxford Anthology of American Literature*, New York 1938. This was a time when the 'decentering of the subject' was rather more than a preoccupation of academic cultural theory.

16 Wyndham Lewis, 'The Pole' in *The Wild Body*, London 1927, pp. 108–12.

17 *Armed With Madness*, p. 153.

18 See especially the story 'Widdershins' in Mary Butts, *Several Occasions*, London 1932.

19 Mary Butts, *Speed the Plough and Other Stories*, London, 1923, p. 13.

20 *Ashe of Rings*, p. 174.

21 *Armed With Madness*, p. 36.

22 *Speed the Plough*, p. 15.

23 Ibid., p. 16.

24 Mary Butts, *Death of Felicity Taverner*, London 1932, p. 51.

25 Filiation/affiliation—the importance of this polarity in early twentieth century modernism is most interestingly discussed in Edward Said, *The World, the Text and the Critic*, London 1983.

26 See Stephen Graham, *The Gentle Art of Tramping*, London 1927 and Arthur Bryant, *The Spirit of Conservatism*, London 1929, p. 75.

27 See Henry Fairlie, 'The BBC,' in Hugh Thomas (ed.), *The Establishment*, London 1959.

28 See David Elliston Allen, *The Naturalist in Britain: A Social History*, Harmondsworth 1976.

29   J.B. Priestley, Review of *Speed the Plough*, *London Mercury*, Vol.VIII, No.43, May 1923, p. 99.

30   See Jerry Zaslove, 'The Death of Memory: The Memory of Death: Céline's Mourning for the Masses…,' in James Flynn (ed.), *Understanding Céline*, Seattle 1984, pp. 187–243.

31   Arthur Rimbaud, 'Historic Evening' in Louise Varese (tr.), *Illuminations and Other Prose Poems*, New York 1957, p. 113.

32   Journal entry for 9 May 1930 (in Byington and Morgan, p. 175).

33   G.K. Chesterton, *The Napoleon of Notting Hill*, Harmondsworth 1982, p. 23.

34   *Armed With Madness*, p. 13.

35   John Cowper Powys, *Wolf Solent* (1929), Harmondsworth 1978, pp. 13 and 19.

36   *Armed With Madness*, p. 91.

37   See John Bird, *Percy Grainger*, London 1976.

38   As we have seen, Shell issued a series of advertisements on 'green roads' in the early sixties. R. Hippisley Cox, *The Green Roads of England* (London 1914) was being reprinted through to the late forties and, as Martin Wiener points out, Ramsay MacDonald used to dream of 'green roads' while at the front bench in the House of Commons. See M. Wiener, *English Culture and the Decline of the Industrial Spirit 1850–1980*, Cambridge 1981, p. 121.

39   *Armed With Madness*, pp. 104 and 105–6.

40   This theme is repeated in various short stories—particularly one called 'Green' in which a bedroom is described as follows: 'Their bedroom had a rose-brick fireplace and a line of persian prints. Under the mirror, piled in a shell, were strings of glass flowers and fruit. Everything was in order, polished, and very still…There were folded silks, bedroom books: two more murders, a County History…Propriety, simplicity, the routine of country-house life' (*Several Occasions*, p. 174).

41   H.D., 'The Flowering of the Rod' in *Trilogy*, New York 1973, p. 172. The passage quoted from Butts is from *Death of Felicity Taverner*, p. 183.

42   The journal entry opens as follows:

> 'At Gertrude Stein's: Catalogue
> Two cups and saucers of rose porcelain, and medallion heads in profile in the box.
> A blue and white and crystal glass house.
> A gold bird in a gold cage that sings a song or a few notes from time to time
> Two altar monuments, a leaf composed of petals in gold foil,
> And some in enamel black and red…'

> (quoted in Byington and Morgan).

> The Butts passage is quoted from *Death of Felicity Taverner*, p. 80.

43   *Death of Felicity Taverner*, p. 19.

44   *Ashe of Rings*, p. 231.

45   *Armed With Madness*, p. 44.

46 *Death of Felicity Taverner*, p. 191.

47 *Imaginary Letters*, p. 53.

48 Jane Harrison, *Ancient Art and Ritual*, London 1913, p. 199.

49 *Death of Felicity Taverner*, p. 185.

50 Ibid., p. 32 and *Ashe of Rings*, p. 189.

51 Mary Butts, 'The Magic of Person and Place,' *The Bookman*, Vol.85, December 1933, pp. 141–3.

52 See Mary Butts, 'The Art of Montague James,' *London Mercury*, Vol.29, 1934, pp. 306–17.

53 Mary Butts, *Traps for Unbelievers*, London 1932, p. 25.

54 Mary Butts, *Several Occasions*, p. 21.

55 Mary Butts, '"Ghosties and Ghoulies"; Uses of the Supernatural in English Fiction,' *The Bookman*, February 1933, p. 435.

56 *Ashe of Rings*, p. 59.

57 Such demonisation—the creation of a malevolent or inadequate 'outside' principle against which a precious Englishness is defined—need not be confined to the perspectives of race or class. For T.H. White the left-wing intellectual could play the part amply:

> It is astonishing to see the intellectuals, who know all about communism and the European situation, trying to live their own lives, even indoors. They lean against the mantel-piece; at the wrong angle, and the fender slips, and bang goes one of the candlesticks—broken. They can't cope even with their own centres of gravity. I saw a presumably 'modern' boy the other day who was so little conscious of the position of his own body that he fell backwards off a chair while thinking of something else. All truly good and great men are interested in laying and lighting fires...Get your communist to light a fire in an English interior grate. He clumsily lumps on, criss-cross and anyhow, a few random logs and hunks, applies half a dozen matches, and finally has to go for the paraffin...The trouble is that they don't do enough things with their bodies...How safe would Karl Marx have been, I wonder, walking in a line of guns. Would he have mooned along star-gazing, and left a loaded gun against the wall at lunch, and shot his own foot off climbing over a stile? I don't mind a great man being a communist, so long as he is a great man...

See T.H. White, *England Have My Bones* (1936), London 1981, p. 194.

58 *Warning to Hikers*, p. 13.

59 Mary Butts, *Several Occasions*, pp. 57–70.

60 *Ashe of Rings*, p. 181.

61 *Warning to Hikers*, p. 26.

62 Simone Weil, *The Need for Roots* (1949), London 1952.

63 Eric Gill, *Autobiography*, London 1940. A reference to Gill's work informs the journalism of the underrated Colin Ward. See, for example, 'Making the best of it,' *New Society*, 22 March 1984.

64 *Warning to Hikers*, p. 6.

65 Ibid., p. 12.

66 See Eric Hobsbawm, *Industry and Empire*, Harmondsworth 1977, p. 169.

67 This early and short-lived marriage left bad feelings and was followed by a long period of mutual recrimination. Rodker had been firing away at Mary Butts—veiled accusations of addiction, suggestions that she was the neglectful mother of his daughter etc—for years before *Death of Felicity Taverner* was published. Readers who would follow this story in its dubious *à clef* presentation might consider Rodker's *Adolphe 1920* (London, 1929) with its portrayal of 'Angela,' a fast-moving figure who is said to live in the past while at the same time craving the future, and who feels no responsibility to the present except to take it as a passing moment of excitation. 'Merciful forgetfulness,' writes a man who himself might be asked a question or two, 'how much she had to be grateful to it.' The real attack comes later; it can be found in Rodker's anonymously published *Memoirs of Other Fronts* (London 1932). This doleful book contains an interesting account of Rodker's own experience as a 'deserter' and imprisoned conscientious objector during the First World War. In its closing section, however, the book launches into 'Muriel', and here there is muck enough for the largest appetite. If Kralin is in any sense the retaliation, then at least part of the counter-accusation seems to have been that if Butts herself is indeed committed to culture (the 'meaning of meaning' which Kralin denies) of a bourgeois kind, at least she didn't turn herself into a Soviet apologist. By this time Rodker the anarchist (who was to be a member of Freud's London circle during the Second World War) was more interested in psychoanalysis. But this too could probably have been grist to Butts's grinding mill—more alien 'abstraction' against the essential green world of belonging.

68 *Death of Felicity Taverner*, p. 52.

69 C.E.M. Joad, 'The People's Claim' in Clough Williams-Ellis (ed.), *Britain and the Beast*, London 1938, p. 72.

70 *Death of Felicity Taverner*, pp. 40, 69.

71 Ibid., p. 104.

72 Ibid., p. 24.

73 Jean Paul Sartre, *Anti-Semite and Jew*, New York 1948. M. Wiener mentions a comparable British anti-Semitism of the thirties. See his *English Culture and the Decline of the Industrial Spirit*, p. 107.

74 Ibid., p. 18.

75 For the British version see any issue of *The Salisbury Review*.

76 See the letter to F.J. Warburg (October 22, 1948) in *The Collected Essays, Journalism and Letters of George Orwell; Volume Four: In Front of Your Nose 1945–1950*, Harmondsworth 1984, p. 507. The review of Sartre's *Portrait of the Antisemite* is in the same volume, pp. 511–13.

77 In *Armed With Madness* Butts complains of 'a pretence made that all is for the best inside the vast, roaring, fortuitous wilderness: that Epping Forrest (sic) is the true green-wood, and Southend virgin sea' (p. 167). Too bad for H.V. Morton, or more accurately for the 'little London factory hand' Morton met in the First World War—a man who, when prompted, visualised the England of the 'England Wants You' poster not

as London, 'not as his own street, but as Epping Forest, the green place where he spent Bank Holidays.' See H.V. Morton, *In Search of England*, London 1927, p. 2.

78 Appropriately Butts's writings found a secret readership in North America, although not one which was necessarily complicit in their more dubious nationalist resonances. They were taken up in the fifties by a group of poets based in Berkeley, California (Robert Duncan, Jack Spicer, Robin Blaser, Helen Adam among others). These poets may have found in Mary Butts a charismatic literary lineage—a figure and a writing which had not been disenchanted by academic exegesis—but with an interest in the styles of magic they also discovered a source for their own poetics in the sudden and transformational quality of Butts's unstable world. As Duncan has put it, 'Mary Butts's *Armed With Madness* incited us all to traffic in myths and to derive a "scene" by charging every possibility with overtones and undertones, to make thunderheads, storm weather—but to hold it unreleased, for the power's sake, living in actual life as if it were a dream' (quoted in Ekbert Faas, *Young Robert Duncan: Portrait of the Poet as Homosexual in Society*, Santa Barbara 1983, p. 227). Meanwhile back in the old country, where a very different reading becomes necessary, all the indications are that the thunderhead has broken. I owe thanks to Robin Blaser who once gave me an old copy of *Armed With Madness*, thus causing the curiosity which, six years later, occasioned this essay. I should also make the point—hopefully an obvious one—that a poetics which works with the particular is not necessarily 'particularistic.'

79 I am concerned here with what I take to be the weakest aspect, or rather the fatal flaw, of Martin Wiener's *English Culture and the Decline of the Industrial Spirit 1850–1980*.

This essay started as a talk which I gave at a History Workshop Conference on Patriotism, 11 March 1984. While my thanks are due to the people who took part in the discussion on that day, and also to Raphael Samuel who made some useful suggestions subsequently, my greatest debt is certainly to Camilla Bagg, daughter of Mary Butts, without whose generous conversation I would have been unable to get even as far as I have towards an understanding of these writings.

4 A Blue Plaque for the Labour Movement

1 Wal Hannington, *Unemployed Struggles 1919–1936*, London 1977, pp. 77–8.

2 Quoted in Kevin Lynch, *What Time is this Place?* Cambridge (Massachusetts) 1976, p. 36.

3 I am drawing from Jürgen Habermas here. See especially *Legitimation Crisis*, London 1976.

4 J.H. Plumb, *The Death of the Past*, London 1969, p. 17.

5 In her *A Theory of History* Agnes Heller describes 'the sense of historical existence' as follows: 'We experience change in values and institutions,

we experience our fate and the fate of others, even of remote peoples, as being interwoven. New events and experiences happen to us, and we participate in new undertakings or we suffer because established ones are shaken. We are the victims of world-catastrophes and we turn our faces towards the first glimmers of the dawn. We cherish hopes concerning the years to come and we despair when they betray our expectations. We ask: what is the sense of all this? We ask whether our children will live in a different world, in one better or worse than ours. We ask whether a better future is possible at all; and if the answer is in the affirmative, what we can do for it, if in the negative, when and how we "missed the bus"' (p. 218).

6 Edward Shils, *Tradition*, London 1981, p. 59.

7 Valerie Chancellor, *History for their Masters*, Bath 1970.

8 Frances Fitzgerald, *America Revised: History Schoolbooks in the Twentieth Century*, New York 1980, p. 17.

9 Heller, *A Theory of History*, p. 67.

10 I follow Agnes Heller's critical definition of 'philosophy of history' here. 'All philosophies raise the question of the sense of human existence. Human existence over the last two hundred years is experienced as historical experience. Philosophies of history answer the questions about the sense of historical existence and so they satisfy the needs of our times. But they claim to answer another question as well, a question about the sense of history. In this claim resides the ambiguity of all philosophies of history: they equate the sense of historical existence with the "sense of history"' (*A Theory of History*, p. 218).

11 See Martin Walker, 'The lord of the manor sets up house,' *Guardian*, 28 December 1983.

12 Heller, *A Theory of History*, p. 42.

An earlier version of this essay was first published in *Formations of Nation and People* (London 1984).

5 Falling Back Together in the 1980s

1 Quoted from Thomas Hobbes, 'Elements of Philosophy' in W. Molesworth (ed.), *The English Works of Thomas Hobbes*, London 1839, Vol.1, pp. 136–7.

2 I quote this from Chronicle's review of 'The year they raised the *Mary Rose*,' BBC2, December 24 1982.

3 Ernle Bradford, *The Story of the Mary Rose*, London 1982, p. 197.

4 This speech is reprinted as an appendix in Anthony Barnett, *Iron Britannia*, London 1982, pp. 149–53.

5 Theodor Adorno, 'Requiem for Odette' in *Minima Moralia*, London 1974, p. 189.

6 On this crisis of 'historicity'—of 'society's placing of its own reference to its own temporality'—see Cornelius Castoriadis, 'The Crisis of Western Societies,' *Telos* 53, Fall 1982, pp. 17–28. As Castoriadis has argued

elsewhere, a major political effect of the crisis of 'progress' is to discredit the existing potentials for an alternative future. Camped out on the edge of the abyss, crisis becomes a form of government.

7   See Heller, *A Theory of History*, pp. 218 and 328–33.

8   On 'Co-presence' see A. Giddens, *The Constitution of Society*, Cambridge 1984, pp. 64–8.

9   While this generalised sense of national identity casts its accommodating net widely, it still operates on a principle of exclusion rather than only inclusion. That some groups are constituted as 'other' and outside the 'homogeneous we' (Enoch Powell's phrase) is clearly evident in the links connecting nationalism and racism.

10 Alexander McKee, *How We Found the Mary Rose*, London 1982; Ernle Bradford, *The Story of the Mary Rose*; Margaret Rule, *The Mary Rose: The Excavation and Raising of Henry VIII's Flagship*, London 1982.

11 McKee, p. 38.

12 Rule, pp. 33–4.

13 For a useful discussion of Gramsci's concept see David Forgacs, 'National–Popular: Genealogy of a Concept' in *Formations of Nation and People*, London 1984, pp. 83–98.

14 McKee, p. 37.

15 Ibid., p. 121.

16 Bradford, p. 101.

17 This question of *action* finds its cultural equivalent in the related terms of *adventure*. Imperialist ideologies of adventure (the Rider Haggard tradition) remain active in historical memory even though the prospects of realisation are less good these days. Opportunities for mercenaries and 'soldiers of fortune' exist in too many places, but round-the-world-sailing and diving after wrecks (for Second World War 'Russian Gold' or for 'History') are becoming increasingly prominent as bearers of such ideas of adventure.

18 Bradford, p. 114.

19 Arthur Bryant, *The Story of England: Makers of the Realm*, Arthur Bryant 1953, pp. 13–14.

20 Heller, *A Theory of History*, p. 201.

21 Quoted from 'The Kingfishers' in Charles Olson, *In Cold Hell, in Thicket*, San Francisco 1967, p. 13.

22 Ernst Bloch's path-breaking work—arguing against the orthodox Marxism of the time—on the emerging culture of National Socialism, written in the 1920s and early 1930s, was published as *Erbschaft Dieser Zeit* ('Heritage of these Times') in 1935. No full English translation has been published, although a useful excerpt appeared as 'Non-synchronism and dialectics' in *New German Critique* No.11, Spring 1977. A full French translation has been published as *Héritage de ce Temps*, Paris 1978.

23 Ralph Miliband, 'The New Revisionism in Britain,' *New Left Review* 150, March/April 1985, p. 18.

24 Anthony Barnett, *Iron Britannia*, p. 80.

25 See Jeremy Seabrook's *What Went Wrong? Working People and the Ideals of the Labour Movement* (London 1978), *Unemployment* (London 1982), *Working*

Class Childhood (London 1982). A good (and representatively) critical review of the last of these three books is by Jerry White and published in *History Workshop Journal* No.15, Spring 1983, pp. 183–7. In my reading, Seabrook's work testifies with considerable accuracy to a much wider crisis in the labour movement's relation to history and its own historical memory. It does not, therefore, seem fully adequate just to vilify Seabrook himself—as if all this hankering was only the unfortunate result of personal or stylistic perspective. The question 'What went wrong?' was a good one to ask of the post-war Labour Party, and it is not just Seabrook who is badly in need of a future-orientated sequel. Seabrook dislikes attempts to portray socialism as a 'project,' but that is exactly what it must become if it is to achieve a theory of history and also a politics which will take it beyond romantic and mournful yearning for the dislocated traditions of a far from universal working class constituency.

26 Zygmunt Bauman, *Memories of Class: The Pre-History and After-Life of Class*, London 1982. I draw especially on pp. 192–4. I am also influenced here by a conversation which I had with Bauman shortly after the strike collapsed.

27 Alain Touraine quoted in Bauman, p. 162.

    Parts of this essay were first published in *The Ethical Record* (publication of the South Place Ethical Society), Vol.88, No.7, July/August 1983.

6 Moving House in a Welfare State

1 *Miss Savidge* is a film of twenty five minutes in length. Directed by Witold Stok, written and produced by Witold and Danuta Stok, the film was completed in early 1984 and shown at a History Workshop conference on patriotism at Ruskin College, Oxford on March 10th. On May 5th it was screened at the Wells Centre with Miss Savidge herself in attendance. Both screenings were followed by interested discussion. At the time of writing no distribution arrangements have been made (one potential distributor, apparently echoing the words of a commissioning editor for Channel Four, found the film very good but 'insufficiently political'...).

2 Quoted from Robert Bly (tr.), *Selected Poems of Rainer Maria Rilke*, New York 1981, p. 47.

3 When we talked in Wells on May 6th, Miss Savidge described how in the war she had been employed making technical drawings of De Havilland and Mosquito warplanes. She commented that there were scarcely any right angles in these designs, and that she was well prepared, therefore, when it came to mapping her equally erratic pre-technological house. At a later meeting (28/7/84), it also emerged that Miss Savidge had attended evening classes at a London art college and that her first employment had been in wallpaper and silk design.

4 Edmund Husserl, *The Crisis of European Sciences and Transcendental Philosophy*, Evanston 1970, p. 105.

5 I quote Ernst Bloch's 'Small Town (1924)' from the French translation of Bloch's *Héritage de ce Temps*, Paris 1978, p. 26.

6   On these 'model dwellings' see Gareth Stedman Jones, *Outcast London*, Harmondsworth, 1984. Also Jerry White, *Rothschild Buildings, Life in an East End Tenement Block 1887–1920*, London 1980.

7   Alvin Gouldner, 'The Secrets of Organisations,' *Social Welfare Forum*, New York 1963, pp. 163–77.

8   See Claus Offe, *Contradictions of the Welfare State*, London 1984. The same arguments are considered in Zygmunt Bauman, *Memories of Class: The Pre-History and After-Life of Class*, London 1982.

7 The Ghosting of the Inner City

1   George Orwell, *Nineteen Eighty-Four*, Harmondsworth 1983.

2   J.H. Plumb, *The Death of the Past*, London 1969.

3   Raymond Williams, *Towards 2000*, London 1983.

4   Sir Walter Besant, *London North of the Thames*, London 1911, pp. 573–87.

5   See Agnes Heller, *A Radical Philosophy*, Oxford 1984, pp. 15–17.

6   Twenty-one year old Colin Roach died of shotgun wounds in the foyer of Stoke Newington police station late on January 12th 1983. Considerable protest followed and demands were made for a full public enquiry into the incident. Roach's death raised, once again, serious questions about police conduct towards the black population in the area. Was this another case like that of the White family who in 1982 were awarded £50,000 exemplary damages against the Stoke Newington police who illegally entered their home in 1976, beat them up and prosecuted them on rigged charges? While the inquest into Roach's death (held after considerable controversy in June '83) delivered a verdict of suicide, the jurors wrote to the Home Secretary expressing their 'deep distress' at the police's handling of the case. True to form, Leon Brittan decided against a public enquiry, referring the letter instead to the police so that they could investigate themselves.

7   See Charles Thompson, 'Putting them back the way they were,' *Heritage Outlook*, Vol.4, No.3 (May/June 1984), pp. 58–9.

8   Paul Joyce's *A Guide to Abney Park Cemetery* was published in 1984 by the London Borough of Hackney and a voluntary association of fairly recent origin called Save Abney Park Cemetery. Joyce's booklet treats the cemetery as part historical testimony and part wilderness—preservation and conservation together. The Hackney Society has also found occasion to comment on Abney Park Cemetery in its survey of the *Parks and Open Spaces in Hackney* (London 1980). There is little satisfaction here for those who make the error of mistaking this 'open space' for a cemetery rather than a park. As it is put, 'any attempt to "tidy up" this park should be treated with suspicion. Yet soon after Hackney took the cemetery over, flowerbeds were inserted into its main avenues as if no public park could be complete without them, thus displaying a simplistic and uniform attitude to park design which it is hoped will in future be avoided' (p. 7). The real point, however, is not to do with 'park design' so much as with the

use of this 'park' as a cemetery at all. The Hackney Society laments the fact that burials have taken place 'on the grass verges and other unsuitable positions' and hopes with winning sympathy that 'these could perhaps be deprived of their headstones in due course' (p. 18). Fortunately, however, no burials are now taking place 'except for insertions into existing family graves,' so the era of disgraceful and predominantly working-class indiscretion is coming to an end. In future, strolling incomers will be less and less disturbed in their musings by the vulgar glare of new stone, crudely exposed soil, plastic flowers or any well-trimmed and excessively decorous verge. As somebody who enjoys the occasional Gothic stroll himself, I find the Hackney Society's aesthetic remarkably sympathetic. What remains problematic is the way this aesthetic is forced over other forms of life with such stunning disregard for what it would disconnect. With blithe confidence the Hackney Society elevates its own particular choice to the level of aesthetic and universal law. 'In the name of memory history has been abolished.'

9   Michael Hunter, *The Victorian Villas of Hackney*, The Hackney Society, 1981.
10 See Amanda Root, 'The Return of the Nanny,' *New Socialist* No.22, December 1984, pp. 16–19. A good riposte to this article came from Susan Black, *New Socialist* No.24, February 1985, p. 47.
11 Paul Harrison, *Inside the Inner City*, Harmondsworth 1983.
12 Paul Johnson, 'The poverty myth that can make us all paupers,' *Daily Mail*, August 30th, 1983.
13 David Walker in *The Times*, 25 August 1983.
14 Philippa Toomey, 'Hooray for Hackney,' *The Times*, 26 August 1983.
15 Henri Lefebvre, *Everyday Life in the Modern World*, London 1971, p. 158.
16 Charles Moore, *The Old People of Lambeth*, Salisbury Papers 9, 1982.
17 Zygmunt Bauman, *Memories of Class: The Pre-History and After-Life of Class*, London 1982, p. 179.
18 Agnes Heller, *A Radical Philosophy*, Oxford 1984, pp. 135–6.
    Parts of this chapter appeared in C. Aubrey and P. Chilton (eds.), *Nineteen Eighty-Four in 1984*, London 1983.

Afterword

1   Philippe Hoyau, 'L'année du patrimoine ou la société de conservation,' *Les Révoltes Logiques* No.12, Summer 1980, pp. 70–7.
2   I agree here with Pauline Johnson who has argued that the recent emphasis on popular culture can be problematic in its apparent egalitarianism: 'Whilst avoiding the overt elitism of much of the classical tradition this project can lend itself to an insidious, covert elitism which loses the far-reaching claims of a humanistic perspective on emancipation and is content to claim only the satisfaction of those needs realisable within the terms of the present.' See Pauline Johnson, *Marxist Aesthetics: The Foundations within Everyday Life for an Enlightened Consciousness*, London 1984, p. 148.

3 This passage from Habermas's *Legitimation Crisis* is quoted and discussed in Martin Jay, 'Habermas and Modernity,' *Praxis International*, Vol.4, No.1, April 1984, pp. 1–14. In Agnes Heller's recent work 'aura' is described as a characteristic of actions or forms which articulate the person as a whole. See the later sections of the essay 'Everyday Life, Rationality of Reason, Rationality of Intellect,' in Heller's *The Power of Shame: A Rational Perspective*, London 1985. Readers concerned about the apparent 'essentialism' of 'the person as a whole' may find Heller's account of the sphere of objectivation 'in itself' especially useful.

4 The Conservative appropriation of the 'lifeworld' is indicated by the recent publication of V. Havel's essay 'Politics and Conscience' in *The Salisbury Review*, January 1985, pp. 31–8. While Havel—whose essay makes its moving plea for a pastoral *lebenswelt* in terms of the Czech experience of Soviet domination—is certainly not to be judged by the company his writings end up keeping in the West, exactly such an iden- tification is presumably willed by the Salisbury Group. Roger Scruton translated this article together with E. Kohak and some indication of what the 'lifeworld' means on the far right is provided by the fact that in the English article *lebenswelt* becomes 'the *natural* world' rather than the lifeworld. While it would be interesting to know whether this slip- page is characteristic of the English translation alone, the main point is that when the idea of the lifeworld becomes a vague metaphor it could indeed be applied just as easily to the 'common-sense' of Quinlan Terry's classical architecture or to the morbid experience of Charles Moore's essentialised 'old people of Lambeth' as to the sufferers of Soviet dom- ination. Precisely here—where an originally philosophical concept starts its career as a vague and emotive, if not always ideological, metaphor— there is reason to justify Heller's apparently rather formal restriction of the term 'lifeworld' to its philosophical definition as a phenomenological attitude.

5 Ernst Bloch's *Heritage of Our Times* (Erbschaft dieser Zeit) was first pub- lished in 1935. See Anson Rabinbach, 'Ernst Bloch's *Heritage of Our Times* and the Theory of Fascism' and also the translated excerpt from Bloch's book 'Non-synchronism and the Obligation to its Dialectics,' both of which appear in *New German Critique*, No.11, Spring 1977.

6 See Agnes Heller, *A Theory of History*, London 1982, pp. 277–338. Heller discusses the counterfactual nature of utopia in 'A socialist in exile,' *New Socialist* No.29, July/August 1985.

Index